P144

**Business Planning**
An Approach to Strategic Management

Second Edition

KU-589-662

Leeds Metropolitan University

17 0181924 8

# Business Planning
# An Approach to
# Strategic Management

SECOND EDITION

**Bill Richardson · Roy Richardson**

Pitman Publishing
128 Long Acre, London WC2E 9AN

A Division of Pearson Professional Limited

First published in 1989
Second edition 1992

© W Richardson 1992

**British Library Cataloguing in Publication Data**
A catalogue record for this book is available
from the British Library

ISBN 0 273 03720 X

All rights reserved; no part of this publication may be
reproduced, stored in a retrieval system, or transmitted in any
form or by any means, electronic, mechanical, photocopying,
recording, or otherwise without either the prior written
permission of the Publishers or a licence permitting restricted
copying issued by the Copyright Licensing Agency Ltd,
90 Tottenham Court Road, London W1P 9HE. This book may not
be lent, resold, hired out or otherwise disposed of by way of trade
in any form of binding or cover other than that in which it is
published, without the prior consent of the Publishers.

10 9 8 7 6 5

Printed in England by Clays Ltd, St Ives plc

LEEDS METROPOLITAN
UNIVERSITY LIBRARY ✓
1708192248
BTB
659440
658.4012 RIC
10.10.97 £21.99

# Contents

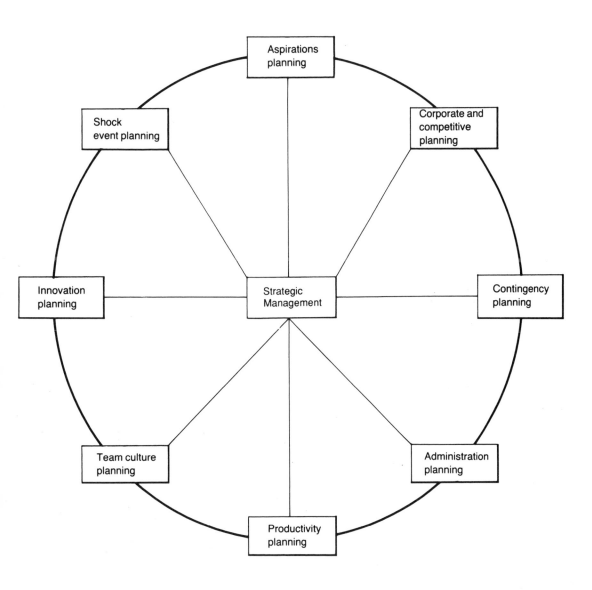

**Figure 1 A total approach to planning strategic success**

# Preface to first edition

Plans, decisions and actions help us look forward to and negotiate our futures. Organisations bring people together to take part in planning, decision-making and action processes. Collectively these organisational decision-making processes determine whether the organisation will survive and/or grow through time. They also determine the success achieved by the enterprise in satisfying the aspirations of the people who come to it.

As a strategy for maintaining its own existence and for satisfying the needs of people the organisation seeks to create wealth through interactions with its environments. Its planning/deciding/acting processes, therefore, take place within the context of this need to 'earn a living' from environments. Today's environments, however, are dynamic, turbulent and hostile. Organisations which continue to use only traditional planning systems in these modern environments will fail. Today a more active and systematic approach to creating organisational success is required.

It is the job of the management strategist to make sure that his or her organisation is, in totality, an effective planning system. The management strategist takes responsibility for ensuring that the enterprise survives and continues to satisfy those involved with it.

The theory of management strategy has developed (and is developing) to help the management strategist, in these difficult times, to do his or her job more effectively. As a body of theory it contains concepts, frameworks and techniques to help these top decision makers plan and create organisations as effective planning/decision-making/acting systems.

In this book we provide a *complete planning* model of the organisation. This model identifies a range of interactive, critical planning problems and infers that greater organisational success is to be had through a proactive and systematic approach to their resolutions. Briefly, these critical planning problems are:

- How to identify and manipulate important organisational stakeholders.
- How to anticipate longer term futures and decide on appropriate product or market developments and other organisational changes, including changes to enhance competitive prowess.
- How to plan for things which might foreseeably go wrong with mainstream plans.
- How to administrate product market 'dreams' into operational 'reality' via organisational functions and through a system of management by objectives.
- How to make organisational changes which significantly improve performance through finding and working on major cost cutting or profit-making drives.
- How to create a responsive team culture where *everybody* inside the organisation changes the way they do their jobs, incrementally, to accommodate changing circumstances and where *everybody* seeks, continuously, to be more efficient and more customer responsive.

- How to create a specialist force for innovation – to intensify, and then harness, the enterprise's ability to make and do effective new things.
- How to grab unexpected opportunities and/or to respond positively to shock events.

The model also provides a framework for considering the organisation as a complete planning system performing a range of planning activities which collectively determine how successfully the organisation adapts to its environments as they unfold or are created. Pertinent prescriptions, models and other aids from the theory of management strategy are introduced as the book progresses through its exploration of each subsystem of the complete planning system. Introduced, too, are case studies, exercises and points for thought and discussion. Together, these constituents offer business practitioners and students the opportunity to think through – and to practise – how they might improve organisational performance in critical areas. Knowledge of management strategy's theory together with skill developed through practice might therefore lead to enhanced competence in the practice of management strategy.

Many books view 'strategy-making' as that planning process conducted by top management and directed at making those big one-off decisions which have long-term, major resource implications. This book provides a different view of strategy-making. Here *the organisation*, through its many types of plans and decisions is the strategy for success. Organisations, naturally, are planning/decision-making/acting systems. Management strategists need to take on the role of planning architects – to plan and implement activities which enhance the performance of the organisation as a complete planning system. Action to improve the range of planning subsystems identified in this book will generate a collective and synergistic system for the attainment of greater strategic success.

The nature of much strategy-making requires that decisions should be customised to the situation they address and should rely, to a large extent, on the strategist's own judgement. More than anything, this book seeks to stimulate, in readers, the desire to improve their own business strategic skills. At the same time it also aims to provide a vehicle for the development of these skills. Such skills seem set to assume massive importance in increasingly hostile and uncertain real world business situations.

## Acknowledgements to first edition

Many people have helped in the creation of this book. In particular, colleagues at Sheffield, including Maurice Brown, Peter Jennings, Colin Gilligan, David Hawley, Janet Kirkham, John Patterson and Kevan Scholes have provided much advice, direction and stimulation. Chris Roscoe and Margaret Marks deserve special mention for their help and guidance on typing, presentation and grammar. Annie Robinson has been especially helpful in the process of refining and clarifying the script. More generally, clients, students and work colleagues from our range of organisational occupations have helped develop our interests in, and understandings of, management strategy – as have those who contribute to the literature of management. Finally, of course, debts of gratitude are owed to Susan, Sarah and Lesley and to Margaret, Rachel and Rebecca for living with preoccupied 'strategists'.

Bill Richardson
Roy Richardson
Sheffield 1989

# Preface to second edition

In the three year since the publication of the first edition of this book, the job of the management strategist has become even more difficult and critical. For *all* managers, from organisations big and small, public and private, profit- and non-profit-making, at *all* levels, and studying in a company or in a university/college, there is an even greater need to improve skills in business planning and strategic management.

This revised edition maintains its central objective of providing comprehensive and effective help for the development of these skills in these people. New sections have been added to reflect the growing importance to modern managers of the topics of strategy-making processes, business ethics, strategic alliances and global strategies, and vision management. A companion volume, *Case Studies in Business Planning*, 2nd edition, (Pitman, 1992), is referred to throughout the text. This supplements the cases and 'thought/ discussion' stimulators in the main text.

The first edition of this book has been used successfully to underpin strategy and decision-making programmes of study at HND, BABS and postgraduate levels and in Training and Enterprise Council sponsored programmes of management and organisational development. My hope is that the second edition continues to be useful.

## Acknowledgements

Many people take the credit for helping in the development of this book. Thanks offered in the acknowledgements to the first edition remain current. Additionally, Sheffield Business School colleagues Claire Capon, Rene Hayes and Ted Johns deserve mention for their contributions to the development and testing of book material. Penelope Woolf and Suzanne Dempsey of Pitman Publishing have also provided valuable help and advice. A special place must be reserved for my students, clients and colleagues, generally – our shared relationships and common interest in management strategy have been invaluable to my own development.

Bill Richardson
Sheffield 1992

# 1 An introduction to business planning and management strategy

In this chapter we examine the nature of planning and decision-making and discuss how a range of different types of plan contribute to a 'strategic theme' underpinning organisational success. A model of the organisation as a complete business planning system is introduced and the component parts of the complete system are described. Readers are also introduced to the theory of management strategy – that body of theory most concerned with organisational plans, decisions and success. These issues are discussed under the following headings:

- Plans, decisions and personal success
- Basic organisational strategy – the strategic theme
- Critical planning problems in the 'today' environment
- Complete planning systems
- Defining management strategy
- Models of the strategy-making process
- A 'contingency' approach to planning strategic success
- Limitations of management strategy

## Case example: plans, decisions and personal success

Joe and his family had been looking forward to their holiday for months. As the departure date drew near the kids were brought into the holiday planning process. They were dispatched to the shops to find a 'decent map book'. Together, the family planned the route. 'I think we should aim to be at Coventry by 10.00 am and, all being well, we should by-pass Bristol around 1.00 pm', ventured Joe.

The day before departure everybody got down to their holiday jobs. The kids washed the car (and made a good job of it for a change). Joe gave the car and the tool kit a final checkover .... Most of the journey had been fairly uneventful. A two-mile 'tailback' on the M1 (due to road works) and a wrong turn had added ten miles – and extra time – to the journey but, for the most part it had simply been a routine drive. They were not too far away from the planned 50 miles per hour average speed, either; they were in no hurry and could save a few pounds at that sort of speed. Just after Bristol, however, and going well according to schedule, disaster almost struck. Travelling at around 55 mph, in the nearside lane, the windscreen suddenly shattered. As Joe instinctively applied the brakes the car started drifting towards the centre lane. Within a split second he had made sense of what had happened, searched desperately for – and found – an area of clear windscreen, checked his rear view mirror and regulated the drift of the car. Totally shut off from the sounds of his family, Joe indicated left and eased onto the hard shoulder. Two hundred yards on he brought the car to a halt, pulled on the handbrake, checked to see that everyone was alright ... and said a little prayer.

Fortunately, they were members of the AA. Before too long a new screen had been fitted and the journey was resumed. Four hours late, but safe and sound, they checked into their hotel.

## Plans, decisions and personal success

*Planning* has been defined as 'the design of a desired future and of effective ways of bringing it about' (1) and, as 'examining the future and drawing up a plan of action' (2). From these definitions, therefore, we can identify planning as something which:

(a)  designs, and precedes, action;

(b)  attempts to fit appropriate actions to something we have to make sense of before it happens (and of which we can never be entirely certain), i.e. the future;

(c)  is directed at achieving desired results (objectives);

(d)  is a response to the pessimistic belief that unless something is done a desired future state will not occur, and to the optimistic belief that we can do things to improve our chances of achieving the desired state.

*Decision-making* has been isolated, within the overall planning process, as that activity which makes the choice of which activity to pursue given that we often have a number of alternative action options. Thus, a decision has been defined as 'a commitment to action' (3, 4).

Of course, as Drucker (5) has pointed out 'a plan is useless unless it degenerates into action'. Figure 1.1 describes a comprehensive planning/decision-making process in the form of a complete activity, encompassing planning, deciding and acting.

### Think and discuss
Looking at the model in Fig. 1.1, identify some of the planning activities which helped the family in the previous case example arrive at its destination.

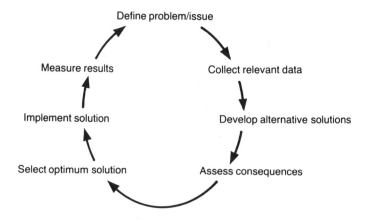

Many writers point to the iterative nature of much decision-making and find this model too sequential to represent reality. Writers also question the use of the word 'optimum' and ask whether we really do choose, or whether we can measure 'optimum' solutions.

**Figure 1.1  The planning/decision-making cycle**

Planning (in its comprehensive planning/deciding/acting role), therefore, is the most fundamental and important of all our life skills. Fortunately, planning is, for the most part, a common sense, second nature activity. The simple family holiday illustration offered above reminds us that:

(a) Living is planning and expertise in planning is usually essential to success in life. Effective planning is a prerequisite to negotiating our environments and getting safely into our futures.

(b) It is the *combined* effect of a range of different sorts of plans which determines how successful we are. Joe's holiday activities, for example, produced plans to take account of:

- the family's aspirations, needs and wants;
- the destination and route;
- family contributions to the holiday effort;
- the family budget and cost efficiency;
- things which might foreseeably go wrong – a breakdown, perhaps;
- shock events that demanded 'on the spot' responses;
- 'second nature' responses (braking, steering, indicating, etc.) to those common occurrences which the experienced driver tends to take in his or her stride.

On the face of it, some of these plans are more important than others. Deciding the destination, for example, is likely to have been of greater consequence than deciding which route to take. Effective reaction to the windscreen crisis was obviously more critical than, say, a decision on when to change gear. Nevertheless, an ill-informed choice of route might have added time, cost and frustration to the journey. Persistent failure to change gear at appropriate points could, conceivably, have produced mechanical breakdown and consequential costs and problems. The success of Joe's family holiday was, in total, down to good all round planning. The family's ability in implementing solutions to a range of perceived problems manoeuvred it successfully into its future.

## Basic organisational strategy – the strategic theme

Organisations, like families, are 'groups of people who co-ordinate their activities in pursuit of a common purpose' (6). The strategic *theme* for any organisation (or family or individual, for that matter) is concerned with the effective adaptation of the organisation to its environment through time. The term 'strategy' is freely used in management literature without any consensus over its definition (7). In fact 'strategy' is any means to achieve anything. In this book we portray the organisation's *underlying* strategy for success as effective adaptation to environments over time. The book then sets out to identify how all the organisation's sub-sets of plans, decisions and activities might be undertaken to enhance this 'strategic theme'.

While the things an organisation does might change markedly over time the need for these things to contribute to this basic, unchanging, strategy remains constant. The success with which this basic strategy of effective adaptation is achieved, therefore, depends upon the contributions made by 'all those sets of *plans*, *decisions* and *actions* which lead to the development of an effective strategy' (8). Underlying this book is the premise that while this proposition has always been true, today, more than ever, environmental forces require organisations to be more sophisticated in *all* planning activities. A growing catalogue of published case studies offers witness to success through effectiveness across a *range* of planning fronts. The rejuvenation of manufacturing organisations such as Courtauld, Lucas and Jaguar illustrates how success is being recreated through the planning of new product/market developments, through the removal of 'slack' via the instigation of efficiency drives and through restructurings towards more sensitive and responsive interactions with customers and other societal stakeholders. Newer strategic situations facing formerly 'steady state' institutions such as local authorities, banks, building societies, solicitors, and nationalised corporations are also demanding effective *total* planning systems. Those in charge of these organisations are having to come to terms with more difficult, decartelised or privatised, market situations. They are having to plan more carefully their desired, longer term futures (and ways of achieving them). At the same time they are responding to pressure to improve productivity on an ongoing basis. More attention is being paid to the provision of attractive organisational offers to customers. Further, organisations confronted by competitors keen to attract the benefits of information technology (IT) and by a society which now *expects* improving goods and services, dare not opt out of the IT-led process of continuous innovation. Political turbulence in a 'global village' world and the increasing risk of manmade disasters (as in Chernobyl, for example) means also that today's enterprises need to be capable of reacting favourably to shock events.

## Critical planning problems in the 'today' environment

Organisations today are experiencing a range of critical planning problems. The task of the 'today' management strategist, therefore, is to improve his or her organisation's total planning capability so that it might continue to adapt successfully through time.

Below is a list of critical planning problems arising from the 'today' environment. This is based on an analysis of management strategy research, on case studies describing the strategic problems and practices of organisations operating in the 1980s and 1990s, and on our own practical experiences of organisations. It indicates eight critical planning problems which confront enterprises seeking strategic success in modern, dynamic, turbulent and hostile business environments. This book explores the nature of these problems and how they might be resolved.

(a)  How to identify and manipulate important organisational stakeholders.

(b)  How to anticipate longer term futures and decide on appropriate product or market developments and other organisational changes, including changes to enhance competitiveness.

(c)  How to plan for things which might foreseeably go wrong with mainstream plans.

(d)  How to administrate product/market 'dreams' into organisational reality.

(e)  How to seek out major cost cutting and contribution creating opportunities and to make the required changes to enhance productivity.

(f)  How to create a responsive team culture wherein everybody in the organisation adapts to meet changing circumstances and where everybody seeks, continuously, to improve their own contributions to efficiency and customer satisfaction.

(g) How to create a specialist base for innovation: to intensify and then to harness the ability of the enterprise to change effectively its products, services and processes.

(h) How to make the most of unexpected opportunities and respond positively to shock events.

# Complete business planning systems

The successful 'today' organisation, then, is likely to be performing well across a range of planning fronts. This book explains and explores a series of planning activities, which together determine the level of strategic success achieved by an organisation. It thus offers a more comprehensive approach to the study of planning strategic success than is found in many more specialised books on strategic management.

We have categorised the organisation's strategic planning activities under the following headings:

- Aspirations planning
- Corporate and competitive planning
- Contingency planning
- Administration planning
- Productivity planning
- Team culture planning
- Innovation planning
- Shock event planning

## Aspirations planning

Organisations interact with a variety of 'stakeholders' (owners, managers, workers, customers, etc.) all of whom come to the organisation in pursuit of their own desired outcomes. The organisation has to be able to decide which aspirations it should satisfy and what it should offer in order to continue to attract important contributions from its stakeholders. In recent years, for example, British Telecom has needed to become much more sensitive to the needs of its private and governmental owners, its customers and its employees.

## Corporate and competitive planning

Corporate planning activities seek to align the entire organisation with its markets of the future through effective anticipation. Also, some organisation projects (for example, the building of a new factory or the acquisition of a rival company) require initial heavy investment in the hope of receiving worthwhile paybacks over future years. Such major, long-term projects call for long-term planning to try to establish whether conditions over a protracted period of time will remain conducive to the realisation of these paybacks. The adoption of longer term perspectives and keeping 'half an eye' on the future – and its potential threats and opportunities – seem intuitively to be simply good common sense. Corporate planning helps the enterprise to make sound long-term decisions. Critical decisions associated with the corporate planning process are ones which determine where and how the organisation is to compete.

## Contingency planning

Planning is about deciding *future* actions. Contingency planning accedes to the reality of futures not always being as envisaged at initial planning stages. Contingency planning, consequently, seeks to minimise the costs which might arise if unlikely (and undesirable) events occur. In the family holiday illustration, for example, Joe planned to reduce the adverse impact of any breakdown which might have occurred.

## Administration planning

Plans and planning activities have to be co-ordinated and controlled if they are to relate to each other in such a way as to enhance the total organisational planning effort – if they are to achieve successfully the strategic theme. Organisations, too, are full of people who need to be motivated, controlled and co-ordinated. Administration planning is concerned with ensuring that events happen in the correct sequence, that activities are synchronised and that people are motivated and controlled to ensure that things happen according to plan. For example, organisations constantly change their organisational structures (the jobs and grouping/reporting relationship of jobs) as they attempt to improve co-ordination and control of the enterprise as it grows and/or confronts changing environments.

## Productivity planning

Over time all organisations have to make profits or meet budgets. The enterprise which consistently fails to be productive (to produce, or to be perceived as producing, greater benefits than costs), eventually runs out of resources and has to cease operating. Productivity/efficiency planning seeks to maintain and improve cost/benefit situations. Many of our manufacturing companies have, during the 1980s, reduced energy, manpower and stock holding costs (for example) while attempting to hold or increase sales levels. Local authorities, receiving fewer central government resource inputs, have also been planning ways of 'getting more for less'. The early 1990s has been an era of major reductions in the workforces of high street banks, insurance companies and many other organisations. A systematic approach to 'getting more for less' is, for many firms, a pre-condition of survival.

## Team culture planning

This form of planning is concerned with achieving incremental responsiveness via an organisation which is capable of – and happy to make – the day-to-day adjustments necessary to continue to satisfy customers and to do its present jobs better. Here the aim is to create a 'team culture' where *all* personnel commit themselves to 'trying for 1 per cent work improvement each day'. In this way organisations such as IBM, Havant, have gained 'quality' reputations and claim to have created a collective force for attaining competitive advantage.

## Innovation planning

This type of planning is responsible for the success demonstrated by the firm in creating and implementing new and improved ways of operating and in producing and distributing new and better products and services. Innovations have been a major source of success in computer, travel and retail industries, for example, as new products and processes have changed the shape of industries in favour of the innovative organisations.

## Shock event planning

Turbulent, hostile and dynamic environments throw up many new opportunities which need to be spotted and 'grabbed' as and when they arise. They tend also to throw up major 'shock events' which can hit the organisation without warning and which require effective and spontaneous reaction. Increasingly, it seems, organisations are having to deal with incidents similar in nature to Joe's windscreen crisis, illustrated at the beginning of the chapter.

Today's environments demand more sophisticated and effective approaches to the full range of interrelated and over-lapping organisational planning activities. Enterprises which achieve effectiveness across the planning board have the total planning approach which holds all the aces in the strategic success game. This book explores, for the benefit of practising and student management strategists, each component of the complete business planning system illustrated in Fig. 1.2.

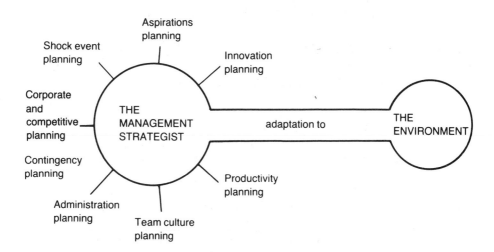

**Figure 1.2  The management strategist at the centre of the complete planning system and strategic adaptation**

## Defining management strategy

'Strategy' and 'management strategy' are terms which appear regularly throughout this book. The following list describes some of the meanings we may seek to convey when using these terms.

(a) 'Strategy' is a means of achieving a desired end.

(b) 'The strategy' – as far as this text is concerned – is *the organisation itself* as a means of achieving two basic strategic objectives: sustaining its own existence; and enhancing the lives of the people who interact with it.

(c) 'Management strategy' can be:

- a process, ultimately of organisational adaptation to environments through time;
- a job for the management strategist, who has overall responsibility for the way in which the organisation adapts to its environment and satisfies people;
- a job for everyone in the organisation, because their plans, decisions and actions collectively create the level of success achieved by the organisation as *the* strategy;
- a collection of critical planning tasks (see Fig. 1.2) which management strategists might undertake to maintain or improve organisational success;
- a body of theory which seeks, particularly, to help management strategists tackle critical planning tasks and, consequently, to do their jobs better.

By and large, we leave readers to find for themselves the relevant meanings which apply to these terms as they appear at particular points of the text.

The theory of management strategy is 'a field of study concerned with the management of the total organisation with particular emphasis on its decisional behaviour' (9). At the heart of this field of study is the search for understanding of what creates organisational success. Numerous theorists have been motivated to develop and publicise their own findings (and those of others working in business-associated disciplines such as economics, accountancy, marketing, operations management and sociology) on how to solve organisational problems.

## Models of the strategy-making process

The theory of management strategy contains many models of strategic decision-making *at work* in organisations. Figure 1.3 illustrates some of these models in the context of a continuum of strategic decision-making processes. These models and the nature of the continuum they form are discussed in greater detail in this section.

The *corporate planning* model is *prescriptive* as to how strategic decision-making processes *should be* undertaken. The view projected by this model emphasises a linear-sequential sequence of decision-making which involves top management in seeking out and utilising all relevant information before generating, evaluating and choosing the way(s) forward for the organisation.

Strategic analysis, therefore, leads to strategic *choice* and onto strategic *implementation*. An underlying concern of this model is the quest to achieve a state of global rationality wherefrom best choices of strategic developments can be made from a base of perfect information. Strategic decision-making, in this view, is seen to be the province of top management who *deliberately* and *systematically pre-plan* developments to ensure that the organisation develops, through people working to the 'blueprint', in closely defined, *intended* ways. It also emphasises strategic decision-making as a process concerned with choices on long-term effect, major resource committing, developments. Corporate planning models and processes are central, particularly, to Chapters 3, 4, 5 and 6 of this book.

The *logical incrementalism* view of strategic decision-making is more *descriptive* than it is prescriptive. Theorists such as James Brian Quinn (10) have been concerned to find out how strategy making *actually takes place* in organisations. (Descriptions, of course, lead to enhanced understanding and so provide a better basis from which to become a more skilful interventionist in decision-making processes – they help us better prescribe how to make change towards our preferred outcomes.)

In contrast to the corporate planning model the logical incrementalist view sees top managers using political and social skills to pick up, re-form, check out, gather support for, modify and test strategies. Quinn's study of strategic change processes in major companies emphasises the role of top managers as opportunistic and incremental blenders of strategies which 'surface' from different parts of the organisation and which, before being 'blended', deal with more specific strategic problems. A senior executive, quoted by Quinn (11), explains this approach to strategy making ... 'Typically, you start with general concerns, vaguely felt. Next you roll an issue around in your mind till you think you have a conclusion that makes sense for the company. You than go out and sort of post the idea without being too wedded to its details. You then start hearing the arguments pro and con, and some very good refinements of the idea usually emerge. Then you pull an idea in and put some resources together to study it so that it can be put forward as more of a formal presentation. You wait for the 'stimuli occurrences' or 'crises' and launch pieces of the idea to help in these situations. But they lead towards your ultimate aim. You'd like to get there in six months, but it may take three years, or you may not get there, and when you get there, you don't know whether it was originally your own idea or somebody else had reached the same conclusion before you and just got you on board for it. You never know.'

This more incremental view of strategy nevertheless maintains top managers as the architects of strategic developments. This incrementalist manager, too, is rational and logical. He/she creates a situation where a coherent strategy can emerge based on better, more up-to-date information, and on the commitment of staff. Here, *deliberate* strategies are formulated in iterative fashion and helped to *emerge* in a *broadly intended* way. Chapters 11, 12 and 13 of this book are concerned, particularly, with the design of organisations for the achievement of incremental, broadly intended strategy.

The *'muddling through'* model of strategic decision-making (12) is akin to the logical incrementalism model except that the central decision-making is not endowed with the same level of purposiveness. In this mode the decision-making proceeds via small steps which are expected only partially to achieve goals. The decision-maker is committed to repeating endlessly these small steps and to making adjustments as conditions and aspirations dictate. Often decisions get taken in a 'disjointed incrementalist' manner – the decision-maker *accedes* to options linked to existing activities, to 'righting wrongs' and to trials and retrials. Processes of objectives setting, information analysis and strategy evaluation are intertwined – goals and strategies to achieve the goals are chosen simultaneously. The result is a few simple and global objectives that provide little direction. The central decision-maker, here, uses less logic, purposefulness and influence than the logical incrementalist manager. Rather, he/she 'muddles through' decision-making life, *acceding* to an *emergent* strategy which is *intended* only to the extent that it is a continuation or refinement of existing, traditional operations. Defenders of this approach to strategic decision-making claim that its reliance on past experience and its propensity towards small steps forward (and its *deliberate* exclusion of wider drawn, less certain factors) makes it a more rational approach to strategy-making than that provided by the allegedly rational approach of the linear-sequential model.

Critics of this approach to strategy-making, however, are able to point to a history of organisational crises which have been seen to occur as a consequence of 'strategic drift' (13) – organisations which have failed to challenge and change existing recipes for doing business become misaligned with the nature and needs of their environments until their survival is threatened. Chapter 11 considers, in more detail, the concept of strategic drift.

In the *'garbage can'* model (14) strategic choice decisions are outcomes of the interplay between problems, solutions, participants and choices, all of which arise independently of one another. Problems can arise anywhere, at any time. Solutions exist irrespective of whether problems exist (for example, people with preferences wait for their moment to come, computers wait for questions they can answer). Participants in decision-making processes move in and out. Opportunities for choices occur any time a decision has to be made (for example, when a budgetary schedule demands that money be spent before a specified date). Most decisions get made in an *oversight* mode – the choice is made quickly, incidentally to other choices being made – or under *flight* conditions (the original problem has 'flown' away and a choice which solves nothing is made). Fewer decisions actually produce *resolutions* to strategic problems.

In this model, therefore, many, if not most, organisational decisions are little more than coincidences. Decisions happen due to the 'temporal proximity' of what has streamed into the garbage can during a particular period of time. Decisions appear out of 'foggy emergent contexts when people, problems and solutions find themselves sharing the same bed' (15).

The garbage can model of strategic decision-making, therefore, stands at the opposite extreme of the decision-making continuum to that of the rational corporate planning model. The garbage can view has people sometimes acting before they think. Top managers might have little or no involvement and/or little or no purposive, rational involvement in important decision-making situations. Here, strategies can simply *emerge* in *unintended* ways from different parts of the organisation.

In providing a model of the *organisation itself* as the strategy (for wealth creation and wealth distribution) this book emphasises the importance of *all* the plans, decisions and actions which are taken throughout the organisation. Each decision, from whoever and from wherever, contributes to (or detracts from) the nature and effectiveness of the organisation as a wealth breeder/distributor. This book aims to help strategists improve their skills for linear-sequential type activities and for creating organisations which help incremental and garbage can situations produce strategic outcomes which emerge in broadly intended ways.

A key concept underpinning this book's attempt to help organisation designers is that of *social enactment*. Chapters 10, 11, 12 and 13 in particular, are concerned with the issue of how to design organisations as social systems which transmit and embed shared meanings about the appropriate ways in which people of the organisation should behave. Through this means, organisation culture can direct the people of the organisation to use their decision-making discretionary powers to enact strategy for the 'common good' of the organisation, see Fig. 1.3.

struggle to find a generally applicable planning approach which has even greater pertinence for the strategic theme problems of the 1990s and the twenty-first century.

Faced with the need to understand how to design and implement 'complete planning' organisation systems, modern management strategists can take heart and help from looking back over the history of strategic planning theory. Useful theoretical contributions are available from the body of management strategy to help the strategist think through his or her organisation as a total planning system and to improve each planning activity therein (17). With this help the strategist can plan improved strategic success and decide those organisational changes for successful adaptation to and/or manipulations of the organisation's environment. This book will draw heavily from these sources.

## A 'contingency' approach to planning strategic success

A danger inherent in any search for new prescriptions for organisational success lies in the propensity for older models to be *inappropriately* discarded or disregarded. Over the course of this century, in fact, many branches of organisation theory (for example, leadership theory and motivation theory) have progressed to become embedded in a *contingency* era. A contingency approach to problem-solving acknowledges the need to find customised responses to particular problems and accepts that often the most appropriate solution is to be found through reference to a range of theories. Contingency solutions, too, often attack problems on a number of fronts. Traditionally, theoretical approaches to decision-making in organisations emanated from the disciplines of economics, mathematics and statistics, which were concerned with the issue of how rational choices might be made to maximise profit or utility. More recently, psychologists, sociologists and organisation theorists have contributed models and theories more concerned with the understanding of people and their less than rational behaviour.

The aims (and structure) of this book owe much to our belief that practical success will, within the foreseeable future, depend increasingly on a contingency, 'across all fronts' planning sophistication underpinned by an eclectic use of theory. In fact, later chapters of this work reveal that organisations are recruiting 'superman strategists' – managers who have expertise in a range of planning styles and approaches – and who are consequently achieving success through attention to *total* planning systems. Through the provision of a complete planning framework and a text which draws from the work of management theorists, practitioners and students alike should be able to improve their own understanding of, and contributions to successful business planning. Certainly the effectiveness with which business planning is performed in an era which promises 'the prospect of increasing uncertainty, more intense competition, and even more dramatic change' (18) will determine the wealth (or otherwise) we enjoy personally, organisationally and nationally.

The remaining chapters of the book introduce and discuss concepts, theories and techniques relative to each strand of the complete business planning framework identified in Fig. 1.2. At the end of many of these chapters is case study and other material together with points for thought and discussion. These are intended to provide 'real life' orientated opportunities to review material already covered and to create a *complete text and work book* for students studying this important subject area.

## Case study: running a town centre travel agency

You own and manage a town centre travel agency. Besides working in the agency yourself you also employ three full-time staff – Wendy, Joy and Phil – who enjoy equal status and who do similar jobs, i.e. they all contribute to clerical, typing and customer reception duties.

The tour operators and clerical and administrative staff have just announced a one-day strike over pay for Thursday and no bookings can be made on that day. It is Monday now and you are mulling over the work schedule changes you should make. Some of your thoughts include:

- Wednesday is your usual 'closed' day.
- The local Chamber of Commerce (of which you are a member) needs helpers for a charity 'bring and buy' sale to be held in a nearby church hall on Thursday. It is your busy season and although for both commercial and socially responsible reasons you would like to have been seen to contribute you have already advised the Chamber that you can not help on this occasion.
- Phil's wife has just had a baby and you know that he would appreciate some extra time off work.
- Your wife insists that working hard each day in the office and then bringing work home is straining your health and your family life. You need a break.
- As usual at this time of the year when all hands are on the receptions/bookings 'deck' there is a substantial backlog of clerical and financial accounting work.
- All your staff are highly capable at each aspect of their jobs and they appreciate the variety of work involved. If you had to differentiate, however, you would say that Phil is particularly efficient at the clerical side of things while Wendy is particularly adept at customer relations and reception.
- When you are not in the office the staff manage on a consensus basis without any problems or conflicts.

### Think and discuss

1   Refer to the town centre travel agency case study.

(a) Assuming that it is Monday now plan outline work schedules for the coming Thursday.

(b) Rework your decision in the context of the planning/decision-making cycle (see Fig. 1.1).

(c) What type of 'complete planning' activity did you undertake in reaching your decision?

2   Think about your own organisation (or one of your choosing). Which planning activities does it perform well and/or poorly?

### For further study

Refer to the 'Crossed wires at British Telecom' case study in the accompanying volume, *Case Studies in Business Planning*, second edition, Pitman, 1992.

Use the 'complete planning' framework to reach an opinion on whether BT was, in 1987, a successful 'across the board' planner. Which planning subsystems seem successful and/or less successful? Assess BT's strategic sophistication as at 1990. Comment on any changes you perceive as having occurred between 1987 and 1990.

# References

1  R L Ackoff, *A Concept of Corporate Planning*, Wiley Interscience, 1970, p 1

2  H Fayol, *General and Industrial Management*, Pitman, 1949

3  H Mintzberg, *Power in and Around Organisations*, Prentice-Hall International, 1983, p 4

4  E F Harrison, *The Managerial Decision-Making Process*, 3rd edn, Houghton Mifflin, 1987, pp 3 and 4

5  P F Drucker, *The Practice of Management*, Pan Piper, 1968, p 400

6  J G Capey and N R Carr, *People and Work Organisations*, Holt, Rinehart & Winston, 1982

7  For a discussion on the lack of consensus over what 'strategy' is, see E E Chaffee, 'Three Models of Strategy', *Academy of Management Review*, 10 (1), 1985, pp 89–96

8  This is a definition of 'strategic planning' provided by W F Glueck, in *Business Policy: Strategy Formation and Management Action*, McGraw-Hill, 1976, p 3

9  H Mintzberg, op. cit., p *x*

10  J B Quinn, *Strategies for Change: Logical Incrementalism*, Irwin, Homewood, Ill., 1980

11  J B Quinn 'Managing Strategic Change' in *Readings in Strategic Management*, D Asch and C Bowman (eds), Macmillan, 1989, p 21

12  C E Lindblom, 'The Science of Muddling Through', *Public Administration Review*, 19, 1959, pp 79–88

13  G Johnson, in 'Rethinking Incrementalism' *Strategic Management Journal*, 9, 1988, pp 75–91, discusses the concept of strategic drift.

14  M D Cohen, J G March and J P Olsen, 'A Garbage Can Model of Organisational Choice', *Administrative Science Quarterly*, 17, 1972, pp 1–25

15  A Pettigrew, *The Awakening Giant, Continuity and Change in ICI*, Basil Blackwell, 1985, p 22

16  C B Handy, *Understanding Organisations*, Penguin, 1976, p 14

17  F E Kast and J E Rosenzweig, *Organisation and Management*, 4th edn, Tokyo, McGraw-Hill, 1985, Chs 3–5, provide a discussion on the origins and nature of management theory.

18  D E Hussey, *Corporate Planning Theory and Practice*, 2nd edn, Pergamon Press, 1982, p v

# Recommended reading

H I Ansoff, *Implementing Strategic Management*, New York, Prentice-Hall International, 1984

E E Chaffee, 'Three Models of Strategy', *Academy of Management Review*, 10 (1), 1985, pp 89–96

S Cooke and N Slack, *Making Management Decisions*, Prentice-Hall International, 1984

G Morgan, *Images of Organisation*, Sage, 1986

G Johnson, *Strategic Change and the Management Process*, Basil Blackwell, 1987, Ch 2

# 2 The impact of environmental change and the critical role of business planning

In Chapter 1 we defined planning as 'the design of a desired *future*' and the basic organisational strategy as being one of 'effective adaptations to *environments*'. Strategic planning/management, is concerned with making sure that the organisation has the capability to interact efficiently with its environments as they unfurl.

This chapter addresses a fundamental business planning problem – the development of awareness of the *need to plan* in a more proactive and systematic manner. We provide a classification of the nature of the environment and examine how environmental change has made effective strategic planning more difficult and, at the same time, more critical. We also discuss how today's environments raise, simultaneously, a range of planning problems and why, consequently, there is a call for a 'complete planning' response. Our discussion proceeds under the following headings:

- The open system view of organisations in society
- Dynamism, diversity, difficulty and danger
- Planning to achieve objectives in modern environments

## The open system view of organisations in society

Most businesses develop and endure – some for years, decades, even centuries. Implicitly, therefore, businesses have, in the main, successfully negotiated their futures.

On the other hand, however, issues of business planning, corporate strategy and organisational decision-making have only recently taken openly important places within business and academia. While the need for businesses to undertake business planning activities has always been with us, this need is now taking an increasingly overt position as business theorists and practitioners focus on business planning and strategic management as the core of organisational, industrial and national success.

Why, then, is there now all this fuss about business planning? The answer is to be found in the nature of today's business environments. Planning is crucial to organisation success and continued existence. The crucial activity of planning only becomes critical, however, when it becomes difficult and when changes taking place in the environment threaten the success and survival of the enterprise. We shall see that modern environments are, generally, difficult and threatening.

Help is at hand, however. The body of theory on management strategy can help us to gain understanding of how organisational environments have changed and can help us be more alert to the dangers (and opportunities) of new situations. Understanding theory can help organisations to achieve success despite the adverse nature of today's environments.

In Chapter 1 we described the ongoing strategic theme for all organisations as being one of continuous adaptation to the nature and demands of their particular environments. 'Systems' theory dictates that organisational 'life' is maintained through a process of taking resource inputs from the environment, converting them within the organisation and then releasing outputs in the form of goods, services, information and waste back into the environment (1). Success in this process ensures that the organisation achieves 'dynamic equilibrium' (2), i.e. it moves forward in a reasonably orderly fashion, into the future (see Fig. 2.1).

**Figure 2.1 The open system model of organisation**

If, then, planning is about the design of *future* outcomes and if the primary strategic task for any organisation is to achieve a 'fit' with its environment it follows that major difficulties in planning and implementing desired futures are likely if planners are uncertain about what the future nature, components and demands of their business environments will be. Environments which are turbulent, dynamic and unpredictable present bigger planning problems than do those which change only slowly and predictably.

When nothing much changes and when change that does occur is easy to spot, understand and respond to, then forecasting future environmental situations (and thence planning the appropriate organisational response) presents no great problem. The planning process in such circumstances is likely to be so natural and evolutionary in nature that people inside the organisation tend to forget that it is actually taking place. It presents no problems and so it warrants little attention. For some years, in the 1950s and early 1960s life seemed, for many British businesses, to exhibit this sleepy, slow and secure pattern. Environments appeared to be *static*.

Many organisations operated in just one product/market area and naturally had great expertise and experience therein. Environmental variables at work in other market areas seldom broke through market boundaries. So, organisations tended to operate in what we can describe as *single* environments. Given these *static* and *single* environmental properties, firms found the understanding of past, present and future environments *simple*. Organisational life in these conditions was *safe*.

The fact is that organisations are finding successful development hard to maintain. In Britain, particularly, our manufacturing base continues to decline and falling shares of our *home* markets indicate that even our own people find foreign products to be more in line with their needs and demands. Traditionally secure professions, too, such as in local authorities, building societies, estate agencies and the legal and banking professions are having to come to terms with the impact of decartelisation and free markets. As Peter Drucker has observed 'The only thing we can be sure about the future is that it will arrive and that it will be different.'(3) All too suddenly it seems that firms and institutions from all sectors of our economy are having to deal with environmental conditions of increasing *dynamism*, *diversity*, *difficulty* and *danger*.

To help us plan for such environments management strategy makes available a major source of discussions and illustrations which can help us to understand why poor business performance prevails – and why greater attention to business planning is now required. These contributions help us to examine how the nature of business environments has changed and to understand better the implications this change holds for the design and implementation of effective planning/decision making systems.

## Dynamism, diversity, difficulty and danger

### Dynamism

Planning problems are compounded when environmental change is rapid. Byars (4) sums up how the speed of environmental change is accelerating for everyone: 'If we compress the entire span of human development into just 50 years we could say that ... it took man 49 years to get over being a nomad and settle down into established communities. It took a bit longer than that for us to get our first pair of pants. Only six months ago we learned to read and write. Two weeks ago the first printing press was built. And only in the last three or four days we learned how to use electricity. Yesterday was a very busy day. We developed radio, television, diesel power, rayon, nylon, motion pictures and high octane gasoline. Since breakfast this morning we have released atomic energy, built jet planes and produced several new antibiotics. We may now add that a few minutes ago we sent a man to the moon.'

Of course, business exists in this rapidly changing environment. The growth of consumer law within the past couple of decades, for example, following centuries of few and minor developments has suddenly (it seems) produced an era which many commentators have labelled 'the era of vendor emptor' (in contrast to the traditionally prevailing maxim of 'caveat emptor'). Organisations used to decades of trading from powerful bargaining positions have seen the legal environment make rapid and substantial inroads into traditional market power situations. Rapid change in the legal environment has been matched, too, by social, technological and economic change.

#### Case example: the living/changing law
The Consumer Transactions Restrictions on Statements Order has made illegal certain notices and statements which had been used by some traders to mislead shoppers of their rights. To trace its history is to watch a piece of English law grow. We have to go back, initially, hundreds of years to the start of modern law. In those days the buying and selling of goods was conducted largely between traders and the goods themselves were very basic. There were no electrical consumer goods, for example, and, of course, no mass markets. Trade was freely competitive. Economies were not subject to significant government intervention and 'caveat emptor' (let the buyer beware) was the legal maxim of the time. So, if you bought a horse which turned out to be lame it was just a case of 'tough luck' even if the seller had implied the horse was in good condition. The seller actually had to use the words 'I promise that the horse is in good condition' before you could expect any chance of a successful legal action.

Slowly as the centuries passed the law started to change. Some judges in some cases recognised that the concept of freedom of contract was not always fair to the buyer and that often the buyer had little alternative but to accept the seller's terms. Further, goods were becoming more complicated and their characteristics not so easily checked at the time of sale.

In 1893 the first Sale of Goods Act became law. It was written by Sir Mackenzie Chalmers, a Birmingham judge who incorporated a mixture of rules which judges had been making up to that time. The Act therefore reflected to a large extent, society as it then was. The newer attitudes were evident in the important provisions that goods must correspond to their description, must be fit for their purpose and be of merchantable quality. These conditions were to apply even if no specific promises over these characteristics had been made. However, importantly, the Act also incorporated some of the older legal attitudes which still prevailed. The freedom of contract philosophy had its say in the rule which enabled the implied conditions of description, fitness and merchantable quality to be expressly written out of a contract. Of course, what happened was that sellers wrote exclusion clauses into their contracts and the buyer lost his legal protection. This situation lasted for another 80 years. In the meantime society continued to change. Mass production of increasingly technical goods was based on a new mass consumer demand. The injustices created by exclusion clauses resulted in more court cases and judges like Lord Denning spoke of 'the inequalities of bargaining power' in contracts.

In 1973 the law gave way again to the changing demands of society. The Supply of Goods Implied Terms Act 1973 said that exclusion clauses were void if they sought to take away buyers' implied rights under the Sale of Goods Act 1893. Unfortunately, because the law now simply said that these exclusion clauses had no effect this didn't stop sellers from continuing to include them in sale contracts. The vast majority of buyers (who did not know the law, anyway) continued to be misled. The sellers 'preferred position' remained intact.

So we arrive at the present legal situation. The Consumer Transactions Order now makes certain types of exclusion clause *illegal*. Notices which are displayed on business premises, on boxes, carrier bags and other containers and on documents such as receipts, guarantees and finance agreements and which attempt to take away buyers' implied rights are illegal. Common examples of such notices are 'No refunds given' or 'Goods will not be exchanged'. However, other statements less bluntly worded might still be illegal if they mislead a customer as to his or her rights. In the 1960s and 1970s traders experienced great difficulty in coming to terms with a rapid influx of consumer legislation seeking, in similar vein, to change the balance of power in favour of the customer.

When things change fast the future is harder to predict and we have less time to spot and respond to new situations as they arise. More attention has to be paid to the issue of strategic planning if planning systems are to continue to be pertinent and successful. Such attention includes, for example, the search for a new organisational alertness.

## Diversity

The expansionist times of the 1950s and 1960s gave rise to strategic developments which emphasised growth and diversification. More recently, in a more generally stagnant economic situation, organisations have embarked on rounds of 'merger mania'. In many cases, product/market bases have expanded to encompass a portfolio of varied product/market operations. Keeping tabs on a range of business situations and stances is difficult. Also, a growing range of environmental forces are ever more active in attempting to influence all types of enterprises. As we can see in Fig. 2.2, modern businesses have many environmental factors to take into account.

**Figure 2.2  Some environmental influences on organisations**

These environmental influences have been classified by strategy theorists under headings of *specific* and *general* environmental influences. The *specific* environment has direct and more immediate effect on the enterprise. It is comprised of those parties such as customers, suppliers, legal agencies, community groups and competitors who interact with, or otherwise influence, the firm regularly and directly. *General* environmental conditions are the concern of whole classes of organisations and include technological, legal, political, economic, demographic, ecological and cultural conditions.

## Think and discuss

Refer to Fig. 2.2. Categorise the variables illustrated under 'general' and/or 'specific' headings.

The organisation is not typically in touch with elements in the general environment on a day-to-day basis and yet these remote areas which are often difficult to spot and understand are the root cause of many organisational problems. Back in 1965 Emery and Trist (5) argued that it is the combined effect of previously unrelated influences, arising from within the obscure general environment, which poses most organisational threat. The Swiss watch industry, for example, was almost decimated by competition arising from a new location and using technology not previously endemic to the watch industry. Many issues on social responsibility demonstrate how, increasingly, problems arise from completely unconnected, remote environments. The controversy over the Sellafield 'escapes', for example, indicates how a variety of previously remote and unconnected stakeholders can join forces to demand organisational change. Emery and Trist have termed those environments which exhibit unrelated/

interrelated general environmental factors *and* dynamism as 'turbulent fields'. These contrast with easy to plan for 'placid-randomised' environments where environmental transactors remain independent of each other and where change is slow. (The large British manufacturers of the 1950s, for example, supplying numerous small retailers in unchanging circumstances could, to a large extent, control their environments and their futures.) Most observers agree (see for example, 5) that 'turbulent fields' are now commonplace. Naisbitt (6) has spent more than a decade analysing newspaper clippings from the USA to identify ten major trends that are reshaping the most basic form and structure of our society (see Table 2.1).

**Table 2.1  Megatrends: ten new directions transforming our lives**

1  **The decentralisation alternative** – the more pervasive and dominant of the ten trends identified. Decision-making authority is being pushed down to the lowest practical levels. This is in contrast to the trend between 1900 and 1960.
2  **The north to south drift of major industries and the general population** – this is a USA specific finding, of course, although a similar trend has been apparent in Great Britain.
3  **The deinstitutionalisation** into smaller, less centrally controlled public goods and services organisations in industries such as health care, telephones, airlines and education.
4  **The information economy** wherein most workers are paid to process data or information. This trend is more profound than the shift last century from an agricultural to an industrial society.
5  **Biology as the dominant science** replacing the dominating positions of physics and electronics and evidenced by technologies such as genetic engineering.
6  **Multiple options** are available to a greater degree than ever before. For example, we have an increasing number of higher education courses to choose from and more brands of cigarette than ever before. We have a freedom of choice never before imagined.
7  **High tech/high touch** refers to a learning trend. Technology reduces the need for visibility and interaction between people. This trend is a reaction to the acknowledgement that personal contact is important and that a balance between social and rational aspects of life needs to be struck.
8  **The computer as liberator** – computers are being adapted to the social and psychological needs of people and will influence the behaviour of almost every segment of our society.
9  **The organisation man to entrepreneur** trend is being fuelled by the computer as liberator. Old management patterns are being replaced by those that see and reward entrepreneurial efforts and enable unprecedented autonomy in defining the nature of the work place. Bureaucracies continue to be subject to review, organisations as 'loosely coupled systems' are now possible.
10  **The true global economy** trend has created a real and apparent economic interdependency between nations on a global scale. This offers more hope than worry. Emerging transnational economic arrangements will advance international relations more than the existing traditional political structures.

Taken from J Naisbitt, *Megatrends: Ten New Directions Transforming our Lives,* Panthon, Bristol, Futura, 1984

# Case study: Sellafield and social responsibility

In early 1986 a series of radioactive leaks at the government-owned British Nuclear Fuels Ltd (BNFL) Sellafield plant produced a much publicised crisis for the organisation and the government. One worker had received a dose of radioactivity at the level of the yearly acceptable maximum when he had inhaled plutonium gas which had escaped in a building on the site. Others received a tenth of the yearly acceptable dose. Later, 250 gallons of contaminated water had gushed from a broken pipe creating 'an increase in radioactivity in the immediate vicinity', according to the plant's operators.

News of the accidents produced a variety of reactions from different pressure groups. A spokesman for Greenpeace, the international conservation group, called for Sellafield to be shut down 'so investigations can be carried out by the Nuclear Installations Inspectorate and the Radio-chemical Inspectorate into the state of the plant and machinery involved within the Sellafield complex'. The spokesman continued 'Greenpeace believes we can no longer depend on the management of British Nuclear Fuels to safeguard the public from the radioactive hazards posed by the plant and therefore calls for the removal of the senior management team immediately... BNFL public relations department has shown in the past that it has misled and deceived the public about the true nature of accidents and the government must step in.'

Friends of the Earth, the British-based environmentalist group said BNFL had shown itself incapable of running the plant without exposing workers and the public to unacceptable levels of risk.

The leader of the Irish Opposition, Mr Charles Haughey urged the Irish Premier, Dr Garret FitzGerald, during his forthcoming meeting with the British Prime Minister, Margaret Thatcher, to demand the closure of Sellafield. Dublin's Lord Mayor, Mr Jim Tunney, announced plans for a meeting of all Irish local authorities along the country's east coast to discuss the growing concern about possible dangers from Sellafield. Mr Paddy Lalor, an Irish MEP, raised the Sellafield issue in the European Parliament in Strasbourg and obtained a vote in favour of closing it.

Pressure grew in the Isle of Man for a substantial compensation claim to be made against the British government in respect of environmental and tourism industry damage attributed to the Sellafield leaks. Within the Sellafield organisation workers had staged a half-day protest strike. Interviewed leaving the plant gates one worker had commented 'Sure I'd work somewhere else, but you tell me where.'

The Environment Secretary of State, Mr Kenneth Baker, interviewed on BBC's 'This Week, Next Week' described the incidents as 'minor' and denied any sort of secrecy: 'I think they are very open.' He also made the point that 'the reprocessing has to go on. You simply just could not close it', and that 'I think if the people of Sellafield were asked they might vote to close the European Parliament.' Fears of radiation were likened to 'fears of witchcraft in the Middle Ages'.

Both the government and the Sellafield management emphasised the 'minor' nature of the incidents, the national need for a civil nuclear power industry and the great concern and practical steps taken to ensure safety. 'This is the most regulated industry in the country.'

The Alliance suggested that the plant should remain open but called for an impartial public enquiry into the incidents which had 'chipped away at public confidence'.

The Labour Shadow Environment Secretary, Mr Jack Cunningham, whose constituency included Sellafield said that the application of the Official Secrets Act had bedevilled the nuclear industry and called for its use to be dropped. He criticised plant management and demanded a more independent means of overseeing the nuclear industry.

The government's attempts to 'ride out the Sellafield storm' were damaged by revelations from a physicist and former Sellafield employee, Dr Derek Jakeman, who furnished information showing radioactive pollution in the 1950s up to 40 times higher than had been previously acknowledged. According to one report, in 1955 Dr Jakeman and a colleague had taken geiger counters home to measure radiation levels there. Alarmed at the high readings they had asked for further information but had been refused and threatened with dismissal.

The Chernobyl disaster of a few months later maintained nuclear safety as a central public issue.

Government Inspectors were brought into the plant, some managerial reorganisation was effected and during the summer of 1986 a TV advertisement showing groups of school children at Sellafield invited the public to visit the plant and 'find out the truth'.

(This case study is intended as an aid to class discussion rather than as a comment on the handling of a business situation.)

## Think and discuss
1   Model Sellafield in the context of general and specific environments. (Fig. 2.2)
2   Describe how Sellafield's environment has become more diverse over the past 30 years.
3   What are the problems which this diversity creates for Sellafield planners?

## Difficulty

The interactive blend of wider environments, more change, remote origins of change and faster rates of change means that understanding and planning to meet the environments of the future and/or understanding and reacting effectively to things that are happening now are, for organisations in such environments, immensely *difficult* tasks. Difficult tasks, of course, require greater attention if they are to be performed well. Local authorities, for example, have been traditionally concerned with the specifics of their localities. Now, however, they need to devote more time and resources to planning effectively in a national and international context and to spotting and understanding the various political, economic, social and technological changes taking place in these wider environments.

## Danger

The trend we have identified so far is one which shows planning organisational success becoming more *difficult*. A further aspect of the trend in the nature of business environments – that from *safe* to *dangerous* – is largely responsible for making business planning activities *critical*. Difficulties in understanding the future only become *critically* problematical if the organisation has neither the *power* nor the *time* with which to nullify and/or otherwise react to changing environmental demands. The leading banks and building societies, for example, might have sufficient resource strengths and strong market positions to facilitate learning periods long enough for them to come to terms with the implications of their presently changing environments. However, in an increasingly competitive world (a situation fuelled by the impact of foreign competition and governmental free market directed strategies) organisations are losing their traditional power bases. Britain's cutlery, motorbike, and clothing industries provide examples of how, in competitive conditions, organisational survival is threatened.

Allison (7) has described power as 'an elusive blend of bargaining advantages and skill and will in using bargaining advantages'. Hirschman (8) has said that stakeholders in any system have three basic options:

(a)  to stay and contribute as expected (to exercise 'loyalty');

(b)  to leave (or 'exit');

(c)  to stay and try to change the system (to use 'voice').

Society, through its external stakeholder constituents is gathering power and, in its dealings with organisations, exercising 'voice' more regularly, forcefully and skilfully. In the context of a 'horseshoe of influence strategies' (see Fig. 2.3) we can see how, in particular, society is actively seeking to 'regulate it' (note the plethora of consumer legislation in the 1960s and 1970s and more current demands); to 'pressure it' (consider everyday media reports of social responsibility issues); and to 'restore it' (again, refer to recent governmental free market policies towards professions such as public utilities, local authorities, solicitors, opticians, etc.).

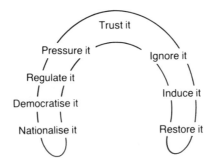

| | |
|---|---|
| *Nationalise it:* | impose social obligations through government ownership |
| *Democratise it:* | install workers, consumers, etc., into the organisation's decision making machinery |
| *Regulate it:* | control via legislation |
| *Pressure it:* | utilise pressure group campaigns, etc. |
| *Trust it:* | rely on the businessman's natural altruism |
| *Ignore it:* | rely on business adoption of the 'it pays to be good' maxim |
| *Induce it:* | pay the organisation the economic cost of its socially responsible behaviour |
| *Restore it:* | create perfect market conditions to stimulate self regulation based on consumer sovereignty |

**Figure 2.3  A conceptual horseshoe of societal influence strategies (adapted from Mintzberg,** *Power in and Around Organisations***, Prentice-Hall International, 1983)**

'Exit', however, provides the *major* reason for organisational change today. External stakeholders are 'exiting' critical resources. The government's rate-capping activities provide one example of critical exit. So, too, does the growing trend for shareholders and potential shareholders to make investment decisions on *social* as well as economic grounds. Today's customers, assisted by effective competition, show a growing propensity to 'vote with their feet' – to walk away taking their contributions to the competition. This newer tendency for external stakeholders to take their organisational transactions – and contributions – elsewhere, presents the major threat to our organisations (and the major impetus towards the adoption of new planning approaches). Tebbit (9) sums up today's 'exit' scenarios: 'As Chief Executives know very well, competition in world markets has never been fiercer than it is today. If we want to expand sales we have not only to attract customers but to keep them ... With so much on offer it becomes clearer every day that purchasers are becoming more and more discriminating. Wherever they are and whatever they want price is no longer the sole consideration. What they seek above all is reliability, fitness for purpose and value for money. In short they want quality.'

A changed stakeholder power balance between the organisation and its external stakeholders makes the need for effective business planning and strategic management critical. External stakeholders now have the power, will and skill with which to exercise effective 'voice' and/or 'exit'. (We discuss 'stakeholders' and 'power' more fully in our next chapter.)

Fewer business enterprises are able to rely on having the power or the time to realign, slowly, strategic misfits. The nature of today's environments, the direct opposite of the '4S' environments of 25 years ago (see Fig. 2.4) demands that practising management strategists pay due regard to the need to sophisticate their organisation's planning systems – to spot, understand and plan better effective adaptations to the changes taking place. Planning sophistication will be a major factor behind organisational success in the '4D' 1990s.

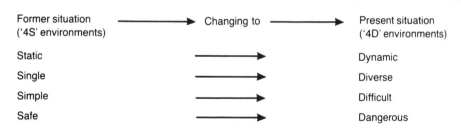

**Figure 2.4  The changing nature of business environments**

# Planning to achieve objectives in modern environments

Achieving effective planning systems for '4D' conditions is a very different task to that pertinent for '4S' environments. Planning for the '4S' environment can be likened to planning for a leisurely barge trip. We do not have to spend too much time pre-planning. It is almost enough simply to have a destination in mind when we set off. Once embarked on the trip we can remain fairly confident that with one reasonably diligent person at the wheel we can set course for a slow, uneventful and enjoyable journey. If things go wrong we are never too far away from dry land and a telephone. Each day is much like the last. Thus doing things successfully tomorrow can be achieved (perhaps with the help of some extrapolative forecasting) in a similar manner to how we have done things successfully today.

The '4D' environment, however, requires a planning approach more analogous with shooting uncharted rapids. In this case planning prior to departure is likely to be very important. Faced with such situations we will put a premium on whatever information might be available on what to expect on – and from – our journey. In the absence of sufficiently perfect information we would have to make 'best assumptions' based on any experience we might have of similar waterways. Perhaps we would solicit the opinions of other canoeing experts. Also we would spend much time on preparing the canoe and on carefully checking our safety equipment. Skilful and motivated crew members would be necessary to form a successful team and we would most likely spend much time training to sharpen up our minds and bodies so that as the course unfurls *every* member will be equipped to sense and react to the threats and opportunities which present themselves. We would embark on our journey with one underlying assumption clear – the environment in which we will be operating will have the capability to destroy us. Everyone would understand the need for effort towards adapting our positions to suit the changing demands of the environment unfurling before us.

In '4D' environments, therefore, it makes sense for organisations to develop planning skills in *anticipating* what is 'around the corner', *adapting* to what is 'happening now' and *responding* to shock events. It also makes sense to train *all* organisational members to contribute better to the ongoing quest for survival and success.

For our business organisations of today the messages arising from management strategy and day-to-day practice are clear, if largely ignored or unheeded. Business planning is the basic means of achieving organisational success and consequentially personal satisfaction. Today's environments make critical the design and implementation of 'today' planning systems. Management strategists who value their existing organisational tenures should already be utilising formal, sophisticated and comprehensive planning approaches towards this state. Fortunately, the theory of management strategy offers us many 'tips' on how organisational planners can design and implement 'complete' planning systems.

## Case study: Dunlop's rescue package

Christmas of 1983 saw the formerly great Dunlop Tyre & Rubber Company in less than festive mood. With profitability devastated by the slump in tyre sales and huge borrowings of £435 million Dunlop's somewhat perverse seasonal gift to its shareholders and bankers was the offer of the opportunity to invest further in the organisation and the promise of no dividend declaration in 1984 and 1985.

The proposed complete reorganisation of the company depended upon a prerequisite financial reconstruction. The plan, here, was to raise £72 million in new capital by a rights issue to existing shareholders and a share placing to institutional investors (all at 14p a share) and the conversion of £40 million in bank debt into 14p shares. A further £30 million raised by way of preference capital would complete the financial reconstruction and hopefully provide the foundation for renewed organisational success.

The banks involved in the rescue had also brought in to head the new Dunlop, Sir Michael Edwardes, Robin Biggam and Roger Holmes – all of whom joined Dunlop from the computer firm ICL. Sir Michael, who was to be Executive Chairman, was appointed on an annual salary of £156,000. Like Biggam (Finance Director) and Holmes (Director in Charge of Strategic Planning), Edwardes was also offered an option to buy millions of shares at the reconstruction price of 14p and thereby take a significant slice of the ownership of Dunlop – and the potential to net a paper profit of £2 million (if, following Stock Exchange suspension, the share prices returned to their pre-suspension price of 25p each).

Sir Michael stressed the theoretical nature of this profit at that time and said 'The banks have asked us to come in and do a good job and they want us to be highly motivated to do it.' The new team expected to get Dunlop back on the road to success through a mixture of cost cutting, better marketing and more capital spending. Borrowings were to be further reduced by asset sales. Sir Michael, at a press conference, stated that while reorganisation at Dunlop would be far more dramatic in terms of changing the nature of the business than had been the case during his leadership of British Leyland the impact on the people of the organisation would be far less dramatic.

Although the intention was to change the size and structure of the company, Sir Michael did not expect a large number of redundancies. David Warburton, National Officer of the General, Municipal Boilermakers & Allied Trades Union – the largest union in Dunlop – remained sceptical. His union was anxious to secure a viable and expanding future for Dunlop but, noting the complete absence of any consultation since the arrival of Edwardes, said, 'I can assure him that there will be no blank cheques from us on his reorganisation plans.'

(Before the above plans could be fully implemented BTR [formerly Birmingham Tyre & Rubber Co.], an organisation which had previously been a 'minnow' in the tyre and rubber industry of Dunlop's 'glory' days but which had since developed into one of Britain's biggest and most successful companies, 'stepped in' and after extensive negotiations with Edwardes and other Dunlop personnel, acquired ownership and management of the organisation.)

## Think and discuss

1    Refer to the 'Dunlop's Rescue Package' case study. Which stakeholder 'exit' has been mainly responsible for the demise of Dunlop? Was this action indicative of a failure in planning at Dunlop? Which groups at Dunlop are exercising 'voice'. Which of these are the most successful 'voice' exercisers and why? Which environmental variables have combined to cause Dunlop's demise?

2    Refer to your own organisation/industry (or one of your choosing). Use the '4S' to '4D' framework to identify changes in the nature of the environment which might have taken place over the past years. How would you describe the nature of your organisation's present environment?

# References

1    See, for example, F E Kast and J E Rosenzweig, *Organisation and Management*, 4th edn, Tokyo, McGraw-Hill, Kogan Kusha Ltd, 1985, Ch 6

2    D Katz and R L Khan, *The Social Psychology of Organisations*, John Wiley, New York, 1964

3    P F Drucker, *Managing for Results*, Heinemann, 1964, (as quoted in D E Hussey *Corporate Planning Theory and Practice*, 2nd edn, Pergamon Press, 1982, p 43)

4    L L Byars, *Strategic Management, Planning and Implementation Concepts and Cases*, New York, Harper & Row, 1984, p 59

5    For a discussion of Emery and Trist's environmental models and of pertinent organisational approaches for handling modern environments see C Stubbart, 'Why We Need a Revolution in Strategic Planning', *Long Range Planning*, 18 (6), December 1986, pp 68–76

6.   J Naisbitt, *Megatrends: Ten New Directions Transforming Our Lives*, Panthon, Bristol, Futura, 1984

7    G T Allison, *Essence of Decision: Explaining the Cuban Missile Crisis*, Boston, Little, Brown, 1971

8    A O Hirschman, *Exit Voice and Loyalty: Responses to Decline in Firms, Organisations and States*, Cambridge, Mass., Harvard University Press, 1970

9    N Tebbit, in *National Campaign for Quality*, DoT, 1983

## Recommended reading

T J Peters, *Thriving on Chaos*, Macmillan, 1988, particularly Chs 1 & 2

C Stubbart, 'Why We Need a Revolution in Strategic Planning', *Long Range Planning*, 18 (6), December 1986, pp 68–76

# 3 Aspirations planning

We begin our journey through the complete business planning system with an exploration of aspirations planning. In this chapter we seek to stimulate insight into the critical business planning problem of how to identify, understand and manipulate the aspirations of stakeholders within an organisation.

Organisations attract people – people who see the organisation as a source of satisfaction for their aspirations. These people have things to give to – as well as to receive from – the organisation. Aspirations planning, for our purposes, is 'planning to attract and to satisfy people, through organisational activity, as the means for ensuring the ongoing attainment of the strategic theme'. (In Chapter 1 we described the strategic theme as effective adaptations to environments through time.) We will also assume that 'an associated aim of the aspirations *planner* is that the organisation's activities should more nearly reflect his or her personal objectives'.

This chapter presents a number of models to help readers become more effective aspirations planners. The aim is to help readers to perform the aspirations planning tasks of:

(a) identifying the important people within an organisation;

(b) understanding their needs; and

(c) understanding their power and influence potential.

Finally, and importantly, this chapter should help readers design appropriate political bargaining strategies for creating and controlling interactions with stakeholders.

Our discussion proceeds as follows:

- The rationale for organisations and planning
- Stakeholders, aspirations and proxy payments
- Management strategy models of the rationale for organising
- The organisation as a political arena
- Systems goals within an organisation
- The stakeholder satisfaction cycle: benefits for everyone
- Business ethics, social responsibilities and management strategy
- Problems associated with stakeholder analysis
- Steps in aspirations planning

## The rationale for organisations and planning

The organisation (and its planners) are judged on how well desired outcomes have been achieved. The answer to the question 'Why do businesses plan?', therefore, is inextricably linked to the question 'Why are organisations created?'. Both answers can, as we shall see, be found in the context of people seeking to attain personal satisfaction. Organisations and the business planning systems which create and support them are fundamentally concerned with the creation and distribution of wealth and personal satisfaction. The essence of aspirations planning is that people form and associate with organisations to achieve personal objectives.

## Stakeholders, aspirations and proxy payments

Fundamental to management strategy is this assumption that people interact with organisations as a means of satisfying personal aspirations. This is often forgotten or ignored until the threat of organisational failure reminds its members of the relationship between organisational survival and the quality of personal life-styles. Motivation theorists such as Abraham Maslow (1) suggest that life itself is driven by a constant search to find ways of satisfying basic 'life' objectives. According to Maslow, for example, we move up a hierarchy of needs, step by step, after satisfying the more fundamental needs of the previous level (see Fig. 3.1).

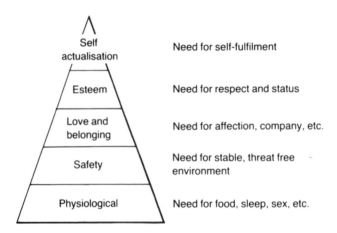

**Figure 3.1 Maslow's hierarchy of needs**

The attractive thing about organisations is that they help people to satisfy these basic needs. *Everyone* associated with an organisation can look forward to a wealth/satisfaction generating interaction. As Ansoff (2) says: 'In recent years, much interest has been excited by the atomic breeder reactor which appears to violate the law of conservation of energy by producing more fuel than it consumes. But the firm, an invention of the mid 19th century, was a similar miraculous breeder "reactor" except that, instead of breeding fuel, it was a breeder of wealth. It has several impressive features:

(a) it generates both goods and the buying power for goods;

(b) it creates jobs in three ways: in the firm itself; in the suppliers to the firm; and in the public sector;

(c) it supports the expansion of the social infrastructure, and provides a return to the investors (and to its other contributors).'

Figure 3.2 superimposes onto the Maslow pyramid some of the 'proxy' payments which managers and other workers receive and which relate to more basic aspirations. Other categories of people connected with the organisation can also be seen to take 'proxy' payments. The customer who buys a Rolls Royce, for example, might be seeking to satisfy a status-based objective. The near-bankrupt supplier who wins an important new customer might be delighted to have attained greater security. Thus the organisation attracts stakeholders (those people who have an interest in the organisation and see it as a satisfier of their aspirations).

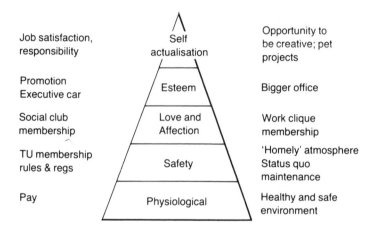

**Figure 3.2 Basic human needs and 'proxy payments'**

# Management strategy models of the rationale for organising

Those standing at the middle of this arena – the management strategists – have to decide what the ultimate objectives of the organisation are and who these objectives must serve. For whose benefit does the organisation exist? A number of alternatives heve been described in the theory:

(a) the organisation exists for the benefit of particular *categories of stakeholders;*

(b) the organisation exists for the benefit of those stakeholders who have the *power* to choose its objectives and influence its activities;

(c) the organisation exists for those stakeholders perceived to be *inside* the organisation;

(d) the organisation exists for *everybody* who contributes to its continued prosperity and survival.

For those involved in the planning of organisational objectives, the discussion which follows is intended to stimulate thought on such issues as:

- How might I identify important organisational stakeholders within an organisation?
- How might I understand what they seek from the organisation?
- Who are the important stakeholders (in terms of their ability to support or damage the organisation and my position therein)?
- Why and how should I cater for their needs and/or demands?

## Who are the stakeholders?

Over the past 30 years or so a number of different theorists have painted particular theoretical 'pictures' to describe and explain why and how organisations create objectives. One consequence of these works is the availability to management strategy of a catalogue of theories of the firm which, in totality, illustrates the organisation as a satisfier of the aspirations of a range of stakeholders. These stakeholders include:

(a)  owners

(b)  managers

(c)  workers

(d)  customers

(e)  suppliers

(f)  society and the public

We will next take a closer look at how theory has portrayed the positions of these six categories of stakeholder.

### Owners

Until comparatively recent times the neoclassical economic theory of the firm represented the most widely accepted picture for describing and explaining the objectives setting procedures in business. This theory owes much to the work of the nineteenth century economists such as Jeavons and Marshall and to the even earlier contributions of classical economists such as Adam Smith (3). This model of objectives setting reality is based on a variety of assumptions such as:

(a)  the firm exists solely for the benefit of its owner(s);

(b)  the owner's sole objective is to maximise his or her own financial wealth;

(c)  this sole stakeholder objective is achieved by the setting and attaining of a single organisation objective – profit maximisation.

Profit maximisation is assumed to be possible because:

(a)  the owner has total control and makes all the decisions – others merely carry out instructions;

(b)  the owner's decisions and all subsequent activity within the organisation are based on perfect knowledge and unbounded cognitive ability.

It is thus presumed that the owner knows all about present and future business conditions and can calculate mathematically all the permutations between all the factors involved in determining production costs, and sales levels and revenues. The owner can therefore work out and plan exactly that level of production where the cost of producing the last unit of output is equal to the extra sales revenue it will bring in. At this point the owner stops producing more. Up until now the sale price of each good has been more than the additional (marginal) costs incurred in producing it. Thus profits have been increasing. At the point where marginal cost equals marginal (additional) revenue, however, the firm stops producing. It has reached the point of profit maximisation. Increasing output further will produce greater comparative marginal costs. Because the organisation cannot increase the price it charges for its goods and services (in the marginalist theory price is assumed to be set by the forces of perfect competition and are thus outside the control of the firm) then further outputs will start to eat away profits already earned. Figure 3.3 illustrates the profit maximising activity.

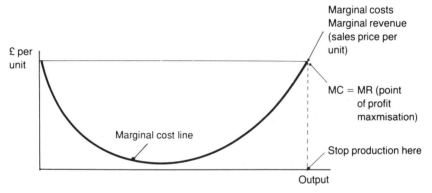

**Figure 3.3 The profit maximisation marginalist model**

## Managers

Neoclassical economists have provided us with a base model from which to develop more realistic models of the processes of objectives planning within organisations. In the 1950s 'managerialist' economists such as William Baumol (4) noted from first-hand experience in business consultancy that, for many organisations a more realistic picture would show that top managers, not owners, have most power over the distribution of organisational wealth and over the activities of the organisation. Theorists argue that in many commercial organisations – particularly the bigger ones – ownership and control do not necessarily go hand in hand. Many owners, for example, do not attend annual general meetings, let alone take part in more regular strategic decision making activities. In many enterprises, therefore, ownership and control are divorced. Top managers can thus attend to their *own* aspirations. For example, their position within the organisation enables them to acquire bigger salaries and bigger departments, they can instigate 'pet projects' and can benefit from a range of further 'perks'. This 'satisfaction package' can be well in excess of that market price (just enough to attract employees to join and work with the firm) assumed by the profit maximiser to be the price payable to managers.

Thus, managerialists have chipped away at the concept of the one, all powerful, owner stakeholder. The concept of maximisation did, however, remain: the managerialist's manager seeks to maximise his or her 'utility' (satisfaction) *subject to a minimum profit constraint*. The top management team in 'managerialist' organisations is aware of the need to keep shareholders (and bankers) happy if its members are to maintain personal security and a relatively trouble-free continuance of control. Baumol, for example, saw top managers pursuing their aspirations through an organisational objective of sales *revenue* (not volume) maximisation.

Growing sales means greater prestige, higher salaries, better bargaining positions with financiers and a more easily managed staff. However, such sales revenue maximisation objectives could only be followed to a point. Managers were assumed to be able to calculate that point at which profits may be so adversely affected that shareholders are dissatisfied. Figure 3.4 illustrates the sales revenue maximisation objective.

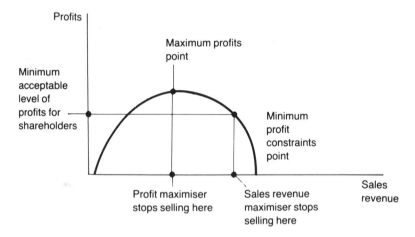

**Figure 3.4 Baumol's sales revenue maximisation model**

## Workers

Cyert and March's work in the early 1960s provided us with yet a further view of the process of goal formation in business (5). Their 'behaviouralism' model took us even further down the road away from the neoclassical, marginalist perspective. Behavioural theory sees the firm as a coalition of stakeholder groups. Inside the organisation shareholders, managers and *workers* have their own sets of objectives. Top management has the task of *satisfying* each group of stakeholders. Maximisation is impossible, according to Cyert and March, because decision-makers have neither the time, the resources nor the information and cognitive ability to make maximising decisions. Rather, top management seeks to provide acceptable levels of satisfaction to everybody. Stakeholders amend their aspirations and expectations according to their perceptions on matters such as how well other stakeholders are being treated, how well the firm is performing economically and how environmental conditions are likely to affect the organisation's economic performance. They realise that the organisation has limited resources and so 'filter' their demands so that at any one time each group is presenting only its list of most important, feasible objectives for the attention of top management.

Cyert and March see the firm pursuing objectives and activities in response to the influence and activities of departmental personnel (for example, the sales, production and finance departments each aim to attract their 'share' of the firm's budget allocation).

Mintzberg (6) refers to management and the workforce as 'the internal coalition' and categorises them into six groups of influencers:

(a)  the top, or general management (in our terms the management strategist and his or her close aides);

(b)  the operators (those workers who actually produce the products and services);

(c)  the line managers who stand in the hierarchy of line authority from the Chief Executive down to the first-line supervisors;

(d)  the analysts of the technostructure (staff specialists involved in the design of planning and control systems);

(e)  the support staff, comprising those staff specialists who provide indirect support to the operators and the rest of the organisation (the legal and public relations specialists, for example);

(f)  the ideology of the organisation which, Mintzberg suggests, although technically inanimate shows every indication of having a life of its own. The ideology is that set of beliefs shared by the people inside the organisation. Often referred to as the 'culture' of the organisation we shall spend more time with this influencer in Chapters 11 and 12 on team culture planning.

## Customers

Systems theorists see the organisation as an open social system transacting with people from outside the organisation. As long ago as 1954 Peter Drucker reminded us that high on the list of important external stakeholders is the customer: 'If we want to know what a business is we have to start with its purpose. And its purpose must lie outside the business itself. In fact it must lie in society since a business organisation is an organisation of society. There is only one valid definition of business purpose: to create a customer.'(7) Customers look to the organisation for products and services which offer value for money – commodities which, in the judgement of the customer, add to the overall quality of life bearing in mind the price paid. In recent decades the marketing concept has permeated much of business. Central to this concept is the belief that organisational success depends upon the production and delivery of desired satisfactions to customers. The achievement of value for money products/services is a major objective of the 'marketing led' organisation.

## Suppliers

Suppliers associate with the organisation in the hope of achieving contracts which produce profits and security. Thus, the business enterprise has to ensure that it has the capability to reward suppliers in order to acquire vital resources. Little theoretical attention has been paid to the organisation/supplier situation although concern over dwindling resources and a growing awareness of the impact suppliers can have on competitive positions means that this stakeholder is moving into sharp focus in the 1990s.

## Society and the public

More widely drawn societal stakeholders such as the media, governmental personnel and special interest pressure groups are increasingly exerting influence on today's organisations. Their demands require organisations to introduce objectives to ensure adequate standards of social, legal and moral responsibility. Aspirations towards the firm acting as a 'responsible corporate citizen' have been reflected in the amendment of the 'marketing concept' to a 'societal marketing concept'. The issue of social responsibility tends to confirm many writers' views that the organisation is now most clearly to be seen as a socio-economic instrument of society. It is also illustrative of how environments and environmental change have become the most critical issues with which organisations, management strategists, and business planning systems are having to deal.

## The organisation as a political arena

The preceding discussion of stakeholder positions introduced stakeholder groups as separate and discrete entities, each group, from owners to society, pursuing their demands of the organisation independently. A related progression of theoretical thought has, however, also developed from its profit maximising, rational/all powerful owner model into a contingency ('it depends') era. The newer, contingency theory of the firm sees the management strategist taking centre stage of a political arena (the organisation). It is the management strategist and top managers who have to manage a variety of changing stakeholder aspirations and power positions (see Fig. 3.5).

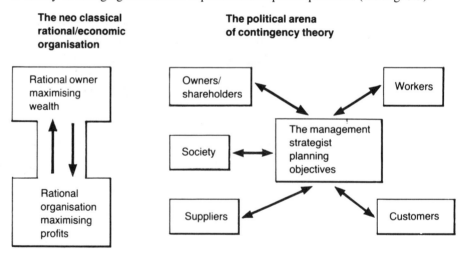

**Figure 3.5 Neo classical and political theories of the organisation**

## Power and influence

At the heart of the organisation as a political arena are the power relationships of its people. Power, according to Johnson and Scholes (8) is 'the extent to which individuals or groups are able to persuade, induce or coerce others into following certain courses of action'. If the management strategist is to introduce pertinent objectives and activities he or she needs to understand the power relationships which exist within the organisation and the factors which underlie the creation and the exercising of power. This section will examine, briefly, some management strategy insights into this subject area.

## Exit, voice and loyalty

Stakeholders might, at any one time, feel satisfied or dissatisfied with the way the organisation is treating them. In Chapter 2 we noted how, according to Hirschman (9), stakeholders have three basic options:

(a) to stay and contribute as expected (to exercise loyalty). We might expect this option to be taken more readily by those who feel happy with the way the organisation is conducting its affairs.

(b) to leave or 'exit'. The stakeholder who feels unable to influence significantly a change of organisational activity and who can see better options open elsewhere may leave the organisation.

(c) to stay and try and change the system – to exercise 'voice'. Here, the dissatisfied stakeholder decides to change, rather than acquiesce to or escape from organisational activities.

## Power, will and skill

Those stakeholders who wish to influence the process of planning objectives have to make the organisation responsive to their demands. If changes are to be made then the stakeholder needs to present his or her position of power and its associated demands in such a way that the decision-making body of the firm perceives the need to acquiesce to the demands made. Allison (10) suggests that the extent to which any stakeholder will influence change will depend upon a blend of:

(a) the power exhibited by the stakeholder;

(b) the stakeholder's will to be heard and achieve personal objectives;

(c) political skill used in making contact with and presenting a useful case to the decision-makers concerned.

We will take a look at each of these attributes in turn.

### Exchange dependency power

The first source of power available to a stakeholder is that created by *exchange dependency*. A stakeholder will have much exchange power if he/she has *control* of a resource, a technical skill and/or a body of knowledge which is *essential* to the functioning of the organisation or to the ongoing satisfaction of its decision-makers. Such essentials also need to be *concentrated* (in short supply or not readily available elsewhere) and non-substitutable (irreplaceable). Stakeholders with insufficiently concentrated power often form alliances with other change-seeking stakeholders to create more powerful *coalitions*. Of course, *countervailing* power can be exercised by the organisation in those cases where organisational inducements are also concentrated and non-substitutable.

## Case examples: powerful exchange dependency positions

(a) Questioned on TV about the size of his annual salary from ICI, the then Chief Executive Sir John Harvey-Jones referred to ICI's recovery and continuing success record under his leadership. He further suggested that his rare management strategist skills were transferable and that such skills might command three times his present salary in the USA.

(b) Many suppliers hold their relationship with Marks & Spencer in high regard. Others are wary of becoming embroiled in a dependent relationship which necessitates giving up control of decisions in areas such as factory layout and decor and the provision of staff welfare.

(c) When oil producers raised their prices dramatically in the early 1970s oil dependent users, generally, had no alternative but to pay up.

(d) Appointed to Tesco's board of directors at only 34, Barry Grange felt that the appointment reflected the growing importance of the computer division and the skills of its computer specialists. 'It's central to business. If the computer division doesn't deliver, then the company doesn't deliver.' Suppliers were aware of the new power structure within Tesco's ranks: 'You don't talk to my chairman' Grange told them, 'You talk to me.'

## Case example: using countervailing power

In 1988, the Canadian Foreign Minister, Mr Joe Clark, met the British Foreign Secretary, Sir Geoffrey Howe, to protest at a proposed law which would label fur garments 'caught in leg traps'. Mr Clark said the law would mean the extinction of Canada's arctic trappers. The Canadian Liberal Party urged Canada to scrap plans to buy nuclear-powered submarines from Britain if the British Parliament supported the labelling proposition.

## Social power

French and Raven have provided a further social power model which is based, largely, on an exchange dependency theme. Their framework reminds us particularly of how position power (for example that possessed by the owner or the manager) often affords the possessor the ability to reward or punish (even dismiss) those lower down the organisational hierarchy. It also introduces the concept of charisma – inherent persuasive power – as an influence source. French and Raven's social power typology (11) describes:

(a) *Legitimate or position power*. Power here is based on the position or office held by the individual.

(b) *Reward power*. People obey because they believe they will be rewarded in some way – psychologically or financially.

(c) *Coercive power*. Compliance is induced by fear of punishment or removal of rewards.

(d) *Expert power*. The expert is believed to possess more expertise or knowledge, and can therefore successfully influence others.

(e) *Referrent or charismatic power.* The initiator is perceived as having status, prestige, or an element of charisma.

## Perceived power

The more attractive the exchange being offered or, alternatively, the more damaging the effect of the exchange not taking place (due to stakeholder exit, for example) the more amenable will be the decision-maker to the demands being made, *provided the decision-maker perceives the stakeholder to possess power.*

The will and skill exhibited by stakeholders in their power struggles will be important here. For example, Salancik and Pfeffer (12) discuss how chief executives, once installed, build up a power base which can maintain their image of irreplaceability long after their particular skills are no longer pertinent to new environmental situations and/or problems. By publicising their importance managers can indoctrinate the organisation into implicit acceptance of it. In a similar way, traditionally important customers often continue to be afforded special terms and treatment despite the dwindling financial value of their accounts.

Other, more inherently powerful stakeholders, sometimes fail to persuade organisational decision makers of their real worth.

## The power of 'being there'

An additional source of power to exchange dependence is the power of 'being there'. Woody Allen makes the point that '90 per cent of success is being there'. Those with resource power have to present their demands to the decision-makers. Access to decision-making machinery and decision-makers is a necessary prerequisite to influencing organisational activities. However, such access can be a source of power in itself.

The people on the decision-making committee, often without any strong exchange power, nevertheless become important influencers simply by virtue of their being involved in the decision-making process. Polytechnics and local authorities provide ready examples of how those prepared to work at gaining access to committees can personally influence the policies of the organisation.

*Access to those who have power* is also a power source in itself. The wife of the chief executive, a friend of the government minister, the 'That's Life' presenter with access to the homes of customers, all can – and do – use their proximity to influence decisions.

## Will

Having a basis for power is not enough in itself. Many laws are ignored and broken, for example, because resources have not been expended towards their enforcement. Stakeholders who are happy with their lot and are thus inactive power players might find their positions worsening as other more active players take advantage of their absence. Even powerful stakeholders have to expend energy towards bolstering their perceived power positions and presenting their demands.

## Skill

Unsuccessful job applicants might take solace from the notion that the best person for the job perhaps only rarely gets it. Highly suitable candidates often fail to attract the attention of potential employers because of an inadequately prepared application form. Others, having overcome this first hurdle, might then fail to convince the selection committee of their real worth. So it is with the organisation's political power struggles. The important factor in controlling organisation activity is *perceived* power. Skilful union negotiators, as an example, have undoubtedly, on occasions, won better deals than their inherently weak positions deserved. Experts with stronger, more rationally based arguments often lose decisions in committees to more charismatic and eloquent opponents. Power and will must be supplemented by skill if they are to influence the planning of organisational objectives.

## Political bargaining strategies

A major purpose of the aspirations planning process is to reach decisions and consequent action through which objectives and associated strategies will be adopted. Current theory emphasises the central role of the management strategist and his or her colleagues (together often referred to as the 'dominant coalition') in this process. Thus, Ansoff (13), for example, sees strategic developments starting from and biased towards the management strategist's own preferred courses of action. Ansoff suggests that eventual 'legitimacy strategies' should be developed by the management strategists through a process which takes account of the aspirations and power positions of the organisation's stakeholders, to determine:

(a) the objectives and strategies which seem most pertinent after analysis of the total stakeholder situation;

(b) the management strategist's own preferred objectives and activities;

(c) appropriate 'bargaining strategies' which, with skilful execution seem likely to narrow the gap between the 'most pertinent' and the 'most preferred', as in (a) and (b) above.

The ability to choose pertinent 'bargaining strategies' is, of course, a characteristic enjoyed by the skilful power influencer. Mitroff (14) offers the following categorisations of 'bargaining strategies':

(a) Convert (change) the stakeholder by means of:

- making demands of the stakeholder through the exercise of power and authority;
- persuading the stakeholder by appealing to reason, values and emotions;
- bargaining with the stakeholder by means of economic exchange;
- negotiating with the stakeholder to reach 'give and take' compromise;
- problem solving with the stakeholder by means of sharing, debating, and arriving at agreed upon mutual perceptions.

(b) Fight the stakeholder and politic to overpower him or her by means of:

- securing and marshalling the organisation's resources;
- forming coalitions with other stakeholders;
- destroying the stakeholder.

(c) Absorb aspects of stakeholder demands by incorporating them by means of co-optation.

(d) Coalesce with the stakeholder by forming a coalition with joint decision-making powers.

(e) Avoid or ignore the stakeholder.

(f) Appease the stakeholder by giving in to some demands.

(g) Surrender to the stakeholder.

(h) 'Love' the stakeholder by forming an emotional bond or special relationship.

(i) Be or become the stakeholder by transforming the organisation into the stakeholder through merger, imitation, idolatry, or role modelling.

Mitroff views this *one* (political only) aspect of the management strategist's job as a highly difficult and creative task: 'Little wonder, having identified these different ways of changing stakeholders, that analysts of a social system and policy makers often advocate such different policies. All of the properties regarding stakeholders and their ability to change through a certain means are highly volatile, changing, and subject to debate. It is exceedingly easy to assume very different capabilities with regard to each stakeholder's ability to change.'

His comments in this context remind us of the immensely difficult and creative total role of the practising management strategist. It is perhaps small wonder that strategists who continue to exercise skill in their jobs often command a high premium in the form of expensive organisational inducements.

## Think and discuss
Refer to the Sellafield case study illustrated in Chapter 2, p 21.

1  Model Sellafield as a political arena.
2  Identify stakeholder coalitions/potential stakeholder coalitions.
3  Use Maslow's hierarchy of needs to identify the aspirations of the stakeholders involved.
4  Which stakeholders are most powerful and why?
5  Identify any political bargaining strategies which BNFL has employed. Suggest potential bargaining strategies for the future.

# Systems goals within an organisation

Henry Mintzberg (15), who defines a goal as 'the intention behind a decision or action', identified four *systems goals*, 'those goals that organisations as systems to themselves pursue'. These systems goals are:

(a) growth;

(b) survival;

(c) efficiency;

(d) control of the environment.

The achievement of these goals is of common interest to all internal members of the organisation. The strategist, presumably, decides which stakeholders are 'inside' the organisation. 'Inside' might be viewed, for example, as comprising family members only in a tightly knit family firm or as comprising owners, managers, workers and perhaps suppliers, too, in an organisation which sees a wide common interest being served by the provision of effective service to customers.

## Growth

Generally, large organisations are safer than smaller ones. They have more 'slack' to fall back on and more resources with which to respond to adverse environmental trends. Often, 'big' means 'powerful' in relation to external stakeholders. Government support is more readily available in cases of survival crises in large enterprises. Smaller firms are more readily left to 'go to the wall'.

Lower costs of production associated with economies of scale and learning curve effects also tend to flow to the giants of industry. Because growth improves the level of benefits available to the people inside the organisation it becomes a basic system objective of the organisation.

## Survival

Any organisation set up for other than a limited period or a specific objective has to take ongoing steps to ensure its survival. Failure to ensure the attainment of this basic objective means, of course, that the organisation ceases to be a source of satisfaction for its members. Long organisational life often blurs the fundamental importance of this objective. Anyone who has worked under the cloud of imminent organisational failure, however, will be well aware of the relationship between this goal and personal life objectives.

## Efficiency

Over time every organisation must be efficient. Otherwise it will run out of resources and fail to survive. Even 'not for profit' enterprises such as charitable institutions and socially orientated governmental bodies have to work within budgets. The very essence of organisations, as we have seen, is their ability to create more from less. While the fanatical search for maximum economic efficiency might be neither desirable nor possible, it is within every organisation members' interest to work towards at least a break-even situation.

## Control of the environment

The organisation earns its living from its environment. It has to adapt to the changes taking place there. The control objective is concerned with achieving a strong bargaining position with environmental stakeholders and with creating stable operating conditions.

## The stakeholder satisfaction cycle: benefits for everyone

An enduring (but only more recently clearly evident) primary objective for management strategists, at the helms of their planning systems, is the achievement of a *stakeholder satisfaction cycle*. The key to the attainment of this objective lies in the

LEEDS METROPOLITAN UNIVERSITY LIBRARY

design and implementation of activities which *efficiently satisfy external stakeholders.* Thus, contributions (payment from customers, materials from suppliers), *non*-interventions from society's publics (pressure groups and government agencies, etc.) are attracted and the organisation earns 'excess money' – the means with which to satisfy *internal* stakeholders and so maintain their contributions to the external stakeholder satisfaction effort. Thus the organisation is a system for mutually beneficial exchanges.

Effective reallocation of 'excess money' (perhaps through investment in product service improvements and/or in staff welfare improvements) has, for successful organisations, stimulated a stakeholder satisfaction cycle which spins ever more successfully into the future. If the organisation gets the distribution process wrong, however, a damaging *dis*satisfaction cycle can ensue. As one manager from a large heating supplier firm told us: 'We cut back on the quality of our product. A major customer realised what we had done and cancelled its order. We're still trying to get over the effects of that move.' At Jaguar Cars, previously supportive workers threatened costly strikes because they felt that the firm's 1989 wage offer did not reflect a fair share of the company's recently enlarged 'success cake'. A dissatisfaction cycle which perpetuates rounds of decreasing stakeholder contributions eventually results in total organisational failure and exhaustion of the enterprise's capacity to offer personal aspirations satisfactions. However, successful 'today' management strategists (and Britain has a number of them) are planning their organisations on the understanding that business planning is not about the implementation of begrudged responses to the pressures of external stakeholders but rather about the creation and maintenance of an effective stakeholder satisfaction cycle.

## Case example: a clash of business rationale philosophies

In 1986/87 BTR and Pilkington fought out a 'takeover' battle. BTR appealed directly to Pilkington's shareholders; its offer document confined itself to providing statistics for the 1980s which showed growth in earnings per share, dividends, increases in share price and increases in return on sales. BTR accused the Pilkington management of being too complacent, insufficiently competitive in outlook and insufficiently concerned with profitability and the aspirations of shareholders. A change to the more aggressive, management controlled culture that was BTR's was necessary, according to the document, to improve financial performance.

Pilkington, in defending its position, appealed to a wider range of stakeholders and defended its philanthropic image and its progressive industrial relations policy which were said to have generated a mini-welfare state in St Helens. A pamphlet issued by Pilkington during the takeover period claimed 'We believe in the creation of wealth, not in the long-term poverty of short-term profit-taking. By wealth we mean the wealth of all those communities in which ... we operate – shareholders, customers, suppliers and employees.  If a company serves the needs of each of those communities and assists in the creation of their wealth then the environment in which it operates will be healthy, and profits, and the wealth of shareholders will follow.'

Pilkington's concern for more than commercial interests was recognised as being a major invisible asset in its successful rebuff of the BTR take over attempt.

(A case study by Claire Capon, covering the BTR/Pilkington take over battle, is available in a companion volume (16).)

## Business ethics, social responsibility and management strategy

The BTR/Pilkington illustration raises the issue of social responsibility. Associated with the concept of social responsibility is the study of *business ethics*. This is the study of morality in and around business organisations – from legal and conscientious standpoints. Morality is concerned with 'goodness' and 'badness' in the context of human conduct towards fellow humans.

De George (17) has traced the evolution of business ethics into an independent interdisciplinary field of study which integrates contributions from business academics and practitioners, philosophers, theologians and social scientists. Ethics as a topic for business strategists will 'come of age' in the 1990s. Presently the study of business ethics focuses on three business areas: the macro economic implications of the free-enterprise system (which increasingly is being studied in a global context); the activities of the corporation in society (the issue of social responsibility); and the morality of individuals in business interactions (the issue of ethics in business).

De George describes how ethics as an area of concern and action in both academia and business organisations is 'mushrooming' in the United States. For example, a number of business ethics institutions are now well established and are actively promoting the institutionalisation of the study. Many organisations conduct social audits as part of regular practice. Big companies such as Chase Manhattan run 'in-house' courses on the subject and numerous 'ethics committees' are operational. In the USA more than 40,000 students study the subject and are served by a growing catalogue of texts and case studies.

Fuelled by heightened awareness of issues such as bribery and corruption in business and government, pollution from business, and the impact on the individual employee and on society generally, of the organisational quest to constantly improve economic productivity, business ethics is becoming a multinational issue of major importance for the 1990s and the 2000s. In this respect Europe once again lags behind the United States but is seeking to catch up.

This section of the book is not intended to provide an in-depth treatment of this increasingly important subject area. Also, we will 'dodge' the normative aspects of business ethics (normative judgements require decision makers to make up their minds about 'what should be', based perhaps more on subjective, social, emotional yardsticks and less on scientific, economic, objective grounds). Rather, in keeping with the thrust of this book we will provide a brief discussion on the ways in which a theoretical principle which underpins the business ethics debate might help management strategists become *better strategic decision makers/implementors.* 'Better' here, does not imply 'more moral', but 'more rational'.

Thus, this discussion suggests that ethical principles can help organisational strategists to bring better information and thought to the decision-making processes of objectives setting, strategic analysis, strategy generation, evaluation and choice and implementation (as per the decision-making cycle shown in Fig. 1.1, p 2). This section concerns itself with just one of the 'ethical principles' which underpins the modern business ethics debate – the *utilitarian principle.*

## Decision-making benefits from the application of the utilitarian principle

The Headingley Library
www.leedsmet.ac.uk/lis/lss

ms on loan

tomer        Esiyok, Elif

                        Due Date

IM study text: Di        10/1/2008,23:59
3028756

trategic marketin        10/1/2008,23:59
4017606

trategic marketin        10/1/2008,23:59
2933705

esearching and wr        10/1/2008,23:59
308063

siness planning          10/1/2008,23:59
819248

18.12.2007 13:54:27

r renewals telephone (0113) 812 6161

Thank you and see you soon!

ally accredited to Jeremy Bentham (1748–1832) who
n and publicly acceptable norm for justifying
al policies and legislations. *Utilities* are benefits – of
nly economic benefits. The utilitarian principle holds
s that one which produces the *greatest amount of net*
d *(or across society)*. It requires that not only should a
ositive benefit/cost balance *but that it should produce
ison to any other alternative potential strategies.* Thus
is concerned with the opportunity costs of strategic
aking process of the systematic and optimising type
ng cycle model illustrated in Fig. 1.1. (p 2). In its aim
ts it is akin to the economist's neoclassical, profit
ational activity. In comparison with a neoclassical
it can be argued that the ethically orientated utilitarian
odern strategist. This is because it generates a better
n which the strategist might make more informed
er he/she or others might consider the ultimate decision
ne). The utilitarian ethical model generates better
cision-makers towards an investigative process which

akeholders being considered. The traditional economic
vironment – merely accepting it as 'being there' and,
perfect market conditions, 'being a consumer powerful
rganisational theorists describe the world as a 'complex
social network' (18) and advocate the need for modern day strategists to make
'stakeholder trawls' of a much wider and deeper nature. In this way, the strategist
might obtain a more comprehensive and longer term view of the opportunities and
threats facing the organisation and might avert disasters which seem to occur with
increasing incidence in modern, 'global village', highly competitive and highly
innovative business situations.

Similarly, the traditional economic model assumes the existence of an all
powerful, owner-entrepreneur *inside* the organisation. This key player is assumed to
be able to buy all internal factors of production, including the workforce, at an exact
market price which, in effect, is the price of a 'fair day's work for a fair day's pay'.
He/she can thus control internal activity to ensure that his/her profit maximising
strategies are operationalised exactly as intended and at a pre-planned, non-changing
cost. The profit maximising entrepreneur, therefore, has little need to consider his/her
internal workforce other than in amorphous, easy to control, terms. In contrast, the
ethical utilitarian model demands that each section and each member of the workforce
should be given separate attention because each section and each member might have
different interests and adopt different positions in the context of a proposed stategy.

In many modern business situations workers seek to influence decisional choices
and the implementation of strategic developments. Thus, the more detailed analysis
implied by the ethical model is likely to be more helpful to the strategic decision-
maker, not only in reaching conclusions from an ethical platform but also in

understanding the power and influence structures at work in his/her political arena and in gaining insights into the opportunities and threats, strengths and weaknesses associated with the developments being considered.

(b) *It widens the catalogue of 'utilities' beyond economic aspirations only.* The neoclassical economic model assumes that man is in pursuit of economic maximisation objectives only. Much theory within management strategy suggests otherwise (1). The managerial economists referred to earlier, for example, have described managers seeking to obtain prestige, status, job security, and 'pet project' satisfaction from their work (4).

If strategic decision-makers can gain better understanding of the real motives at work in and around their organisations then not only will they be better able to make decisions in an ethical context but they will also be better able to design 'political bargaining strategies' which address the real motives and positions of powerful stakeholders. In this way, ethical or not, the strategist will have a better chance of attaining the outcome he or she is seeking to achieve.

(c) *It is based on the view of the organisation as a socio-economic instrument of society.* Whereas the traditional economic model is introverted, and 'closed black boxish' (it concentrates on arranging internal production processes to achieve optimum efficiency and ignores external situations), the utilitarian model clearly requires decision-makers to assess the impact of their decisions on society as a whole – the utilitarian decision would be one which improved society's lot *regardless* of whether the organisation itself benefitted.

Again, regardless of the nature of the decision ultimately taken, such an approach demands a wider and more futuristic information trawl. The information thus gained should be more appropriate to the organisation's own 'systems goals' (15) of growth and survival. The theory of management strategy is now grounded in a model which sees the organisation as an open social system as described in Chapter 2. This model is being increasingly adapted to portray the organisation as a social system which exists *principally for the benefit of society* (19). In order to survive in the longer term, strategists and organisations need to make decisions in this wider context. This will help ensure that organisations continue to achieve productive adaptations to and exchanges with their environments. The making of 'fast bucks' at the expense of societal well-being is increasingly likely to be damaging, ultimately, to the organisation itself.

## Steps in the utilitarian analysis process

The utilitarian approach would require the strategist to take into account:

(a) the full range of stakeholders affected by the decision to be made, many of whom are likely to attempt to influence the decisional processes leading to and from the decision;

(b) the aspirations of the above stakeholders in the context of potential development choices;

(c) an eventual choice of strategic development which maximises total net aspirational satisfaction.

In this section we are suggesting the above process as an aid to decision-making rationality without necessarily prescribing the desirability of the outcome described in (c). In other words, the decision-maker might use the process inferred by the utilitarian model but could reserve ultimately the right to use his/her own judgement and make his/her own decision, on ethical and/or other grounds.

## Problems associated with stakeholder analysis

Notwithstanding the benefits which might flow from the adoption of utilitarian analysis, the process can be fraught with difficulties and requires strong analytical skills. This is the case, more generally, with stakeholder analysis. Skill is required because these analyses necessitate the sorting out of information 'messes' created by:

(a) The need to understand the different power positions of different stakeholders already in or who subsequently enter, the decision-making arena.

(b) The existence of numerous stakeholders, many of which are difficult to perceive. A simple listing of the parties expressing interest in the outcome of the BTR/Pilkington acquisition attempt will indicate the enormity of a task which seeks to identify all parties who might be affected by such a strategic development.

(c) The difficulty in measuring and quantifying interests and aspirations. How can long-term national interest be measured, perhaps from a governmental perspective, for example? – or how do you measure the quality of life changes for workers and managers involved in an acquisition situation? – and how do you measure future outcomes, i.e. before an acquisition strategy has been implemented?

(d) The need to produce an audit of stakeholder interests many of which will be conflicting and changing. The Sellafield case study (p 21) demonstrates how groups of stakeholders perceive the same situation in different cost/benefit 'lights' – one person or group can 'wear a number of stakeholder hats'.

### Think and discuss
Refer again to the Sellafield case study.

1   Identify the stakeholders involved and any coalitions between different groups.
2   Identify the aspirations of each of the stakeholders.
3   Identify the conflicting aspirations *within* groups.

(e) The need to estimate the unknown, in terms of assessing the opportunity costs of alternative ways forward. For most decisional situations there will be a multitude of alternative potential development directions and methods. In the BTR/Pilkington situation these could have included options such as 'Do nothing' (allow each organisation to carry on independently, as before); 'Collaborate' (work together on product/market developments in a manner which falls short of full blown merger/acquisition); and 'Do something completely different' (ultimately, for BTR, this was the strategy pursued).

(f) The need to conduct a stakeholder (and ethical) analysis in situations characterised by shortages of time, people, money and expertise. Small organisations often do not have people with the spare time and/or expertise for sophisticated analyses. Neither might they have the money available with which to buy in appropriate services. Bigger organisations, too, sometimes need to move quickly and to make decisions before the information and insights of a carefully undertaken stakeholder analysis can be made available.

The utilitarian principle does not stand alone in underpinning the business ethics debate. Other principles include those of treating people as ends (as well as means) and of 'only doing to others as you would be done by'. (These principles will be discernible as principles advocated for effective team culture planning in our discussions in Chapters 11 and 12.) The issue of business ethics is moving towards centre stage of the management strategy debate. This brief utilitarian orientated look at the subject of business ethics has been intended as a timely introduction to what will become an important topic of debate for managers and as an indicator of the usefulness (and problematic nature) of introducing an ethical perspective into strategic decision-making.

## Steps in aspirations planning

Someone has to take ultimate responsibility for the creation of organisational wealth and the subsequent distribution of personal satisfactions. The management strategist has this duty. The management strategist is at the centre of the organisation's political arena and its stakeholder satisfaction cycle. The organisation's planning systems are *the* means by which aspirations and objectives are determined and satisfied.

Through their impact on the strategic theme, planning activities determine how successfully the organisation, as a system, survives and/or grows, and, consequently, determine the level of wealth available for distribution to the people of the organisation.

The organisation itself is *the* strategy for achieving the personal aspirations of its stakeholders. This book is an attempt to help those concerned with the attainment of successful organisation to consider how planning systems are fundamental to the setting and achieving of organisational – and, hence, personal – success. The interactive nature of organisational planning systems means that we shall, inevitably, return to the subject of aspirations and objectives again, particularly when we consider the setting of efficiency objectives and the administrative benefits to be had from the system of 'management by objectives'. Before we move on, however, the following checklist of aspirations planning summarises the coverage of this chapter. Most of the benefits from using this checklist will flow from discussions around issues raised. Thus consider:

(a) The organisation as a catalogue of stakeholders present and future. Who are they?

(b) Which of these stakeholders are, or will be, sufficiently powerful to require the further consideration of the planning team?

(c) What aspirations do these powerful stakeholders have in respect of their associations with the organisation?

(d) What are the sources of power and influence available to these stakeholders?

(e) How would a 'pecking order' of important present and future stakeholders appear?

(f) What is the nature and extent of any dissatisfaction experienced by important stakeholders from their organisational outcomes?

(g) What kinds of 'voicing' or 'exit' might these stakeholders undertake if present dissatisfactions remain?

(h) What are the likely consequences of such action on the organisation and on the management strategist(s)?

(i) How might higher and/or new levels of satisfaction improve present contributions and/or attract new contributions from existing or potential stakeholders?

(j) What might be the consequence of such improvements for the organisation and its management strategist(s)?

(k) How has the organisation performed as a stakeholder satisfaction cycle generator?

(l) How has the organisation performed in the context of 'systems goals' attainment?

(m) How has the nature of the organisation's environment changed? How is it likely to change? Which stakeholder influences lie behind these changes?

(n) What bargaining strategies/organisational activities seem to commend themselves in the light of the above deliberations?

(o) Does an ethical perspective generate new information and insights?

The management strategist together with his or her top planning team is responsible for the overall position adopted by the organisation in relation to its stakeholders and for its associated organisational activities and objectives. Planning in this area (as in many other business planning areas) is a complex task and there is no simple course of action. Nevertheless, successful plans, decisions and activities in the context of stakeholder aspirations underpin successful organisations.

## Case study: Lord Sieff's acceptance speech

'I am honoured to receive this award, but this would not have come about without the co-operation and hard work of my many colleagues at Marks & Spencer.

'We at Marks & Spencer co-operate with the British Institute of Management from which, I hope, we mutually benefit. I was delighted to learn that the BIM is expanding its work because strong and enlightened management is essential for economic success on which the health of the nation depends.

'I want to talk a little tonight about the management principles of Marks & Spencer. This year we celebrate our centenary. I doubt whether my grandfather, Michael Marks, when he opened his penny stall in 1884 in the Leeds open market, could have foreseen what that stall would become one hundred years later.

'Such success as we have achieved is due largely to our philosophy and principles to which we adhere. While our policy on merchandise and departments that we run is flexible, our principles are sacrosanct. They are:

(a) We are concerned with high quality and good value, not cheapness; if we cannot get what we want we do not knowingly sell an inferior line. We are not interested in the 'fast buck'.

(b) We buy British goods and manufactured foodstuffs wherever possible. Over 90 per cent of St Michael goods are made or grown in the United Kingdom.

(c) We implement a policy of good human relations at work. And in the last decade we have practised a policy of constructive involvement in the communities in which we operate.

'How do we implement these principles? First, our concern for quality: we work closely with our suppliers at every stage in the production of our goods. That means going back to the suppliers of the raw material so that the raw material producer or farmer works with the manufacturer or food processor and ourselves to supply our customers with what they want. This team work is essential for the production of goods which represent both high quality and good value, and which are profitable to produce and sell.

'Let me give you three examples of goods often largely imported which are profitably produced for us in the United Kingdom:

(a) Men's shirts: In this country 50 per cent of men's shirts are imported and 50 per cent are home-produced – we are the largest sellers of men's shirts in the country and 99 per cent of the shirts we sell are produced here.

(b) Footwear: In this country £2–2.5 billion of footwear is sold each year – 60 per cent imported, 40 per cent home-produced. It is our fastest growing department and with us 20 per cent is imported and 80 per cent home-produced.

(c) Food: Twenty years ago we bought our carrots from Holland. We have the same climate as Holland so I thought we must be able to produce them here. Our first experiments failed. Then a farmer in Lincolnshire said he thought he could produce the Amsterdam forcing carrot. Our first year's turnover with him was £80,000; now it is £13 million.

'The first builders of our business were my uncle, Simon Marks, and my father, Israel Sieff, who learned from that great scientist and Israel's first President, Chaim Weizmann, how science and technology could be applied to maintain and improve the quality of the most ordinary of goods. So we make use of technological developments.

'As well as developing our technologists and design teams, we encourage our suppliers to do likewise and to seek new ideas. We regard our suppliers as partners. We encourage them, like ourselves, to visit our stores and talk to our sales assistants and our customers about their products. Then we both learn what is desirable and what is wanted. We want them to make good profits to be able to invest in new machinery; to pay good wages and reward their shareholders.

'By purchasing all we can in this country we have preserved and increased jobs in traditional industries, all regarded as doomed and by entering new markets we have created new jobs.

'For example, a small woodwork company in Devon, the Carpenters Workshop, who had six skilled workers, approached us four years ago. We made a trial from them of six St Michael bathroom items. They were successful and to meet our demand they acquired and equipped a new factory to produce St Michael goods. The staff has increased from six people in 1981 to 70 now. It will shortly reach 100. Most were recruited from the dole queue. Our turnover with them will be about £2.5 million this year.

'When we cannot obtain at home the quality, value or innovation demanded by our customers, we go abroad. For instance, we import moccasins from Italy – there is little production in this country; apart from moccasins hand made to order at very high prices.

'Once our foreign suppliers have set themselves up to do business with us, providing they produce goods of high quality and good value, and remain innovative, we have a moral obligation to remain with them, as we do with our British suppliers. But the demand for moccasins is increasing. We found a very small group at Norwich who had set up on their own, producing this type of shoe.

'At first they didn't want to deal with us – we were too big. Today they are producing one hundred dozen moccasins a week of high quality and value for us. They now employ 25 people and will grow substantially in the next 12 months.

'This policy of having goods produced or grown at home, whenever possible, entails those at the top not only laying down such a policy but also ensuring that it is understood by all concerned with buying right down the line.

'It needs patience and perseverance but much can be achieved. We also try to persuade our overseas suppliers to open processing and finishing plants in the United Kingdom and to employ British people. So far nine overseas suppliers have invested £12 million here in the United Kingdom and created 1,700 British jobs for our production.

'Now I want to talk about our policy of good human relations at work and in the community.

'Throughout my 50 years with Marks & Spencer I have been involved with the creation of wealth in co-operation with companies in many fields. I have found that too often there is insufficient understanding by top management of the importance of good human relations at work, and ignorance by people generally of the importance of wealth creation for the benefit not only of those immediately concerned but of the community and the country as a whole.

'The British Institute of Management is playing its part in the current campaign by industry and commerce to educate the educators. Your conference last week on schools/industry links will have helped in this respect.

'There will be little or no improvement in the standard of living and the quality of life unless we improve our economic performance. Our future depends on the contributions which industry and commerce can make to increasing wealth, for the benefit of all. We are seeing some progress in certain areas but we have a long way to go.

'We are lucky in this country that we still enjoy a free democratic society. A dynamic free enterprise sector operating within the mixed economy is one of the foundations of democracy. Without a progressive and dynamic free enterprise sector central government will take over more and more and tell us what to do and often, where and how to do it, and democracy as we understand it will disappear.

'The development of good human relations at work is vital for the maintenance of free enterprise. Good human relations at work only develop if top management believes in their importance and sees that such a policy is dynamically implemented.

It costs time, effort and money, as well as determination, but it is time, effort and money well spent.

'At Marks & Spencer we try to keep all our staff informed of proposed developments and take their views into account. At least we try: Unfortunately, too many managers in this country tell employees as little as possible instead of as much as possible.

'Our employees in the United Kingdom number over 50,000 full and part time, of whom over 900 are in personnel, largely spread throughout the stores. The priority of these staff managers is the well-being and progress of 60 or so people for whom each is responsible.

'A policy of good human relations is not something that can be left to the personnel department. The commitment must come from the top. Our senior people in the business spend much time on personnel problems.

'Fostering good human relations means more than just paying good wages. Top management must know how good or bad employees' working conditions and amenities are. If they are not good enough for those in charge they are not good enough for anyone.

'Last year we spent £57 million on welfare benefits – subsidised meals, hairdressing, medical and dental care, pensions, profit sharing. It is my experience that everything we have done in this field because we thought we had a moral obligation has turned out within a few years to be good business as well. Of course everyone must understand or be taught that none of this can happen unless the company concerned is profitable, that without profits there cannot be progress.

'Our staff appreciate our efforts and identify themselves with the business; many consider themselves partners not employees. Most exercise that best form of discipline – self-discipline. They work hard and are open to change. We have a stable and committed staff.

'But in today's difficult economic conditions good human relations with staff, suppliers and customers are not enough. Business cannot progress in isolation from the community in which it operates and in which its staff live. Many communities are suffering from unemployment and inner city decay.

'We donate, as do many other companies, substantial sums to charity; but the responsibility of a successful business to the community goes further. In addition to helping financially we have seconded for periods from six months to three years, some of our most capable people to help develop and direct various worthwhile community projects. Their work has been valuable and constructive. At any one time some 15 people are seconded along with people from other major like-minded companies such as IBM, United Biscuits, the high street banks, the oil companies and others.

'Much of the work is concerned with the decayed inner city areas and youth unemployment. While we have not solved the problems, in some areas we have alleviated them.

'If those who lead industry and commerce do not in their buying policies, seek sensibly British sources of supply; if they do not face up to their responsibility to pursue a policy of good human relations at work and constructive involvement in the community; then we must not be surprised if we wake up one morning to find ourselves members of a society that few of us want, where democratic values no longer operate and where there is little freedom, then if that happens we shall have only ourselves to blame.

'Thank you for listening to me. And thank you for honouring me with your gold medal.'

(Source: BIM text of *Gold Medal Award Acceptance Speech*, 1984)

### Think and discuss
Illustrate Marks & Spencer as a political arena and in the context of a stakeholder satisfaction cycle. Is M & S successful at achieving systems goals? Which M & S stakeholders are most and least powerful and why?

## Case study: sharing the cake at Hogarth Hosiery

You started in business on your own account three years ago when, together with two director colleagues, you acquired a small company – Hogarth Hosiery.

The three of you had contributed personal savings and redundancy payments (you had each 'fallen out of' your previous firm's rationalisation programme) and have since earned £10,500 per annum basic salary. Already the business has trebled in size and now generates a turnover of around £1 million and employs 150 people.

There exists an effective 'all round' team spirit and the organisation is already acknowledged externally as a useful contributor to the prosperity of what is a high unemployment area.

Finance, however, has always been a problem and all profits generated have, to date, been retained in the company. Projections made recently suggest that profits will be up 10 per cent on last year's figures and that by the end of the fourth year of trading you are likely to have a cash surplus of around £10,000.

No new investment in plant or machinery is envisaged at this time but the following expenditure alternatives are being contemplated:

(a) Share the surplus, if achieved, between the three directors in the form of a salary bonus.

(b) Spend £4,000 on a full overhaul of the presently dilapidated staff canteen and rest facilities.

(c) Donate £2,000 along with five other local businesses towards a community care project which will, over the next two years, renovate and beautify the nearby, presently polluted, canal complex.

(d) Donate £1,000 to a charity chosen by the directors.

(e) Donate £2,000 – plus the promise of a further £1,000 per annum for the next five years – towards the creation and running of a Chamber of Commerce backed employment advice/creation agency.

(f) Lend, on a three-year repayment basis, at less than bank rate, £5,000 to a financially 'hard up' supplier who has been a major and profitable source of supply but who now needs cash to improve production machinery.

(g) Choose some of the alternatives and share the surplus as a salary bonus.

### Think and discuss
1   Which alternative(s) would you choose?
2   How much bonus does your choice leave you with personally?

3   What further information might help you 'check' the choices made?
4   Would you attach any conditions to any of your alternatives?
5   Rank alternatives (a) to (g) in order of their immediate appeal.
6   Decide how you would allocate your surplus organisational wealth. Is your decision a rational economic one – or a socially biased 'satisficing' one?
7   Model your own organisation (or one of your choosing) as a political arena. Who are the most important stakeholders? What are their aspirations of the organisation? How successful is the organisation at satisfying the different stakeholders?

## For further study
Refer to the 'Crossed wires at British Telecom' case study in the accompanying case study book.

1   Model BT as a political arena.
2   Model BT as a stakeholder satisfaction cycle.
3   Which BT stakeholders are most powerful and why?
4   Is the BT stakeholder power structure changing and, if so, how and why?

# References

1   A H Maslow, *Motivation and Personality*, New York, Harper & Row, 1954
2   H I Ansoff, *Implementing Strategic Management*, New York, Prentice-Hall International, 1984, pp 131–2
3   See A Koutsoyiannis, *Modern Microeconomics*, Heinemann, 1980, Ch 14, for a useful discussion.
4   See A Koutsoyiannis, ibid, Chs 15–17, for useful discussions.
5   See A Koutsoyiannis, ibid, Ch 18, for a useful discussion.
6   H Mintzberg, *Power in and Around Organisations*, Prentice-Hall International, 1983, pp 26-30
7   P F Drucker, *The Practice of Management*, Pan Piper, 1968, p 52
8   G Johnson and K Scholes, *Exploring Corporate Strategy*, Prentice-Hall International, 1984, p 133 and Ch 5, generally.
9   A O Hirschman, *Exit Voice and Loyalty: Responses to Decline in Firms, Organisations and States*, Cambridge, Mass., Harvard University Press, 1970, p 30
10  G T Allison, *Essence of Decision: Explaining the Cuban Missile Crisis*, Boston, Little, Brown, 1971, p 168
11  J R P French and B Raven, *The Bases of Social Power*, in D Cartwright (ed) *Studies in Social Power*, Ann Arbor Institute for Social Research, University of Michigan, pp 150–67
12  G R Salancik and J J Pfeffer, 'Who Gets Power – and How They Hold on to It: A Strategic-Contingency Model of Power' in M L Tushman and W Moore (eds), *Readings in the Management of Innovation*, Pitman 1982
13  H I Ansoff, op. cit., p 146, and Ch 2.5 generally.
14  I I Mitroff, *Stakeholders of the Organisational Mind*, Macmillan, 1984, Ch 3.
15  H Mintzberg, op. cit., p 4 and Ch 16 generally.
16  Richardson, Patterson, Gregory and Leeson, *Case Studies in Business Planning*, 2nd edn, Pitman, 1992
17  R T De George, 'The Status of Business Ethics: Past and Future', *Journal of Business Ethics*, 6, 987, pp 201–11

18  I I Mitroff and R H Kilmann, *Corporate Tragedies*, Praeger, 1984, Ch 2
19  P F Drucker, for example, op. cit., p 453

## Recommended reading

H Mintzberg, *Power in and Around Organisations*, Prentice-Hall International, 1983
I Mitroff, *Stakeholders of the Organisational Mind*, Macmillan, 1984

# 4 Corporate planning and competitive positioning: strategic analysis

Most of us have longer term objectives – visions of how we want to be in the future. Many of us, for example, embark on higher education programmes so that we might be more attractive to future employers and more capable of progressing personally and professionally. Corporate planning is that planning activity most concerned with taking stock of the organisation's present situation, its longer term aspirations and its likely future environments and resource positions. This area of strategic planning is one from which flow major decisions on where and how the organisation will earn its future living. For most organisations this implies the need to choose competitive positions.

According to one corporate planning guru (1), corporate planning is 'planning for the company as a whole', with a long-range perspective. Igor Ansoff (2) records how this planning activity – which seeks to anticipate and respond to change through sophisticated analysis and evaluation – superceded long-range planning as environmental changes became 'progressively discontinuous from the past' and as, consequently, the setting of organisational objectives in the context of extrapolated forecasts became less useful.

Corporate planning, with its longer term perspective, is itself under attack. As we move into the increasingly volatile, unpredictable and competitive environments of the 1990s we need effective planning systems which can deal with today's, as well as tomorrow's, strategic problems. Nevertheless, we recommend the corporate planning process as *the first step* in any attempt to formalise and sophisticate organisational planning systems. The insight to be generated from this process enables sensible choices to be made about short- and longer term organisation changes, including changes to planning systems. For most organisations, too, it is still simply good sense to adopt a longer term planning perspective. In the individual context the adoption of longer term objectives has been correlated with psychological maturity. Extended future planning in the organisational setting is evidence of a collective psychological maturity.

Corporate planning is often modelled as a 'linear-sequential', step-by-step process which starts with strategic analysis and then moves on to the generation, evaluation and choice of strategic developments. In fact, the process is undoubtedly an iterative one where issues are considered and reconsidered as the process unfurls. The total exercise is designed to stimulate insight into such questions as, 'Where are we now?', 'Where are we going to?', 'Where do we want to be?', and 'How do we get there?'

This chapter introduces some of the models and techniques which management strategy has made available for use in the corporate planning process. In particular, it seeks to help readers develop skills in taking a 'health check' of the organisation, in making sense of mid- to longer term futures (and their implications for the enterprise) and in ascertaining stakeholders' preferred future organisational lifestyles. These are the tasks of strategic analysis. (Chapter 5 goes on to describe how the strategic analysis provides a springboard for making choices about strategic developments.)

'Strategic analysis is concerned with providing an understanding of the strategic situation which an organisation faces.'(3) This first chapter on corporate planning, then, will introduce to those strategists new to the techniques of management strategy, the means of developing an understanding through the analysis of three key decision making factors – people, resources and environment.

In this chapter we consider the following strategic analysis topics:

- Aspirations analysis
- Environment nature analysis
- Analysis of the structure of the environment
- Ranking opportunities and threats
- Resource analysis
- Ranking strengths, weaknesses and distinctive competencies

# Aspirations analysis

Chapter 3 on aspirations planning considered the 'people' side of planning and decision-making. We provided a model of organisational strategy-making which showed management strategists planning strategic activity. Organisational developments were shown to reflect the strategists' own preferred developments, modified in the light of the perceived preferences of other important stakeholders (see Fig. 4.1).

**Figure 4.1  The organisation as a political arena**

Important questions to be answered by management strategists seeking to understand the constraints and opportunities associated with stakeholder aspirations include:

(a)  Who are the important organisational stakeholders?

(b)  What are their power bases and what are their reactions to particular strategies likely to be?

(c)  What will be the likely effects of these reactions?

(d)  How should strategies be shaped to take account of stakeholder desires?

Readers are advised to reacquaint themselves with the concepts and techniques of this important part of corporate planning. Of course, attention to potential *future* stakeholders should form part of this aspect of the strategic analysis.

## Environment nature analysis

In Chapter 2 we discussed how the diverse, dynamic, difficult and dangerous natures of current trading environments are providing *the* critical problem sources for most British organisations. An understanding of the *nature* of business environments is essential if management strategists are to make effective change choices. Such understanding helps strategists to make informed choices about the product/market/ competitive positionings most appropriate for future success (this, traditionally, is the major objective of the corporate planning process). However, the process is also useful for considering and making *planning process* changes (changing the ways the enterprise picks up and uses important information) and for considering and making changes to the way the organisation *implements* its product market choices.

Robert Miles (4) has provided a framework for a comprehensive and systematic analysis of environment types. His environmental dimensions model calls for a 'measurement' response by those performing the analysis. Analysis of the environment is structured around the questions below. Here we provide, as an example the environment in which local authorities operate, to illustrate the framework.

(a) *How complex is the environment?* Complexity is a measurement of the number of different environmental forces which have an impact or a potential impact, on the enterprise. In the local authority context, for example, the array of external variables which require the attention of local government institutions is growing. Competition, for example, is providing new inputs into the environmental scene as are increasing interactions with local business and European and international parties.

(b) *How routine are organisational interactions with environmental parties?* Here, again, traditional pre-programmed methods of operating within a local authority seem to be 'moving over' to accommodate more unpredictable, less certain, interactions.

(c) *How interconnected and how remote, initially, are significant environmental variables?* Back in the 1960s Emery and Trist (5) argued that the major modern organisational problem is one created by 'turbulent fields' – environments which produce forces, initially unconnected and remote, which roll across environmental boundaries to form a collective force for organisational change. 'Turbulent field' forces, of course, are difficult to spot and understand until they close in on the organisation. Consumer protection departments, for example, grown out of the old Weights & Measures Inspectorate, are often faced with crises involving foreign manufactured goods which arrive via complex distribution channels. Ever-changing new technology in goods and services, new legislation, and newly important consumer industries such as consumer credit, also combine to produce the need for organising systems and structures very different from those which were effective only 15 or so, years ago.

(d) *How dynamic and how unpredictable are the changes taking place around the organisation?* When changes take place quickly there is little time for them to be absorbed into the enterprise's mechanisms for understanding and reacting to change.

When changes are also unpredictable, then pre-programmed methods of anticipating responses cannot be utilised. Once more, to an observer, local authorities in the 1980s and 1990s seem generally to have been recoiling constantly from the impact of continuous, unpredictable governmental, social and economic shocks.

(e) *How high is input and output receptivity?* When the forces at work in the environment adversely affect the input and output processes of the strategic theme then the need to understand environments becomes critical. We discussed in Chapter 2, the critical impact of dangerous environments. Local authorities can no longer be sure of their traditional customer bases and sources of revenue, following the privatisation, rate-capping and rate system reforms of the 1980s. In such situations environmental analysis is vital.

(f) *How high is flexibility of domain choice?* This question refers to the extent to which organisations are restricted from moving into new areas of operation. Here again we seem to be witnessing a worsening situation for local government. Doncaster councillor, Ron Gillies, summed up what appeared to be an inequitable restriction on the level of flexibility of choice open to local authorities. He called for legislation to allow his works department to tender outside its authority: 'The Tories keep talking about fair competition and they ought to give us the chance to tender against private competition instead of them tendering against us exclusively.'

Corporate planning decision-makers can use the above checklist of questions to establish the environmental positions of their own organisations on a number of continuums (see Fig. 4.2). Most positions recorded are likely to be at, or moving towards, the difficult and critical ends of the continuums – the environment is complex and non-routine. Many of today's strategists can sympathise with those local government strategists who complain of the difficulties of dealing with diverse ranges of legal and administrative matters and of the problems created by 'the inadequacy of time allowed for the submission of responses to an increasing spate of governmental consultative papers on complex and important subjects affecting local authorities'(6).

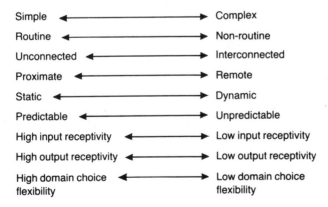

**Figure 4.2 Continuums for evaluating the nature of the organisation's environment**

# Analysis of the structure of the environment

Understanding the nature of the environment is a springboard for the design of more appropriate organising forms for the creation and implementation of product market strategies. Analysis of the *structure* of the environment builds on the insights already developed through *nature* of the environment analysis to establish the present and future opportunities and threats facing the organisation. In this way, better decisions can be made on the most appropriate product/market/competitive developments and positionings for the organisation. Three concepts and their associated models help to build up a picture of those significant structural forces presently at work, and likely to be at work in the future. These are:

(a)  market segmentation analysis;

(b)  competitive structure analysis;

(c)  PEST analysis.

## Market segmentation analysis

Market segmentation analysis draws boundaries around present and potential markets in a way that is meaningful to decision-makers. A number of segmentation approaches can be 'tried' to help the exploration of future areas of opportunity and threat. For example, 'lifestyle' segmentation concepts have provided organisations such as Laura Ashley and Next with the means for appreciating new opportunities to create and capitalise on fashionwear demand. In the mid-1980s Next continued to create opportunities by sub-segmentation (Next for Women became Next Collection and Next Too, for example) and, in the process, demonstrated how sub-segmentation of existing markets into new groups of like-minded buyers can be undertaken for as long as the new group (including any newly attracted buyers) is big enough to provide attractive returns. Alternatively, segmentation analysis can seek to extend product/market boundaries. The building societies in the UK, for example, are no longer restricted to the home loans market but have entered into the financial services sector. Industry structure changes in the health service are pushing service deliverers, therein, to consider choices over where they should focus their effort, expertise and other resources.

Other methods of segmentation include geographical; demographical (based on age, sex, social class, etc.); customer size (some suppliers, for example, find it uneconomical to work for customers who provide orders under a certain size); and quality characteristics (in the car market, for example, some customers are attracted by price, some by durability, some by status, etc.). Michael Porter, as we shall see later, suggests that organisations should decide whether they are to compete in mass markets as price/cost competitors, in mass markets as differentiated/value-adding competitors, or in smaller, more focused markets.

Market segments, once delineated, should then be investigated to determine:

(a)  adequacy of current market size;

(b)  potential for growth;

(c)  threats posed by existing and potential competition;

(d) opportunities for the organisation to gain competitive advantage within the segment (and the capability of the organisation to take these opportunities).

## Competitive structure analysis

Michael Porter (7) has provided a number of useful concepts and frameworks for thinking about the positions of competitive 'players' within any market segment and about the inherent attractiveness of particular segments and the appropriateness of particular competitive moves. He suggests that inherent market attractiveness, potential for growth within that market and the ability to gain competitive advantage therein will depend upon the existing competitive structure of the market and the firm's ability to align itself favourably (in the short and longer term) against the 'five forces of competition'. Thus, for Porter, five forces can be at work in any market – each attempting to take its share of the total profits/wealth available therein.

Understanding the forces at work in any market segment, therefore, is a necessary prerequisite to deducing whether – and, if appropriate, how – the firm should use that segment as a strategic business area. The five forces are:

(a)  new entrants, potential entrants and the threat of entry;

(b)  substitute products/services;

(c)  buyers and buyer power;

(d)  suppliers and supplier power;

(e)  competitors and the nature of inter-firm rivalry.

Figure 4.3 illustrates an application of Porter's model to the oil industry.

The greater the intensity of any of these sources of competition, the harder it will be for an organisation to earn profits and the greater will be the need for strategic sophistication. In the UK the intensity of competition in markets is growing. A checklist of questions can assist strategists in thinking through the strategic implications of the competitive structure of an industry:

(a)  What is the threat of entry into the industry and from where does it arise?

(b)  Where are present and potential substitute products/services located and what is their impact or likely impact on the organisation and the industry?

(c)  Who are our buyers and what is the extent of their power with regard to the organisation?

(d)  Who are our suppliers and what is their power with regard to the organisation?

(e)  Who are our present and potential competitors and how intense is (or will be) present and potential competitive rivalry?

Each of these key areas can in turn be analysed to determine the intensity of competition.

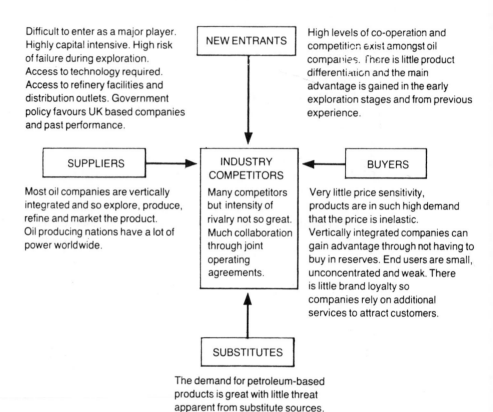

THE OIL INDUSTRY

**NEW ENTRANTS**

Difficult to enter as a major player. Highly capital intensive. High risk of failure during exploration. Access to technology required. Access to refinery facilities and distribution outlets. Government policy favours UK based companies and past performance.

High levels of co-operation and competition exist amongst oil companies. There is little product differentiation and the main advantage is gained in the early exploration stages and from previous experience.

**SUPPLIERS**

**INDUSTRY COMPETITORS**

**BUYERS**

Most oil companies are vertically integrated and so explore, produce, refine and market the product. Oil producing nations have a lot of power worldwide.

Many competitors but intensity of rivalry not so great. Much collaboration through joint operating agreements.

Very little price sensitivity, products are in such high demand that the price is inelastic. Vertically integrated companies can gain advantage through not having to buy in reserves. End users are small, unconcentrated and weak. There is little brand loyalty so companies rely on additional services to attract customers.

**SUBSTITUTES**

The demand for petroleum-based products is great with little threat apparent from substitute sources.

**Figure 4.3 Structural analysis of the oil industry**

(a) *Potential entrants.* Threat of entry depends on the extent of barriers to entry, so:

- Is the potential customer base sufficient to support new operations?
- How heavy is the capital investment requirement in the industry? Is finance available?
- Is there a strong brand image to overcome?
- How costly will be access to distribution channels?
- What operating cost advantages might existing competitors hold (e.g. experienced staff, patent protection, etc.)?
- Is there governmental/legislative protection afforded to existing organisations?
- How vigorously will existing operators react against new entry attempts?

(b) *Substitute products/services* will be more prevalent if:

- customers perceive other offers to perform the same function as ours;
- substitute products offer higher value for money;
- substitute products earn higher profits.

(c) *Buyer power* is likely to be high if:

- there is a concentration of buyers;

- there are alternative sources of supply;
- buyers have access to useful information and tend to shop around;
- there is a threat of backward integration if the buyer does not obtain satisfactory supplies and prices.

(d) *Supplier power* is likely to be high if:

- there is a concentration of suppliers;
- the costs of switching from one supplier to another are high;
- suppliers are likely to integrate forward if they do not obtain the price/profits they seek;
- the organisation has little countervailing power.

(e) *Intensity of rivalry* will be greater if:

- competitors are of equal size and are seeking dominance;
- the market is mature and subject to 'shake out' activities;
- high fixed costs provoke price wars to maintain capacity;
- product homogeneity necessitates activity to maintain share;
- new influxes of capacity have created excess capacity;
- High 'exit' barriers (legal constraints; high cost non-transferable plant and equipment; emotional commitment) exist.

Special mention is warranted at this point of the importance of competitor profile analysis. Here, so far as the organisation's information systems will facilitate, decision makers should perform strategic analyses on each of its significant competitors. The aim of such exercises is to understand the strategic situation of each competitor and, in particular, the way it is likely to react to changes in the market place and the implications of such reactions. Armed with this conjecture the analysing strategists can consider the most appropriate competitive moves to make.

## PEST analysis (USE FOR PRESENTATION)

The major purpose of corporate planning is to facilitate adaptation through anticipation. Analysis of the events and trends occurring on Political, Economic, Social and Technological (PEST) fronts provides strategic decision-makers with a wider, environment-orientated perspective and with a more futuristic view of the organisation's business situation. This more comprehensive view builds on understanding already developed. It thus further facilitates choices of those organisational developments most likely to fit successfully, anticipated near-to long-term futures. The illustration below demonstrates the need to unearth and take account of longer term, general environmental trends and events. A pre-determined categorisation (such as PEST) is a useful stimulus for directing thought. These frameworks, however, need to be customised and extended to highlight all those factors which seem likely to provide future opportunities and threats for the particular organisation.

### Case examples: the significance of particular PEST futures

(a) Social and demographic changes in the age structure of the population means that fewer 18–22 year olds will be around to provide higher education institutions with their traditional customers in the 1990s. Corporate status and privatisation developments, generated by the Conservative Government, seem likely to increase competition in this sector. Growing emphasis on the linking of education with business and on the need for management and worker skills development provides areas of opportunity for those capable of providing training in these areas.

(b)  The 1992 'Europe Open for Business' initiative provides both threat and opportunity for many of our firms.

(c)  Healthy foods and eating trends combine with a growing concern for the welfare of animals to provide major future problems for those involved in meat food industries.

(d)  Growth or decline in economic activity will have significant effects on the power generating industry and its participants as they come to terms with changes to the structure of the industry following legislative changes in the early 1990s.

(e)  The polarisation of society into the 'haves' and the 'have nots' and into the impoverished north and the affluent south provides a source of concern for retailers who have to decide where they will operate, who they will serve and what they will provide.

(f)  Despite the investment costs involved, batch engineering organisations in the UK need to consider carefully whether they can afford *not* to embark on computerisation implementation.

## Case study: the ups and downs of the hotel industry

Behind the spendid red-brick facade of the Hotel Metropole in Leeds, there is a distinct air of faded glory. The hotel has been on the market since September, so far with no takers. The elegant chandeliers, lavishly decorated high ceilings, deep carpets and long corridors at the Victorian Royal York Hotel, next to York Station, hide an equally depressing picture. The three-star Metropole, with 114 rooms and the four-star Royal York are among 12 major hotels, five in Yorkshire, placed in the hands of the receivers this week.

Particularly badly hit have been the country house hotels, one of the phenomena of the 1980s, often rambling piles converted at great expense by people with little experience in the business. They depended heavily on the United States and Japanese trade, which has been wiped out in 1991 by the Gulf War. Even the Holiday Inn, Leeds' newest hotel, owned by the Bass group, has put staff on short-time working.

But the picture is not entirely gloomy. While Eclipsecare Ltd, part of the London-based Crown Hotels group which owns the Metropole, has huge financial problems, with a loan of millions called in by its bankers, another group, Friendly Hotels, this week announced a rise in pre-tax profits of 20 per cent to more than £6 million. Its chairman, Henry Edwards, said the group, which owns Hull's Royal Hotel, intended to take advantage of the glut of properties on the market by making further acquisitions.

One experienced hotelier said 'We have had a wonderful time in the eighties, and now things are returning to normal, we have to re-adjust ourselves. Those who borrowed very heavily are now having to re-group, and this is very difficult under the weight of heavy borrowing at high interest rates.'

Both hoteliers and their customers are suffering from the recession. 'Country house hotels, which sprang up in the last decade, are suffering terribly, because they have to be expensive, and the cost of maintaining them is terrifying', said the hotelier. 'Some of the people who bought these had never owned a hotel, and borrowed up to twice the value of the property to refurbish. Then the market collapsed.'

'Firms are cutting down on their expense accounts, so that conferences, which used to end with a jolly and an overnight stay, are now concluded within the day, people are being asked to use three-star hotels instead of four-star, and city centre locations are being used instead of the country house hotels'.

'When heavy borrowing has been combined with a short-sighted attitude, from people determined to milk the situation until there was nothing left, the problems have been even greater. A lot of people thought it would never end, when there were 97 per cent occupancy rates, and they were not looking to the future'.

'Some have attempted to draw business by halving prices for overnight stays, but Mr Gledhill says that becoming locked in a discounting spiral is damaging to the industry. They are gaining a small short-term advantage, but causing a long-term problem', he says, 'Returning customers will expect to pay the same, or assume the previously high prices were excessive or profiteering.'

While the mid-market hotels suffer, the growth area has been in budget hotels, like Trusthouse Forte's Travelodges, which have had 100 per cent occupancy, offering a basic room for under £30 a night, and taking business away from the city centre three-stars. The short break has also grown in recent years, and hotels are casting their eyes on the growing number of retired people, who spent £19 billion on travel and leisure in Britain last year.

'Hotels are also looking at the potential of the European market, as even before the Gulf War, 49 per cent of foreign trade came from there', says Mr Gledhill.

Historically, the collapse of the US market, as after the Libyan bombing crisis, has been followed by a boom. The question, as Mr Gledhill says, is how many hotels can hang on until then, as banks press harder for repayments.

In such a climate, Jonathan Wix appears to be bucking the trend, as he spends £3 million – some of it industrial development grant – on converting former derelict grain warehouses into a hotel in Leeds which, he says, is the first of its kind in Britain. There is no large reception area – 'It would cost £120 a foot to build, and £18 a year for the interest on that foot of space' – and the hotel cannot technically be classed as a boarding house, as it does not offer evening meals. Instead, guests can choose one of several restaurants, including one next door in which Mr Wix has a substantial but minority shareholding, and place the cost of meals on their hotel bill. There is a breakfast room, overlooking the River Aire, and another innovation is a study room, bookable for 23 hours from 6 pm which can be used as an office throughout the normal working day, with a bed which is folded away behind a false fireplace until needed.

Savings on the dining room and reception areas enable Mr Wix to offer luxury accommodation, tailored to the needs of the business user, with fax machines available in each of the 39 *en suite* bedrooms, at prices £40 to £50 a night cheaper than the average four-star hotel – £74 for the study room, up to £185 for a large director ' suite.

'It h. s worked in Paris, and by hiving off the most awkward part of the operation, I believe we can make it work in England', says Mr Wix, who has experienced both sides of the coin in the past ten years. He has spent £70,000 a bedroom on the hotel in The Calls, Leeds, which opens on 24 April, 'I do not know how you can relax in a room four feet square, where there is hardly room to tie your shoelaces. What we are doing is radically different from the firms who have gone under, but I am backing what I believe is the future of the trade. We have been caught in a pincer movement, as interest rates have hit us and our guests, but there will not be many tears shed for us – this is a very tough and competitive market.'

Larger hotel groups, like Trusthouse Forte, have the resources to ride out the storm, but many smaller operators, some of whom set up in the boom years of the 1980s, have had their dreams shattered.

(Source: extracts from E Roberts, 'No room for sentiment', *Yorkshire Post*, 6 April, 1991)

### Think and discuss

Identify different market segments in the hotel industry. Which factors lie behind the problems being experienced in particular segments?

## Ranking opportunities and threats

One aim of the extended future planning process is to separate the 'wood from the trees'. Many corporate planning experts suggest that only a few (say, four or five) environmental trends or forecasted events will be really important to the firm's future success. Categorisation of opportunities and threats into some simple framework (for example, one which classifies opportunities and threats into 'major', 'moderate', 'minor' and 'no significance' categories) and the subsequent ranking of 'major' and 'moderate' items, can be an extremely useful exercise.

## Resource analysis

Having looked outward to find those significant forces at work in the organisation's environment, the final stage of the strategic analysis exercise involves a more introverted scrutiny of those elements inside the organisation which will be important to future success. Here, via resource analysis, corporate planners recommend the search for significant resource strengths and weaknesses. At the end of this particular process decision-makers should understand what is possible, in product or market positioning terms, given the constraints of resource availability. More generally, the process should indicate how resources might be redirected to improve systems goals achievements (efficiency and control of the environment) and, consequently, to improve the organisation's profit performance.

In this section we provide an overview of some activities which can be performed to build up a comprehensive picture of the firm's resource position.

### Checklist for resource analysis

(a) *Which resources do we have?* A resource audit which does little more than list the tangible and intangible resources of the organisation nevertheless makes a useful start to this stage of the strategic analysis. Here, as in many other areas of strategic analysis, ready-made checklists are available and, provided these aids are amended and extended to fit the specific situation, they can be of great practical value. Figure 4.4 is a checklist provided by Johnson and Scholes (8).

| | Operations | Marketing | Finance | Personnel | R & D | Others |
|---|---|---|---|---|---|---|
| Physical resources | Machines Buildings Materials Location Stock | Products/services Patents, licences Warehouses | Cash Debtors Stock (Equity) (Loans) | Location | Size of R & D Design | Location of buildings |
| Human resources | Operatives Support staff Suppliers | Salesmen Marketing staff Customers | Shareholders Bankers | Adaptability Location Number of employees Age profile | Scientists Technologists Designers | Managementt skills Planners |
| Systems | Quality control Production control Production planning Purchasing | Service system Distribution channels | Costing Cash Management accounting | Working agreements Rewards | Project assessment | Planning and control information |
| Intangibles | Team spirit | Brand name Goodwill Market information Contacts Image | Image in city | Organisational culture Image | Know-how | Image Location |

Figure 4.4  A checklist for resource analysis (adapted from Johnson and Scholes (8) )

(b) *How effective/efficient is our resource utilisation?* The issue of resource utilisation is covered in greater detail in Chapter 10 on productivity planning where the means of measuring and improving the productivity of resource usages are discussed. Briefly, then, resource utilisation is measured by reference to a range of ratios, such as employees to sales, profit to sales, rejects to output, absenteeism to potential staff days, etc. Existing ratios are then compared against a range of criteria such as industry norms, competitors' ratios, and trends over time to generate insight into the levels of performance achieved, into areas of strength and weakness and into areas for productivity improvement activity. Johnson and Scholes (8) recommend that, at this stage, rather than simply measuring and comparing productivity ratios, strategists should also question the existing applications of resource inputs to establish whether they might generate greater wealth if used elsewhere. After resource analysis, planners may decide, for example, how the premises of a town centre cinema might be more profitably deployed as a supermarket.

(c) *How flexible are resources?* Flexibility refers to the effectiveness with which resources can be redeployed and/or rearranged to meet new environmental situations. Strategists need to ask and answer questions such as: 'Do we have a multi-skilled, adaptive workforce?', 'Is our cash tied up in fixed assets?', 'Does management have the attitudes and skills necessary to try new approaches and to create new organisation cultures?', 'Is our plant and machinery useful for existing product/market requirements only?'.

(d) *How balanced are our resources?* Customer bases might be too big (thinly spread) or too small (over-dependent on particular clients). Management teams might be strong in financial expertise but weak in marketing skills. Too many of the firm's products might be aimed at declining markets – too few at growth areas. Too much cash is wasteful, not enough can reduce profit making capability and create the danger of insolvency and liquidation. Strategists need to examine their resource base to gather 'balance' insights.

(e) *How effective is our organising 'fit'?* The concept of fit is one which suggests that the components of organising (for example, the people, jobs, systems, structure and product/market strategies of the organisation) should be mutually supportive of each other and that, in total, the organising mode should be in harmony with the nature and needs of the firm's environment. We cover this concept in much greater detail later (see Chapters 11 and 12). Here, suffice it to suggest that strategists investigating 'fit' should look for the symptoms of 'misfit'. These include a decline in financial performance, customer dissatisfaction, a lack of motivation internally, a sense of 'them and us', and internal conflict. Present organisational arrangements should then be studied to establish the 'misfit roots' of the problem (for example, perhaps the firm's reward systems emphasise individual bonuses for output *quantity* when the product/market strategy demands a team effort emphasising *quality* of output). The investigation should, of course, also move on to consideration of potential remedies.

(f) *What is the extent and nature of any resource slack within our organisation?* Over time, particularly in successful eras, organisations tend to develop 'slack'. Stock levels are maintained at higher levels than might prevail if the firm was operating at maximum efficiency. More than 'just enough' personnel are employed. Salary levels are higher than that level which would be just high enough to maintain employee inputs. Zero based budgeting systems and 'just in time' stock policies are two products of the efficiency conscious 1980s which have demonstrated the extent to which traditional levels of resource inputs can be productively reduced. Efficiency is a wealth creator *and* a means to create competitive advantage. Strategists are well advised to scrutinise their organisation to identify cost improvement areas. (Of course, resource utilisation analysis will already have provided insight into 'slack' problems. Chapter 10 on productivity planning is also designed to help planners improve slack situations.)

A caveat is necessary, however. The search to get 'more for less' can produce a reality of asking for 'too much from too little'. Staff being asked to work with too few resources, for example, can 'switch off'. Customers seeing the effects of efficiency drives in poorer quality goods and services can 'exit'. Further, as we shall see later, creative innovation and shock event planning capabilities rely to a large extent on the existence of surplus resources.

(g) *What is the nature and extent of our strategic standing?* Here we are concerned to establish the power the organisation enjoys in its market place. Environmental analysis should already have provided much information to enable an assessment of strategic standing. The inward look adopted at this time should attempt to establish strategic standing 'drivers' – those things in the organisation's resources which because of their competencies and/or weaknesses, have much to do with the strategic position attained. This investigation, too, should reveal the urgency with which changes to present ways of doing things must be made. The major high street banks have enjoyed much strategic standing power and, arguably, adapted only slowly to the changing needs of banking consumers in the 1970s and 1980s. As the financial services market opened up during the late 1980s, however, so too did the speed and size of the banks' strategy and structural changes.

## Ranking strengths, weaknesses and distinctive competencies

In the same way that environmental analysis is assumed to produce only a few really important opportunities and threats, so too resource analysis is expected to engender only a few significant strengths and weaknesses. Once again, the planners are advised to rank resource characteristics. Lists clarifying the importance of future competitive advantage generators and the importance of competitive advantage detractors are required. These should identify those things which are distinctively good about the organisation and which set the organisation apart from – and at an advantage to – its competitors. They should also identify major weak 'spots'. Future product, market and competitive choices should build on strengths and distinctive competencies and should avoid weaknesses. Organisational changes should attempt to further improve positions of strength and to eradicate areas of weakness.

By now the strategists involved in the corporate planning process should have obtained a strong feel for the types of product/market activities they might successfully employ and the corresponding resource activities which should be implemented. Suggestions as to how the enterprise might improve its cost position and/or its value-adding differentiation capability will inevitably have been already made. Now is the appropriate time to debate more fully such specifics – although actual decisions should be made only after the strategists have undertaken formally the second part of the corporate planning process, i.e. the generation, evaluation and choice of strategic developments. This second stage of the corporate planning process is the concern of the next chapter.

## Strategic analysis: conclusion

It makes sound common sense to think longer term. Living for today, generally, is not a prescription for enduring success. In changing environments, however, it is not wise to extrapolate yesterday's and today's successes. The events of yesterday and today are likely to help only partially in creating a realistic picture of tomorrow. *Environmental analysis* assists planners to anticipate the relevant futures of the short to longer term. *Resource analysis* helps the firm's decision-makers to understand the significance of their resource bases to the achievement of successful ongoing organisational/environmental adaptations. *Aspirations analysis* signals the desires of the enterprise's important stakeholders and helps the management strategists formulate their own desired strategic developments in the light of the aspirations and power positions of others.

Undertaken together these activities provide a *strategic analysis* of the organisation's business situation. If performed effectively, strategic analysis can generate tremendous insight (particularly for first-time users) into the factors which underpin present success/failure levels and into the organisational changes which make greatest sense in the context of the anticipated future.

To recap, we recommend that strategists (with their consultant and/or planning team helpers) conduct strategic analysis in a systematic way as follows:

(a) Conduct an aspirations analysis to determine who the important stakeholders are/will be and to ascertain their power positions, aspirations and propensities for or against alternative potential developments.

(b) Analyse the nature of the environment for the insight this might stimulate on questions of organisational restructuring as well as of potential product/market/competitive developments.

(c) Perform pertinent market segmentation exercises.

(d) Analyse the competitive structure of present – and potential – markets and identify the inherent attractiveness of the markets, and the openings which might exist for the organisation to exploit.

(e) Analyse the wider and more futuristic environment to facilitate a picture of anticipated futures which the organisation might seek to exploit, change or avoid as necessary.

(f) Rank opportunities and threats in the order of their perceived significance.

(g) Conduct a resource analysis including an audit; a resource utilisation check; a flexibility check; a balance check; a 'fit' check; a slack investigation; a strategic standing investigation; a strengths/weaknesses/distinctive competencies ranking; and a value creating debate.

At this stage of the corporate planning process the planning team should be ready to move on to the crucial jobs of generating, evaluating and choosing major strategic developments.

## Case study: breaking into the news

In 1986 Mr Eddie Shah attempted to break into the national daily newspaper industry with his *Today* daily. The newspaper industry to that time had been complacent and non-innovative. Shah brought some life back to the market place, however, as existing 'players' reacted to his full colour offer and his new, less labour intensive, printing technology.

Despite his innovatory approach and his personal enthusiasm, problems soon beset the *Today* venture. Capital entry costs were high – Shah had needed to raise £30 million – but returns were by no means guaranteed. Breakeven sales/production capacity take up had to be wrestled from a declining market already containing too much capacity. With initial revenue coming mainly from cover price rather than advertising and with 60 day payment lags the industry norm, Shah's limited resources were soon strained. Bigger, traditional newspaper organisations seemed better placed in many ways to launch a new daily. Robert Maxwell's Mirror Group, for example, could look to the backing of his Pergamon financial empire.

While some of the big players only talked about future plans for introducing their own new dailies, they reacted more immediately and specifically by producing colour pictures in existing papers. On the day *Today* was launched many of these entries were of better quality than that achieved in Mr Shah's publication. The *Today* threat

**Table 4.1 National newspaper circulation: popular dailies**

| Paper | Circulation | | | Holding company |
|---|---|---|---|---|
| | 1961 (000s) | 1981 (000s) | 1984 (000s) | |
| The Sun | 1,407 | 3,741 | 4,084 | News Corporation |
| Daily Mirror | 4,578 | 3,625 | 3,494 | Mirror Group Newspapers |
| Daily Express | 4,321 | 2,194 | 2,002 | United Newspapers |
| Daily Mail | 2,649 | 1,948 | 1,864 | Associated Newspapers |
| Daily Star | – | 1,034 | 1,633 | United Newspapers |
| TOTALS | 12,955 | 12,542 | 13,077 | |

also quickened Fleet Street's more major developments, both in cost cutting and in colour printing. Before Shah's market penetration Fleet Street was subject to a tight closed shop labelled 'The London Print'. Dominant in this situation were the National Graphical Association and the Society of Graphical and Allied Trades. By using new technology, however, Mr Shah was able to avoid union disputes with those organisations and had to deal only with the electricians union, the EEPTU. Similarly, the journalists were allowed no closed shop and he by-passed the typesetters' and compositors' unions by doing page layouts from the editorial office. It was not long before the Fleet Street operators began to follow suit. Rupert Murdoch, for example, moved his News International operation to Wapping where, with reduced premises and labour costs, savings of £80 million per year were anticipated. Robert Maxwell began installing colour printers and reducing workforce numbers (by one-third to about 4,000 workers).

**Table 4.2 Readership profiles of national daily newspapers**

| MEN | WOMEN | 15–34 | 35+ | ABC1 | C2DE | |
|---|---|---|---|---|---|---|
| 52.8 | 47.2 | 45.4 | 54.5 | 24.1 | 75.9 | THE SUN |
| 54.6 | 45.4 | 39.2 | 60.8 | 26.2 | 73.8 | DAILY MIRROR |
| 51.3 | 48.7 | 34.0 | 66.0 | 56.9 | 43.1 | DAILY MAIL |
| 52.5 | 47.5 | 31.6 | 68.4 | 51.0 | 49.0 | DAILY EXPRESS |
| 58.4 | 41.6 | 50.3 | 49.7 | 19.1 | 80.9 | THE STAR |
| 48.0 | 52.0 | 37.0 | 63.0 | 40.3 | 59.7 | POPULATION |

Some of *Today*'s problems seemed to be due to poor planning. For example, problems over distribution hampered the launch. In some areas people were unable to obtain early copies. This reduced revenue, of course, and also meant that the *Today* organisation had missed out on the chance to capture customers who were interested in the paper initially but who lost interest after the early euphoria of the launch died away.

Advertisers were undoubtedly interested in the very competitive rates the *Today* production costs made possible and were attracted by the opportunity of colour printing. However, once again self-generated problems – poor quality production, patchy distribution and resulting poor circulation figures – caused concern amongst advertising agencies, many of whom demanded their money back.

## Think and discuss
Refer to the case study.

(a)  Perform a competitive structural analysis of the daily newspaper industry.

(b)  Is the industry inherently attractive? Provide reasons for your answer together with supportive examples from the case study.

(c)  Compare the strengths and weaknesses and distinctive competencies of *Today* and the *Daily Mirror*.

## For further study
1    Refer to the case study 'Crossed wires at British Telecom' in the accompanying book. Perform market segmentation analysis, environmental structure analysis and PEST analysis. Identify the major opportunities and threats facing BT.
2    Refer to the case study 'What Next?' in the accompanying book. Apply the resource analysis checklist provided in this chapter to Next in the mid-1980s.

   Identify the company's strengths, weaknesses and any distinctive competencies. Refer to the update appendix to this case study. From your knowledge of high street trading conditions of the late 1980s and early 1990s, identify the major factors behind Next's decline.
3    Refer to the case study 'Silver Wheels Ltd' in the accompanying volume. Advise a friend who has £10,000 capital (a job redundancy payment) whether the coach industry presents an inherently attractive market entry proposition for him. (Your friend already has a Passenger Service Vehicle Licence and is considering buying a second-hand 52-seater coach.)

# References

1    J Argenti, *Practical Corporate Planning*, George Allen & Unwin, 1980, Ch 1
2    H I Ansoff, *Implementing Strategic Management*, Prentice-Hall International, 1984, pp 15–18
3    G Johnson and K Scholes, *Exploring Corporate Strategy*, 2nd edn, Prentice-Hall International, 1988, p 51
4    R E Miles, *Macro Organisational Behavior*, Glenview, Ill., Sutt Foresman & Co., 1980, Ch 8
5    See, for example, C Stubbart, 'Why We Need A Revolution in Strategic Planning', *Long Range Planning*, 18 (6), December 1986, pp 68–76
6    Institute of Chartered Secretaries and Administrators, *The Administrator*, October, 1987
7    M E Porter, *Competitive Strategy*, New York, The Free Press, 1980, Ch 1
8    G Johnson and K Scholes, *Exploring Corporate Strategy*, Prentice-Hall International, 1984, p 91

# Recommended reading

G Johnson and K Scholes, *Exploring Corporate Strategy*, 2nd edn, Prentice-Hall International, 1988

L L Byars, *Strategic Management, Planning and Implementation Concepts and Cases*, New York, Harper & Row, 1984

J Argenti, *Practical Corporate Planning*, George Allen & Unwin, 1980

# 5 Corporate planning and competitive positioning: generating, evaluating, choosing and implementing the ways forward

Strategic analysis exercises are likely to have revealed that existing ways of operating are inappropriate for anticipated future conditions. Corporate planning seeks to ensure effective alignments of the organisation with its mid- to long-term environments. Important decisions, therefore, should flow from this planning process on any changes to be made to products and markets presently served, competitive stances now being taken and to the ways in which the organisation formulates and implements new developments.

The concepts and frameworks introduced in this chapter are generally intended to stimulate thought around the types of change which might be made. Practitioners might thus use these aids to reach choices on specific ways forward for their enterprises. Here our discussion considers the following topics:

- Product/market developments
- Competitive strategies
- Competitive advantage through collaboration: from joint venture to strategic alliance
- Strategy formulation and implementation issues
- Political bargaining strategies
- Generating strategic alternatives: brainstorming
- Evaluating potential strategies and choosing the ways forward
- Corporate planning: strategic generation, evaluation and choice

## Product/market developments

### Developing from a one product/market base

A fundamental strategic choice is that which determines an organisation's strategic business area – the environment from which the organisation will earn its living. Another critical decision is that which establishes the type of product or service the organisation will offer in its chosen business area. Product/market choices must rank amongst the most significant single decisions made within the organisation. Once into a particular business area, however, organisations can follow one of a range of broad developments and thereby amend or add to existing wealth generating activities. These *generic* development strategies can be described in the following terms.

(a) *Vegetate*. This is a 'do nothing' strategy. Organisations which become satisfied with existing ways of doing things fail to consider and implement new ideas and become *passive* reactors to environmental change. Vegetating is often a creator of the need to undertake strategies (b) or (c) below.

(b) *Liquidate*. If organisation owners have lost interest in their firm and no successors are available to take over then the preferred development route might be to liquidate. Family businesses sometimes adopt this strategy when children show little interest in continuing the business. Sometimes, performance predictions suggest that a serious decline is likely to be experienced and that a more economically sound strategy would be to get out while the going is comparatively good. A range of liquidation methods includes selling out, simply letting the business run down, or undertaking a 'final harvest', where products and assets are sold off before final closure.

(c) *Attenuate*. Attenuation is the act of cutting back or shrinking. Organisations might adopt this course of action because important decision-makers prefer to go back to their smaller beginnings and away from the perceived disadvantages of large sized operations. Often, after a period where the firm has failed to compete successfully, attenuation becomes necessary as part of a turnaround strategy. In such cases the aim is to remove excess slack from the system and to hive off unprofitable parts of the business. The leaner, more profitable business that remains can then concentrate on strategies (d) and/or (e) below.

(d) *Consolidate*. Consolidation is a proactive attempt to maintain at least existing wealth-creating capacity. Thus, organisations intent on consolidation seek to improve market share in a declining market (and so maintain levels of business activity). In a growing market the consolidation objective becomes one of maintaining market share (and, consequently, increasing business activity).

(e) *Procreate*. In an organisational context, procreation is a strategic development concerned with the generation of additional wealth producing activity. We have already indicated that efficiency-orientated attenuations and consolidations are wealth producers. Igor Ansoff (1), working on the assumption that additional wealth is to be had from new approaches to products and/or markets, has provided us with a product/market growth vector which enables us to identify other wealth creating product/market strategies (see Fig. 5.1).

## Procreation and balancing products and markets

A useful technique for assessing the wealth-creating potential of products and markets is the growth/share matrix originated by the Boston Consulting Group (BCG). Advocates of the BCG approach to business portfolio analysis (and its derivatives) use a simple matrix which slots individual products (or business units) into four categories:

(a) Stars: products worth developing because of their cash generating potential.

(b) Cash cows: products which have realised their potential, require no further substantial development, and will be the main cash generators of the corporation.

| | PRODUCTS | |
|---|---|---|
| | **EXISTING** | **NEW** |
| **M A R K E T S** — **E X I S T I N G** | Market penetration – going for bigger market share | Product modification and/or new product development – offering new products to existing markets |
| **N E W** | Market development – taking existing products to new users (e.g. geographical expansion) | Diversification, i.e. *related* to present operations (e.g. clothing manufacturers undertaking textile manufacture) and *unrelated* (totally unconnected to present products/markets) |

**Figure 5.1  Product/market developments for the creation of additional wealth**

(c) Question marks: products which may have star quality but which require more investigation to determine whether further development or, alternatively, divestment is justified.

(d) Cash dogs: products which are in secular decline in cash generating terms and should be divested.

A major criticism of this BCG technique is that it concentrates management attention on just two business success factors, i.e. market growth potential and market share position (see Fig. 5.2). In response to this perceived failing a number of other, more multi-variable, models have been put forward.

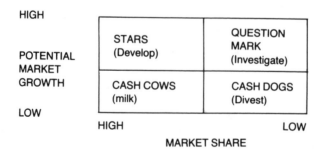

HIGH

POTENTIAL MARKET GROWTH

LOW

| STARS (Develop) | QUESTION MARK (Investigate) |
|---|---|
| CASH COWS (milk) | CASH DOGS (Divest) |

HIGH                                    LOW

MARKET SHARE

**Figure 5.2  BCG product portfolio matrix**

In today's business situations, of course, the most effective method for assessing individual product/business unit potential is through a complete strategic analysis. Nevertheless, the BCG model assists management strategists to assess the earning potential of their existing and potential product/market operations and to make decisions on developments and divestments. It is particularly useful as a concept which identifies the need for a balanced portfolio of products/business units (stars waiting to take over the role of existing cash cows, for example) and as a technique for demonstrating the directions in which cash should be pushed from the centre to the business unit level (see Fig. 5.3).

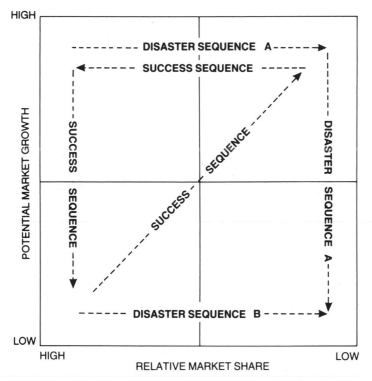

Figure 5.3 Product portfolio growth/share matrix: investment sequences

## Related or unrelated developments

Figure 5.4 illustrates, using management strategy terminology, some continuums of strategic development strategies. These continuums indicate a range of developments from those which relate closely to existing product/market operations to those which have little connection with existing business activities.

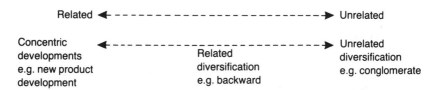

Figure 5.4 Related and unrelated strategic developments

A major strand of management strategy research has been concerned with establishing which side of the related/unrelated continuum offers the greatest success potential.

While much research data is not directly compatible and while results which *might* have accrued from different development approaches to those actually taken remain indeterminable, the research findings suggest that greatest *growth* is to be had through unrelated developments, while greatest return on capital employed is earned through concentric and related diversification policies. The generally prevalent prescription for successfully handling today's environments, too, seems to be one of sticking to known products and markets. Nevertheless, conglomerate stars such as Hanson and BTR continue to produce highly attractive growth *and* profit performances.

Perhaps the appropriateness of any particular development depends more upon the circumstances it addresses and the way in which it is implemented than it does on any generally applicable rule over the inherent pertinence of either related or unrelated development approaches. Of course, sophistication in management strategy implies greater skills in analysing business situations, selecting appropriate developments and implementing effective organisational change.

## Methods of implementing product/market strategies

Product market strategies can be implemented through one (or some) of the following three development methods:

(a) internal development;

(b) joint venture;

(c) acquisition.

### Internal development

Market penetration, product developments, diversification, etc. can be undertaken using a 'go it alone' policy. Advantages of this method of strategy implementation flow from the more incremental approach it usually involves. The organisation can build up expertise in the newer product/market activities over time. Expenditure can be phased. Acquisitions, on the other hand, usually require major cash injections in the short term and can create cash flow problems for the acquirer. Also, of course, a successfully self-developed strategy, compared to a joint venture activity, leaves *all* the profits in the self-developer's coffers. For organisations which attain competitive advantage through their R & D and design capabilities, internal development is the key way of maintaining success.

### Joint venture

In one sense all organisations are joint ventures. The open social system model of organising infers interaction by the organisation with its external stakeholders. The retailer, for example, has a joint venture with the manufacturer in the serving of the end consumer. Joint ventures are inter-organisational poolings of strengths for the effective delivery of product market strategies. *Franchise* arrangements such as those used by Coca Cola and McDonalds, are examples of one type of joint venture. As Britain enters the 'Europe Open for Business' scenario *agencies* between exporters and importers are likely to become an increasingly important joint venture method. The reasons for joint ventures are legion but revolve around a beneficial exchange of resource strengths (the franchisor provides the systems, products, marketing material and image, for example, the franchisee provides local knowledge and expertise, human resource inputs and cash). The 1990s is the era of the strategic alliance and this business trend is the subject of further discussion later in this chapter.

## Acquisition

Acquisition as a development method can make sense for a variety of reasons. In mature markets, for example, acquisition can provide existing players with the means of improving market share (and hence the means of obtaining greater market place power and size-related efficiency contributions). It can also reduce competition and excess production capacity within the industry. Outsiders can use acquisition as a speedy vehicle for gaining a foothold in an industry which might otherwise present high barriers to entry. Such new entrants might also acquire, rather than self-develop, in order to maintain, rather than increase, present levels of production capacity and inter-firm rivalry. New products, too, have a notoriety for failure. Buying established 'winners', rather than developing new products can make sense on risk criteria.

Generally, acquisition should be made for the synergistic benefits its fusion of resources is expected to promote and for the consequentially enhanced achievement of systems goals. We will consider a checklist for evaluating alternative development strategies later in this chapter.

## Case study: W K West Ltd – a century of product/market developments

Below is a summary of how the W K West organisation developed between its establishment in 1884 and the present day.

- 1884: Firm commenced trading as coopers and joiners and specialist packing case (wood) makers serving toolmaking trade within a ten mile radius.
- 1950s: Metal-edged plywood cases introduced into product range.
- 1963: Dealership agency obtained for Tri-Wall cardboard cases; heavy duty cardboard cases introduced; polystyrene casing introduced; markets now covered entire county and included numerous different types of client.
- 1970s: Agency obtained to merchant Sellotape products; moved into supply of packaging-associated products (cushioning and strapping, etc.); now serving Northern England and postal markets.
- 1980s: Significant growth in merchanting operations; firm became 50 per cent manufacturer, 50 per cent merchanter; total turnover in existing markets increased by 150 per cent during decade.
- 1990s: Market place generally is fragmented, highly competitive and price sensitive; customers can shop around, suppliers are powerful, entry into mass market segments is relatively cheap and easy.

Which developments next?

## Think and discuss

Place W K West's product/market developments into the product/market development matrix (Fig. 5.1). Identify the development methods used and suggest reasons why these methods have been adopted.

## Competitive strategies

### How to compete – the basic choices

Any business must make choices as to which products or services to develop and in which business areas to operate. Strategic analysis, including market segmentation, PEST and structural analysis, should have paved the way to these choices by identifying attractive business areas. However, successful strategy also requires decisions on *how to compete* in the chosen market. Michael Porter's major contribution to the theory of management strategy has been through his writings on the means of obtaining competitive advantage. In choosing his firm's competitive strategy, for example, Porter argues that the management strategist must decide the organisation's generic competitive style (2). According to Porter, this choice is between the following competitive stances:

(a) *Least cost producing position.* Adopting this competitive strategy means that the organisation intends to beat the competition through price competitiveness and lower 'bottom line' costs than the competition. In this respect Porter echoes earlier work by the Boston Consultancy Group which advocated the search for mass market leadership to attract learning and scale economies from bigger operations.

(b) *Differentiation.* Adopting this competitive strategy requires the organisation to focus on generating, for customers, value-adding uniqueness in its products and services. Thus, competitive advantage is achieved through improving the 'top line' – the prices the customer will pay.

(c) *Focus.* Porter also draws attention to the need to decide whether to position the organisation in the mass market or whether to *focus* on more specialised markets.

It is essential, according to Porter, for strategists to clarify their chosen generic approaches. While, in accord with systems goal prescriptions, organisations should continually work at efficiency (a least-cost objective) and control of the environment (a differentiation objective), such activities should always be undertaken in the context of their impacts on the chosen generic competitive strategy. Efficiency improvements should not be allowed to dilute differentiation in the organisation pursuing competitive advantage through a unique offer. Conversely, those organisations seeking least-cost positions, should monitor closely the 'bottom line' effects of improving customer offers. Poor performance results from failure to make a clear choice of market focus and generic competitive strategy. Figure 5.5 illustrates Porter's generic competitive strategy model.

The model stimulates insight through thought and discussion generated on:

(a) the parameters which define the market the organisation operates in (or is interested in operating in);

(b) whether the market is a mass market or a focused market (and whether the organisation is to be a broad segment player or a focused player);

(c) the need to improve efficiency and differentiation;

(d) the basic competitive stance the firm should adopt.

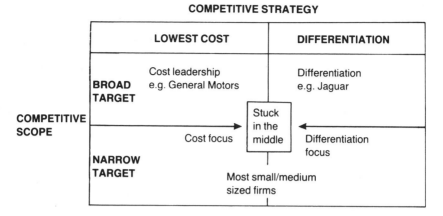

**Figure 5.5 Generic competitive strategies (reprinted with permission of The Free Press, a Division of Macmillan, Inc., from *Competitive Strategy: Techniques for Analyzing Industries and Competitors* by Michael E Porter. Copyright © 1980, The Free Press)**

## Using the value chain to implement competitive advantage

Porter's primary model for explaining how competitive strategy can be translated into competitive advantage is the *value chain*. The value chain consists of organisational activities and margin. Together these ingredients create total value quantified by the price paid by the customer. *Primary* activities consist of *in-bound logistics* (receiving and storing materials, etc); *operations* (activities which transform inputs into final product/service offers); *out-bound logistics* (storage and distribution, etc. of finished goods); *marketing and sales* (the attracting and serving of clients); and *service* (for example, after-sales service). Support activities act as back-up to primary activities and each other. They include *procurement* (purchasing activities); *technology development* (improving processes and products); *human resource deployment* (personnel department and human resource policy activities); and *firm infrastructure* (activities concerned to support the value chain itself, for example, general management, planning and finance).

An important associated concept is that of internal and external *linkages*, (for example between the production and marketing department, and between the organisation and its suppliers, distribution channels and customers). These linkages are important to organisational success and, along with individual activities, provide sources of competitive advantage.

The value chain concept, then, advocates a careful scrutiny of all the firms activities (and their linkages) in order to determine how they might be modified to better support the enterprise's chosen generic competitive strategy. Subsequent chapters on administration planning, productivity planning and team culture planning discuss in some detail how the organisation might create wealth through organisational changes designed to enhance efficiency and differentiation. The understanding of customers' value chains is, of course, necessary to ensure that changes are made in the context of their potential market power structure impacts. Figure 5.6 operationalises the value chain concept in an oil industry organisational setting.

CONOCO (UK) LTD VALUE CHAIN
Primary Activities

|  | Inbound logistics | Operations | Outbound Logistics | Marketing and Sales | Services |
|---|---|---|---|---|---|
| Support activities | Collaborative joint operating agreements (JOA) | Exploration Production Transport | Oil & gas from N.Sea to onshore refinery | Sales of crude oil direct and to Conoco Ltd | Safety standards research & development |
| Technology development | Implementing new systems to increase efficiency & revenue for the company | Development of services & exploration procedures resources capacity | Complex pipeline net-work, Humber refinery one of the most efficient | Production of new products that are in demand e.g. unleaded petrol | Greater capability & service for exploring & producing gas |
| Human resource management | Good image & track record as operator. Backing of Dupont | Skilled & innovative workforce able to undertake & develop operations | Reliable support staff. Flexible use of contract staff. Core workers kept in the company | Sale of crude by skilled staff who have to find buyers in the market at competitive prices | Reputation for high safety standards. Qualified motivated staff |
| Management systems | Organisation & control of raw materials, JOA committee | Well defined role of an operator. Quality systems & co-operation | Good scheduling & fast turnover of crude oil | Efficient internal accounting procedures | High standards offer quality to the partners |
| Procurement | Reputation New licences awarded by the government | Technology for exploration & production. Resources & finance | Co-operation to transport crude to buyers & to the Humber refinery | Knowledge of the market & establishment of regular customers | High priority on safety & research & development |

(Source: Student dissertation, BABS(Hons), 1991)

**Figure 5.6  A value chain in the oil industry**

# Case study: gaining competitive advantage in the holiday trade through IT

In the holiday tours market, Thomson has warned competitors that it will not be beaten on prices and has employed aggressive pricing policies over the past few years. This organisation, however, also concentrates on the more subtle competitive weapon of information technology (IT) – a weapon which Thomson has been developing since 1976 when it introduced its first computerised reservation system. Its present TOP (Thomson Open-line Programme) system was introduced cautiously and meticulously in 1981 via a pilot programme involving several travel agents. Major implementations were made with speed and military precision in 1982. Some

9000 travel agency staff were trained in the use of TOP within the space of a few weeks during that year.

For the travel agent and customer alike, TOP gives instant access to holiday information, freeing them from the delays and frustrations of unanswered telephone calls. Travel agents, too, find a selling tool in the involvement of a prospective client in a holiday booking conversation as the videotex TV screen interacts with the computer centre at Thomson. Communication costs industry wide have been reduced dramatically. For Thomson, the system has produced massive administration cost savings (£28 million between 1982 and 1986). Improved administration and financial control has also provided the database to enable better planning. The TOP system integrates and undertakes a range of activities including the production of invoices, statements, tickets and rooming lists.

Competitively, Thomson used some of the savings generated by TOP to reduce prices in 1986. This action helped stimulate massive new demand (which Thomson knew it could handle with TOP). Other competitors with less effective systems struggled to cater for the upsurge. Thomson's market share grew within the year from 1985 to 1986 by 10 per cent (to 30 per cent of the market). In volume terms, it served 2.6 million customers (compared with 1.4 million in 1985). In 1987 a further 30 per cent volume growth and consolidation of market share resulted. The success of the programme was reflected in Thomson's 1986 announcement that all bookings (with some minor exceptions) would, in future, only be accepted via TOP. Its success is also evident in the 'follow my leader' developments of other tour operators. Continuing attention to improving the TOP system has maintained and improved competitive edge in this area. The TOP system, over time, has been judged to improve Thomson's performance, compared to competitors, in terms of general efficiency and speed of time in accessing and operating reservations systems.

While much interest has been focused on TOP, this system is but one of the Thomson 'technology thrusts'. For example, new systems introduced during the past two or three years cover programme planning, inventory control, financial and management accounts, overseas accounting, personnel, management information, hotel payments, flight operations and in-resort administration. In this last mentioned area, for example, Thomson is now linked directly by computer with Majorca, Ibiza, the Costa Brava, the Costa Blanca and the Costa del Sol. By the summer of 1989 a total of 13 resorts were linked (covering 80 per cent of the company's business). None of the other major operators had anything to compete with these cost saving workload improvers.

A further Thomson IT initiative aimed to reduce costs again for itself and for the trade generally. The Thomson Automatic Banking (TAB) system transfers funds and refunds between agents' and Thomson's bank accounts weekly. Banks charge less for electronic fund transfers than for cheques. Postal costs are eliminated. Staff time is saved and cash flow/forward planning functions enhanced. The writing and processing of one million cheques should become a thing of the past. Payments, of course, would continue to reach Thomson even during postal strikes.

(Source: adapted from a review by W Richardson of C Palmer 'Using IT for Competitive Advantage at Thomson Holidays', *Long Range Planning*, 21 (6), 1988)

## Think and discuss

1   With reference to Porter's five forces of competition, describe how Thomson is changing or has changed the structure of the holiday industry in its favour.

2   Which systems goals (see Chapter 3) is Thomson pursuing through its IT development?

3   Identify the activities which have added value to Thomson's own value system and to its linked value systems.

4   Is Thomson pursuing a least-cost producing strategy or a differentiation strategy?

## Competitive advantage through collaboration: from joint venture to strategic alliance

Figure 5.7 identifies some of the many ways in which organisations have 'come together' to further their respective business objectives. Joint ventures are intended to create *synergy* – together, each partner in the collaboration expects to create a safer and/or wealthier market position than it would have achieved alone.

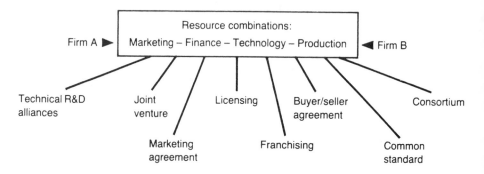

**Figure 5.7  Basic joint ventures (adapted from James (11) )**

In the 1980s and 1990s joint ventures have grown and intensified in terms of their volume, market scope, size of operations and the closeness of the relationships between 'partner' organisations. Joint ventures are increasingly less to do with *tactical, arms length, co-operative* arrangements concerned with *short-term improvements* in performance. Rather, *strategic alliances* have emerged as a newly important means of strategic development. These development vehicles involve 'intense collaborations which take place in the context of competitive long-term strategic plans and which seek to improve or dramatically change competitive positions' (3).

In management strategy terms the 1980s was the era of competitive strategy. The 1990s is the era of competition through strategic collaboration. Rosabeth Moss Kanter describes (and fuels) the trend towards strategic alliances: 'How the times have changed. Today the strategic challenge of doing more with less leads corporations to look outward as well as inward for solutions to the competitiveness dilemma, improving their ability to compete without adding internal capacity. Lean, agile, post-entrepreneurial companies can stretch in three ways. They can *pool* resources with others, *ally* to exploit an opportunity, or *link* systems in a partnership. In short they can become better "PALS" with other organisations – from venture collaborators to suppliers, service contractors, customers and even unions ... distinctions like inside versus outside or us versus them have less meaning when teaming up might produce benefits for each group.' (4)

This section seeks to help managers think through issues related to strategic alliance as a development method. It aims to help decision makers make better decisions over the questions of whether and how their organisations should embark on a strategic alliance. The following discussion examines the questions 'Why choose strategic alliance as a way forward?' and 'Why do strategic alliances sometimes fail?'

## Why choose a strategic alliance?

The above question is directly linked to the more fundamental issue of 'Why organisation?' Benefits expected to flow from a successful strategic alliance contribute to the organisation's own goals of *survival* and/or *growth* through the achievement of operations which create *efficient organisation/environmental transactions*. In competitive strategy parlance, strategic alliances are means for locating *new markets* and for improving *operating cost* and/or *differentiation* capabilities. However, the strategic alliance is a rational choice of way forward only if the business situation favours this method over other development methods of *self-development* or *acquisition*. The following discussion indicates that modern business conditions can be more conducive to the choice of strategic alliance over alternative development methods.

Thus, answers to the question 'Why choose strategic alliance as a preferred development method?' include:

(a) *Big, diverse, global market development opportunities are presenting themselves to organisations lacking the financial and marketing resources to address them with sufficient speed, alone.* In a world where consumer preferences are converging internationally – where quality, price and service are counting for more than country of origin – companies are trying to position themselves on a global scale. Two problems emerge from the adoption of global strategies. First, the cost of building a market presence in many markets simultaneously can be prohibitive. Second, current size of operation and level of marketing sophistication cannot be increased sufficiently quickly – other operators are queuing up to penetrate the new global markets. Strategic alliances thus provide the way forward. VHS videos rapidly became the market standard through a labyrinth of alliances by JVC with, for example, RCA (USA), Telefunken (Germany), Thorn-EMI (UK) and Japanese manufacturers. By the 1990s 80 per cent of videos were VHS machines. Japanese car, computer and telecommunications companies have opened up their respective European markets through joint ventures with European players. Glaxo in the pharmaceutical industry owes much of its success to a network of marketing alliances with organisations such as Roche of the USA who understand their particular health care regulatory systems. Local knowledge can be vitally important. General Motors, for example, was at a disadvantage in its attempt to introduce the Nova car to the South American market. 'No va' means 'no go' in Spanish.

(b) *Some markets are politically protected.* Local company majority equity stakes are required in Indonesia, Malaya, Nigeria and India. Switzerland and Germany prohibit or restrict foreign acquisitions. The European Commission has recently reduced the size level at which mergers require its sanction. Political barriers such as these mean that global players *have* to joint venture in ways that are acceptable not only to their organisational collaborators but also to the governments involved. IBM's co-operative venture with Hyundai for the production of 5,550 personal computers has enabled penetration of the South Korean market. British Aerospace collaborates with foreign defence equipment manufacturers such as McDonnell-Douglas of the USA to ensure sales into their countries' defence industries.

(c) *Many new product opportunities require complex technologies, massive expenditure and rapid development while many of the opportunity seekers, individually, have limited R & D and manufacture capabilities, inadequate finance and comparatively small potential market take-up positions to develop products sufficiently quickly and to acceptable levels of risk.* Projects involving high levels of expenditure, long-term paybacks and multi-aspect, complex technology commend themselves to the strategic alliance. General Electric (USA), Asea (Sweden) and Hitachi and Toshiba (Japan) have collaborated to develop atomic reactors. Rolls-Royce (UK), IHI-Kawasaki-Mitsubishi (Japan), Pratt and Whitney and MTU (Germany), and Fiat (Italy) shared a $3 billion project to power a new generation of 150-seat planes. Renault and Daf Vanguard shared the £200 million development costs of a projected new product range. IBM, once aloof, now joint ventures with smaller organisations in an effort to improve the effectiveness of its traditionally self-contained and massive R & D function. ICL needed resource inputs from Fujitsu for the development of its current generation of mainframes – mainframes can cost up to £500 million to develop and produce.

(d) *The strategic alliance is a competitive advantage bestowing* learning *process, whereby* learning *takes place more quickly than is the case with 'do it alone' methods.* Mitsubishi learned from Acme how to manufacture and sell its machine tools – in Acme market places. Trianju obtained access to Otis Elevator technology, Otis obtained access to and knowledge of the Chinese market. Honda learned about European car making and marketing from its venture with British Leyland. Bull (France) and NEC (Japan) transferred design and production technology knowledge from Honeywell. A contribution of £200,000 to the National and EC Pre-Competitive Collaborative Research Consortium Programme gives access to £4 million worth of research results.

(e) *Governmental incentives make it worthwhile to collaborate.* European research programmes such as Eureka and ESPRIT provide funds to enable research to be undertaken – organisations can *exist and grow* through treating governmental research project backers as customers. However, the formation of an alliance is often a pre-condition of funds allocation. The European Strategic PRogramme in Information Technology (ESPRIT) has more than 450 collaborators, for example.

(f) *Strategic alliance makes sound* defensive *competitive sense.* Multinationals could over run the post-1992 European internal market and smaller, nationally based European firms cannot counter this threat individually. The Airbus Industries consortium of Aerospatiale (France), AerItalia (Italy), British Aerospace (UK), CASA (Spain), Fokker (The Netherlands), SABCA (Belgium), and VWF (Germany) is funded by private companies and by European governments. It attracts multi-skills from its partners and launch orders from major European airlines. It challenges, on behalf of Europe, the exclusive presence of Boeing, McDonnell-Douglas and Lockheed in the medium-sized, wide-bodied jet airlines market. BMW and

Rolls-Royce develop and produce new commercial aero-engines *together* instead of in aggressive competition. Pilkington's decision to license out its float glass technology to 16 major world plate glass manufacturers, forestalled much larger companies from developing competitive technology to rival Pilkington. Ford and Volkswagen formed a single, jointly owned company, Autolatina, with merged German and American management, to effect a rationalisation in 1987, following the collapse of the South American market.

(g) *Strategic alliance can improve* cost *and* differentiation-*based competitive advantages. Joining together to manufacture, for example, can produce scale-based economies. Out-sourcing to organisations capable of performing an important aspect of the product/service value chain more effectively is also likely to improve competitive strategy.* Polaroid, through working *closely* with its suppliers, saved $27 million over two years. Marks & Spencer's collaborations with suppliers, over quality and cost drives, are famous. Bendix transfers its machine tool technology to Murata in Japan and gets back the finished products for sale in the US at 30 per cent less than US manufacturing costs. *Internal* alliances are being developed on the base of quality of working life programmes and quality improvement campaigns which aim to harness the commitment of employees to the quest for improved quality, efficiency and productivity.

(h) *Strategic alliances avoid the problems of merger and acquisition.* Mergers and acquisitions as development methods are notoriously expensive – big premiums over market prices are the norm (5).

Further, they have a tendency to be poor performers on synergy criteria. According to Porter nearly 50 per cent of mergers fail (6). Joint ventures can make more sense because:

- they are less permanent and are easier to get out of;
- there is no obligation to manage all that comes with the package;
- they have less tendency to create organisational rigidity (compared, for example, with the full vertical integration of a supplier which then becomes so secure that it loses the motivation to innovate);
- the alliance allows the smaller partner to maintain its ownership and identity (particularly important to smaller and more entrepreneurial companies);
- the alliance might be the *only* option because anti-competition or nationalistic protective laws might, for example, restrict merger/acquisition;
- there is less impact in terms of organisation re-structuring;
- the learning process for either of the collaborators might be such that over time the collaboration can be phased out, gradually, easily and beneficially;
- the alliance can form a first step towards a 'full blown' merger;
- the alliance is often easier to 'sell' to a potential partner than is the 'bid' approach of the acquisition or merger.

(i) *The supply of strategic alliance partners is running out.* Clarke and Brennan (5) estimate that, in Europe, for every company considering selling, 25 firms are seeking to buy. The European Commission recorded almost 500 mergers in the year to June 1989. Foster (7) reminds us that joint ventures are even more common than mergers. One message behind these statistics is clear – organisations are proactively forging strategic alliances. The best partners are likely to be 'snapped up' first; organisations cannot simply sit back and expect to forge effective strategic alliances 'in due course'.

(j) *Failure to create strategic alliances might result in a* worsening *of competitive position.* Often, new strategic development 'fashions' give most benefits to the early adopters. Not to join the strategic alliance trend might mean being left behind in the competitive race. Also, of course, for smaller organisations dependent on bigger, strategically sophisticated customers or suppliers, a request to join a strategic alliance infers a 'take it' rather than a 'take it or leave it' choice.

Strategic alliances seem set to increase and intensify. Figures 5.8 and 5.9 provide illustrations which indicate the extent of the alliance as a development method in the telecommunications and the motor car industries. They also provide graphic support for the views of particular management theorists who model the historical development of the business world from a 'simple machine' situation to that of a 'complex social network' (8). (This is an issue we will return to in Chapter 14 which examines the subject of shock event planning.) World infrastructural improvements in transport and communications have provided a basis to enable the upsurge in rapidly formed, more intensely liaised collaborations.

## Why do strategic alliances sometimes fail?

Despite the clear strategic logic of the strategic alliance choice, given business situations described above, many – perhaps most – alliances fail to achieve the synergistic benefits hoped for at their outsets (9). Ostensibly, the reason behind alliance failure is simple – the *wrong partners have been chosen*. We will indicate later why this reason for failure is too simplistic by itself. However, at this stage it will be fruitful to consider why strategic alliance partners have sometimes been seen, in hindsight, to have been unsuitable collaborators. Hindsight, of course, can be used to improve future choices. Thus, an unsuitable partner is likely to exhibit one or some of the following characteristics.

(a) *It occupies only a weak competitive position and thereby provides an inadequate contribution to the alliance.* The Siemens-RCA alliance was disbanded when the competitively disadvantaged RCA quit the computer business overnight. Renault invested £654 million in AMC which nevertheless lost £750 million before the partnership was dissolved. The message from such examples is clear – if your organisation is looking for market position, technological skills, marketing or manufacturing expertise, or whatever, *choose a winner*. The choice of strategic partner should be based on an evaluation of the competencies exhibited by the potential partner in the context of their application in your market area of operation.

(b) *It looks to 'stab you in the back'.* Some partners enter into collaborative agreements as a means of 'lulling the competition into a false sense of security before you stab them in the back' (to quote one strategic allying executive) (5). The Acme-Cleveland/Mitsubishi agreement referred to above provides one example of a western corporation providing a stepping stone for a Japanese collaborator to grow into a full blown competitor. In 1970, NEC was only one quarter of the size of Honeywell, its principal foreign partner. In the 1980s the much grown NEC bought its weakened partner. RCA's licensing of TV technology to Japanese companies led to

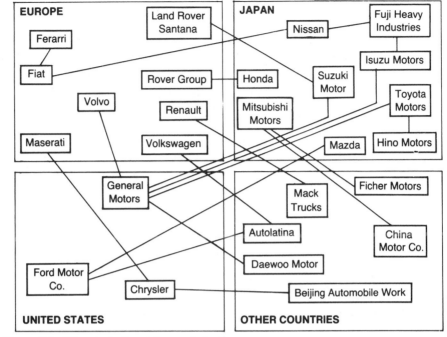

**Figure 5.8  Alliances in the motor car industry**

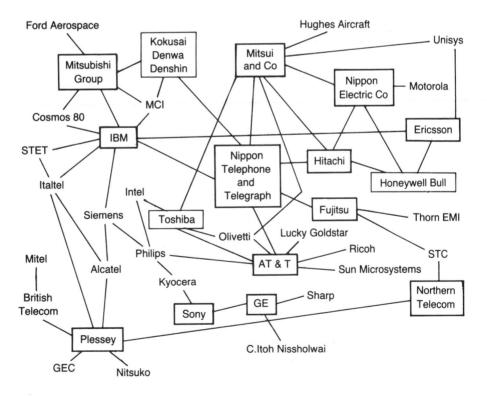

**Figure 5.9  Alliances in the telecommunications industry**

the decimation of its US market by the Japanese in the 1960s and 1970s. More recent Japanese production activity in the US and European small car industries has provided the basis for the development of long-term sustainable positions, for the Japanese.

Collaboration *is for* competition – strategic allying organisations should be aware that for some partners the strategic alliance *will be a means for competing with the allying firms*. Hamel et al. (10) describe the competitive approach to collaboration, adopted, generally, by Japanese organisations: 'Japanese companies see no dichotomy between collaboration and competition; they exploit collaborative agreements in single minded pursuit of their own competitive advantage.' To 'play safe' readers should replace 'Japanese' with 'Most', in the Hamel quotation.

(c) *It learns at your expense.* Associated with the above competitive rationale is the concept of 'transfer of technology'. Western organisations often enter alliances as a means of *avoidance*. They seek, through the alliance, to reduce investment expense and risk. The Japanese (again), however, are more interested in long-term competitive advantage development based on the acquisition of key skills and competencies from their alliance partners. These fundamentally different rationales for strategic alliance are encapsulated in the example below. Precautions are thus necessary to ensure that learning exchanges are balanced. IBM, for example, has built a special site in Japan where collaborators can review its mainframe software developments under *controlled* conditions before deciding whether to license it. Staff working on collaborative projects need to be briefed on what is and what is not to be shared. Asian manufacturer partners often have an advantage over Western designers/ marketers in that the value chain activities which create their manufacturing advantage are often numerous and involve subtle 'excellence' generating linkages. In comparison, their partners' key competencies are often simpler and more transparent. The building of a multi-layered, difficult to unravel, and continually improving base for competitive advantage is one way of achieving its sustainability.

## Case example: different rationales for the same strategic alliance

Senior US executives: 'We complement each other well – our distribution capability and their manufacturing skill. I see no reason to invest up-stream if we can find a secure source of product. This is a comfortable relationship for us.'

Japanese executive: 'When it is necessary to collaborate, I go to my employees and say, "This is bad, I wish we had these skills ourselves." Collaboration is second best. But I will feel worse if after four years, we do not know how to do what our partners know how to do. We must digest their skills.'

(Adapted from G Hamel et al. (10) )

(d) *It seeks dominance – and exercises the power gained to your detriment.* Power balances are crucial elements in determining who gets most out of alliances. If the richer organisation provides resources to strengthen the poorer one it is likely to demand in exchange some control over the poorer firm's decisions. Suppliers dealing with Marks & Spencer, for example, must work to Marks & Spencer's standards. Over time, the dependence of one firm on the other might increase to the extent where, given a downturn in trade, for example, the dependent organisation is required to bear the biggest brunt of the recession. Austin Rover is, perhaps, becoming increasingly reliant on the contribution made by its foreign joint venturers. In such situations the position of the weaker partner might be expected to be most satisfactory during periods of market growth. During these good times, however, the weaker party might be well advised to expect that problem periods are coming and to plan accordingly.

(e) *It is unprepared to match your commitment to the collaboration.* A big organisation might put 1 per cent of its resources into a collaborative venture. Its smaller partner might be inputting 95 per cent of its resource base. Equal levels of commitment might not, therefore apply. This can lead to conflict, frustration and a diversion of attention away from the synergistic rationale which underpinned the creation of the alliance. Hewlett-Packard bought 11 per cent of Cericor Inc. for joint development purposes and was disappointed with the commitment it obtained in return. Cericor, however, had similar relationships with other organisations including Data General, and shared its commitment accordingly. Issues over level of commitment and resource backing need to be sorted out at the outset of the alliance so that people know what to expect and how to judge the inputs that are actually made.

(f) *It procrastinates in decision-making processes.* Who will manage the alliance needs to be sorted out in advance of its implementation. Ownership is not the same as control. Research indicates that a dominant management system, whereby one company takes charge of the operation of the joint venture, or where an independent management is set up and left to get on with its job, is more productive than a joint control management system. The joint management approach delays decision-making in what often needs to be a fast, flexible and responsible decision-making situation. This problem arises because of the perceived need to refer continually to each organisational hierarchy before committing resources to the alliance's development (11).

(g) *It is mistrustful of you and your approach to the alliance.* Much of the above discussion suggests that a degree of mistrust makes sense in the alliance situation. To use a personal analogy the strategic alliance is more akin to a relationship with a mistress than a wife. Nevertheless, winning alliances are forged by organisations (and people) who 'get on' with each other. In contrast, the venture between the Tiny Metheus Corporation and Computer Vision was disbanded allegedly because of a lack of trust between the respective managements. Unidata, a computer venture of Philips, Bull and Siemens collapsed, in part, because the partners couldn't shed corporate and national rivalries. A failure to integrate the managements of Dunlop and Pirelli is similarly held as being a major contributor to the failure of their 1980s collaboration.

(h) *It has objectives and an organisation structure/culture which are mismatched with your own or which do not facilitate an appropriate organisation system for the alliance sub-unit.* The examples of mistrust, cited above, derive from problems of conflicting objectives, structures and cultures. Other examples are available. The Acme-Cleveland/Multi-Arc Vacuum venture failure was attributed in part to differing management styles. This problem of 'culture clash' and conflicting objectives is compounded when more parties are involved. A further difficulty is caused by the need for the alliance to be managed in a more flexible, 'give and take' style than is the norm in more bureaucratically managed parent corporations. Despite the importance of these management issues research indicates that 60 per cent of alliances do not define expectations at the outset, or set commonly agreed objectives (12) and that while half of top management's time goes into *creating* a joint venture less than 10 per cent of its time is spent *addressing management questions and management systems* (13). Alliances need to be adequately resourced and staffed by personnel possessing the skills, information, commitment and interpersonal styles appropriate for their jobs. Insufficient attention to these issues enables Peters to suggest that 'Numerous hastily formed partnerships yielding short-term financial returns have bombed in the long run because time-consuming relationship building was ignored.' (14)

(i)  *It has links with other market place competitors and is careless about passing on your secrets.* As world market places become networks of alliances the danger of loss of proprietary information grows. A look back at Figures 5.8 and 5.9 will help set this problem in context. Some 'free market' economists attack strategic alliances from a general market perspective, claiming that collaboration constrains innovation because collaborators become too secure, lose the motivation to compete with their partners and/or expect innovation secrets to be leaked before the innovations can be marketed to competitive gain. Again, this is a problem which calls for prior thought, clear agreement between parties and mutual trust.

(j)  *It is looking to 'catch up' rather than to 'stay ahead'.* Competitive advantage, like charity, begins at home. *Self-development* activity aimed at improving organisational value chain activities is the fundamental competitive advantage creator. The Japanese haven't so much used the strategic alliance strategy as a means for gaining leading competitive positions directly, so much as they have used strategic alliances to develop *their own ability* to gain competitive advantage. The Japanese approach confirms Porter's view: 'Alliances are no panacea. Improving competitive position ultimately requires that a firm develops its internal capabilities, in areas important to competitive advantage.' (15)

Alliances between organisations simply intent on joining the alliance bandwagon are unlikely to work. Neither are those which are formed as short termist attempts to bolster weak competitive positions. Rather, they are more appropriate as a way forward for organisations *who already enjoy* competitive advantage and who are seeking to sustain or improve their positions. Again, to quote Porter (discussing global competitive situations): 'Alliances are tools for extending or reinforcing competitive advantage but rarely a sustainable means for creating it.' (16)

## Competitive advantage through collaboration – conclusion

This section has indicated that strategic alliance as a development method is particularly pertinent to modern, global market, quickly changing, high technology, big resource requiring, business conditions. We can expect more, rather than less, of the strategic alliance as a generic way forward for our organisations. This discussion, however, has also warned of some of the pitfalls associated with the strategic alliance method. These pitfalls have been described in the context of their arising through the adverse activities of strategic partners. In fact, this view, according to the theory of management strategy is too simplistic. The real problem behind failed strategic alliances is a *lack of rationality* on the part of decision-makers in choosing, negotiating, setting up and managing aspects of the decision processes involved in the alliance creating/managing/process. Greater thought, information analysis and evaluation is required to improve the chances of successfully planning and implementing strategic alliances. To support the above discussion and as a helpful conclusion to this section, Figures 5.10 and 5.11 are offered as aids to a more systematic approach to the achievement of competitive advantage through collaboration.

- The relationship is IMPORTANT, and therefore gets its adequate resources, management attention, and sponsorship.

- There is an agreement for longer term INVESTMENT, which tends to equalise benefits over time.

- The partners are INTERDEPENDENT, which helps to keep power balanced.

- The organisations are INTEGRATED so that appropriate points of contact and communication are managed.

- Each is INFORMED about the plans and directions of the other.

- The partnership is INSTITUTIONALISED – bolstered by a framework of supporting mechanisms, from legal requirements to social ties to share values, all of which in fact make trust possible.

**Figure 5.10  The 'six Is' of successful strategic alliances (source: Kanter (4) )**

# Strategy formulation and implementation issues

Choices on products to sell, markets to serve and competitive strategies to adopt are important decisions. They will affect the future strategic theme performance significantly. Also of importance are, however, choices designed to ensure that the organisation is an effective *implementer* of product/market decisions and a successful *ongoing formulator* of new developments. In this section we present a number of prescriptions and research findings which address the question of how to make pertinent formulation/implementation responses to modern 'right-sided' environments (as per Figure 4.2).

(a) *Divestment*. Igor Ansoff sums up the uncertainty rationale for divestment: 'If the firm's management is reluctant to increase the complexity of the firm's system to a level necessary to make them responsive to the environment, it should simplify the strategic position of the firm by exiting from turbulent business areas.'(17)

(b) *Boundary spanning/environmental scanning*. Specialist marketing, public relations, and research personnel are often necessary to give the required time and expertise to monitoring, understanding and interacting with important aspects of diverse environments. Chapter 7 on administration planning suggests a 'marketing controlled' approach for the creation of a boundary spanning/environmental scanning, organisation-wide response to today's environments.

(c) *Sophisticated communication systems*. Sensing mechanisms have to be supplemented by communicating mechanisms. With so much more important

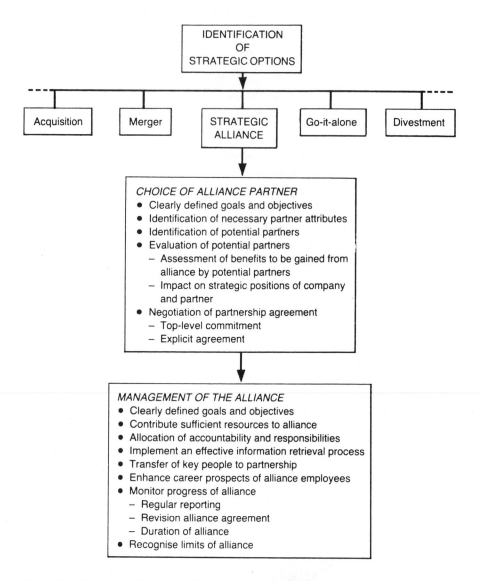

**Figure 5.11 Strategic alliance checklist for success (from James (11) )**

information being generated, larger, more complex (but effective) information systems are needed to ensure that important messages are picked up and communicated to pertinent decision-makers in a timely and clear manner. Too often messages arrive too late or are insufficiently informative. Paradoxically, sophisticated 'today' information systems rely to a large extent on less formal and less controlled mechanisms for communication – people have to be motivated to talk to each other about the things that matter.

(d) *Scenario forecasting.* In seeking to spot future threats and opportunities, scenario forecasting uses a range of internally and externally generated 'pictures' of the future to supplement econometrically derived projections. The various opinions obtained are then used by the decision-makers to engender thought and debate leading to the selection of a range of forecasts, including pessimistic, most likely, and optimistic outcomes. (The role and techniques of forecasting are considered in Chapter 8.)

(e) *Contingency planning.* All organisations need contingency plans to deal with the unexpected. Contingency plans seek to offer alternative arrangements ready for deployment if the blueprint plan proves, in the event, to be unrealistic. Contingency planning is the subject matter for our next chapter.

(f) *Decentralisation.* Large organisations operating in a number of different markets which exhibit hostility and unpredictability have, in the commercial setting, divisionalised for greater success. More successful decentralisations of responsibility have utilised the following procedure (18):

- keeping overall financial and strategic control at the corporate level;
- keeping divisional (compared to operating) units small – in terms of size and decision-making responsibility;
- delegating production and marketing strategy making to those units at 'grass roots' level;
- reallocating finance on a return on investment, rather than on a size of operation, basis.

(g) *Team culture planning.* Strategy is at least as much to do with the thousands of daily decisions and plans as it is to do with major 'one-off' long-term developments. When much is happening quickly, strategy depends particularly upon everybody taking part in sensing and reacting to the changes taking place. In the commercial context organisations are being seen to develop success through harnessing collective effort towards increasing customer satisfaction and productivity. (Team culture planning is covered in Chapters 11 and 12.)

(h) *Innovation planning.* In an era of rapid change, organisations have to innovate to stay in the strategic race. Strategy itself is innovation. It is about the continuous process of forming and implementing new adaptations. Specifically, successful commercial organisations have been seen to employ, within the total framework of a responsive organisation, 'innovation champions' who have led multifunctional teams to invent useful new products, services and new ways of operating. (Innovation planning is covered in Chapter 13.)

(i) *Opportunity and shock event planning.* Even in the most sophisticated strategy-making institution shock events can occur. Local authorities, for example, had to respond instantly to the unforeseen Chernobyl disaster. In a 'global village' world the frequency of such shock events seems likely to increase rather than to diminish. The ability to grab unexpected opportunities and/or to recover effectively from adverse events will depend in no small way on the general sophistication of the organisation's planning system, the availability of slack resources (for deployment to the emergency) and the extent of motivation inherent in the enterprise. (See also Chapter 14.)

(j) *Sophisticated planners.* A number of commercial organisations have, in recent years, undertaken massively expensive management development campaigns. Personnel at all levels of such organisations are being introduced to the theories and practices of successful strategy. Strategy/decision-making/planning courses of study have mushroomed in universities and polytechnics and many 'in company' programmes of this type have been implemented. Many top planners have, themselves, been through management strategy-based programmes of study.

The following section provides information on some research studies into how strategy-making processes might best be designed and implemented for modern day success.

## Differentiation and integration

Following work by Burns and Stalker (19) Lawrence and Lorsch (20), researching in the 1960s, set out to establish the kind of organisation structure most suited to different types of environment. They investigated firms operating in stable, medium-dynamic and diverse-dynamic environments. A major conclusion of their work was that greater commercial success in dynamic and diverse environments is earned by those organisations which are *highly differentiated* (in terms of functions, attitudes and interpersonal styles of personnel, and work time horizon orientations) *and* which are more *intensely integrated*. Integration (the level of collaboration existing among departments) was successfully achieved by these organisations through recourse to a range of 'integrators':

(a)  rules and procedures;

(b)  direct managerial contact;

(c)  appeals to the hierarchy;

(d)  temporary cross-functional teams;

(e)  permanent cross-functional teams;

(f)  individual co-ordinators;

(g)  co-ordinating departments.

In contrast, the successful firms working in *stable* environments were less differentiated and used only the first three of the above integrators. In fact, research evidence suggested that in stable environments the introduction of additional, more sophisticated integrators is likely to be an unhelpful irritant to the administrative system.

## Decentralising for diversity

In his book *Strategy and Structure* (21), Alfred Chandler traced the growth of successful American companies during the first half of the twentieth century. He showed how a typical organisation structure moved through sequential stages of one-man operations/control; functional department structure; and divisional structure as the enterprise grew in size and diversity of operations/environments.

## Achieving excellence

In *In Search of Excellence* (22), Peters and Waterman report on their findings of the organising characteristics of successful American companies. Characteristics which achieved success in ambiguous environments were identified as:

(a) *A bias for action.* Successful organisations showed an ability and desire to try things – to respond to situations rather than to sit back and hope for environments to change in favour of the organisation.

(b) *Close to the customer.* Success for these firms was founded on understanding customers and in serving them well.

(c) *Autonomy and entrepreneurship.* In order to avoid some of the problems of 'bigness' many successful firms pushed responsibility and authority (autonomy) 'down the line' to product managers and venture teams, etc. Further, they encouraged staff to be entrepreneurial.

(d) *Productivity through people.* The 'excellent' companies treated their workers as mature people who would respond better to high expectations and peer group assessment rather than to heavy handed 'boss' control.

(e) *Hands on value-driven.* This characteristic refers to the way that leaders, through personal example and involvement, have indoctrinated their organisations to accept and adhere to those core values that are essential to the organisation's identity and success.

(f) *Sticking to the knitting.* According to Peters and Waterman, organisations that do branch out into new operating areas which are related enough to benefit from existing 'excellent' skills perform more successfully than the 'out and out' conglomerates.

(g) *Simple form, lean staff.* The successful companies had avoided two dangers which expansion creates – complex organisation structures and large numbers of staff personnel. Excellent companies seem to have few people working at corporate level – most are out 'in the field' getting things done. Despite the hugeness of many of these winning organisations staff *knew* their job and their place in the structure – even though jobs and structures might be in a constant state of flux.

(h) *Simultaneous loose–tight properties.* While the excellent firms encouraged autonomy and entrepreneurship, employees knew that discretionary decision-making operated within the constraints of adherence to the organisation's core values. Excellence in these areas was often achieved through attention to, and control of the finest detail.

## Case examples: handling the environment

(a) *Hanson plc.* Hanson's skill at picking acquisitions where parts can be sold off for more than the total cost of the original purchase price is legendary. Its late 1980s purchase of Kaiser Cement in the US was followed by a short period of swift disposals which realised £250 million – exceeding the acquisition price. Similar strategies produced similar outcomes from SCM (the titanium dioxide business).

Both these businesses now stand in the books at nil net cost, yet were producing trading profits in 1988 of more than £300 million. After divesting those parts which do not fit into the Hanson conglomerate portfolio the Hanson 'turnaround' approach, incorporating delegation of responsibility for success of the business unit concerned; centrally administered financial controls; tight management control systems; and staff changes where necessary, soon has return on capital employed growing.

(b) *Sumrie*. The sale by Sumner International of its Sumrie clothes subsidiary to Executex in 1988 made sense for both organisations. Executex expected synergy to flow from the availability of additional suit-making capacity and anticipated that Sumrie would provide an easily integrated acquisition (Sumrie is literally 'just round the corner' from Executex). From Sumner International's perspective the divestment of a unit which was 'requiring too much management time' would enable the organisation to concentrate on its newer, expanding secretarial, management and language learning centres.

(c) *Maxwell*. In 1988, Robert Maxwell explained the sale of the industrial and engineering side of Hollis as being part of his plans to concentrate the company's resources on its professional and financial services interest.

## Think and discuss

Identify whether and, if appropriate, how the above organisations are adopting theoretically prescribed planning process approaches for handling today's environments.

# Political bargaining strategies

In Chapter 3 on aspirations planning we discussed how strategists often need to modify their preferred development strategies to take account of the perceived preferences of powerful stakeholders. In a situation where the strategist perceives his or her preferred course of action to conflict with that of the stakeholder, a number of potential response are possible:

(a)  change the strategy to concur with the stakeholder's wishes;

(b)  bargain to achieve a compromise strategy;

(c)  bargain to obtain the stakeholder's acceptance of the strategist's preferred strategy; or

(d)  ignore the stakeholder and simply press on with the preferred strategy.

A major art in strategy-making is the ability to create pertinent bargaining strategies and implement consequential developments which are both economically effective and politically acceptable. Chapter 3 provided, in greater detail, some political bargaining strategies.

# Generating strategic alternatives: brainstorming

At this stage of the corporate planning process the management strategist should be almost ready to decide the way forward. The strategist has by now assimilated information on:

(a) organisational objectives and aspirations;

(b) resource strengths, weaknesses and distinctive competencies;

(c) environmental opportunities and threats;

(d) strategic standing and strategic 'fit';

(e) potential product/market developments, competitive strategy choices, political situations and organisational change issues.

During the planning process certain potential strategies might have resurfaced time after time. However, before making any strategic development choices a further intermediary step is recommended. Many corporate planning gurus recommend *brainstorming* sessions to generate long lists of potential developments. Corporate planning developments are likely to be of such importance that it is necessary to consider an exhaustive list. It is better, argue the theorists, to raise impractical and/or inconsequential developments for evaluation, than to miss a strategy which would have proved appropriate and beneficial. Brainstorming is best conducted in groups of four to eight for periods of no longer than one hour. Basic guidelines which should be explained to groups before the start of the exercise include:

(a) the more ideas the better;

(b) no idea is too 'outlandish' to be expressed;

(c) laugh *with* contributors but not *at* them;

(d) combinations and modifications of ideas are welcome;

(e) *evaluation* should not be part of the exercise.

At the very least, the final list recorded should counteract the worry expressed by John Argenti who says, 'I have felt it necessary to place so much emphasis on the number and variety of strategies that are available to any company because, in general, the list from which most companies select their final set of strategies is rather brief and unimaginative.' (23) Brainstorming can produce important new development ideas. After generating a plethora of strategic alternatives the planning group needs to 'sort out the wheat from the chaff' via a preliminary evaluation. Following this activity the strategic development list should contain only those potential strategies which the planners consider worthy of more detailed evaluation.

## Evaluating potential strategies and choosing the ways forward

The evaluation of potential strategies uses the very same information that first stimulated each strategy. The corporate planning strategist assesses the appropriateness of particular developments against a backcloth of objectives, strengths, weaknesses, opportunities and threats. Johnson and Scholes (24) have suggested three broad tests of the pertinence of potential strategies:

(a) *Suitability* measures the extent to which a potential development fits the needs of the business situation as identified in the strategic analysis. For example, does the strategy address an opportunity, build on a strength, bolster a weakness or avoid a threat?

(b) *Feasibility* tests the extent to which a strategy can be implemented. A strategy which seeks to make inroads into a new market might be suitable in terms of addressing a perceived opportunity. However, severe cash shortages might make the strategy infeasible.

(c) *Acceptability* criteria demand assessments of whether strategies 'on the table' satisfy stakeholder aspirations. For example, a particular strategy may not satisfy top management's growth aspirations; another might be perceived as too risky for the owners of the business to accept; a strong workforce might be against the significant restructuring that a third option involves, and so on.

No hard and fast rules can be applied in the evaluatory process. Strategists need to design their own framework of criteria for evaluation and test strategies accordingly. Often different criteria have different significance and these have to be taken into account also. It might be that the wishes of owners, for example, are given greater weight than those of the workforce. Sometimes, too, a suitable strategy *must* be implemented despite reservations over its acceptability and feasibility. In the 1980s, for example, redevelopments that were painful and difficult to implement were undertaken to ensure the survival of top British organisations such as Jaguar, Lucas and Courtaulds. A strategic 'score card', as illustrated in Fig. 5.12 can be useful in evaluating, ranking and choosing strategies for implementation: plus and minus points are awarded to each strategy against each evaluation criteria and the totals indicate the potential effectiveness of each option. The example is of a professional association considering entry into new markets (despite the adverse competitive situations in options of going up-market and consolidating, the planners were, in fact, in favour of these two developments).

| Strategy | Resources | Market growth opportunity | Competitive situation | Existing members' aspirations | Total |
|---|---|---|---|---|---|
| Do nothing | 10 | −10 | 0 | −8 | −8 |
| Reduce entry qualifications - go down-market | 5 | 10 | 5 | −10 | +10 |
| Consolidate | 5 | −5 | −2 | 5 | +3 |
| Emphasis qualification exclusivity - move up-market | 5 | 10 | −8 | 10 | +17 |

Figure 5.12 Evaluating product/market for a professional association

## A checklist for evaluating alternative developments

We have already stated that evaluations, like other stages of corporate planning processes, should be customised activities. Model frameworks, however, can assist planners to be more usefully creative in their particular situations, than would have been the case without guidelines to follow. The framework below (25) is presented as a checklist of eight evaluatory questions.

(a) Will the strategy make us more efficient and/or more capable of exploiting/controlling the environment?

(b) Will the strategy afford synergistic opportunities?

(c) Will the strategy promote competitive advantage based on distinctive competence?

(d) Is the potential strategy addressing an inherently attractive market?

(e) Will the cost of the strategy provide us with the opportunity to earn acceptable returns?

(f) Do we have the resources and the commitment to successfully implement the potential strategy?

(g) What are the likely consequences of potential responses by environmental stakeholders to implementation of the potential strategy?

(h) How does the potential strategy compare with other potential strategies?

In the section which follows, this framework is illustrated by application to a general strategy of acquisition.


## Evaluating acquisition choices

### Will the acquisition make us more efficient and/or more capable of controlling/exploiting the environment?

Much debate over the efficiency of acquisition has centred round the fundamental question, 'For whose benefit does the organisation exist?' Shareholders, for example, are often seen to obtain a poor deal from top management in acquisition developments. In terms of organisational survival, however, growth depends on high standards of efficiency (over time the organisation must attract at least as much resource as it spends) and on control and exploitation of the environment. This systems goal concept is central to the premise of management strategy that strategic success, fundamentally, is about organisational adaptation to environments through time. People inside the organisation, particularly, have common vested interests in working toward these system goals. The achievement of system goals sustains and improves the total wealth of the enterprise. As such, distribution of the wealth created presents a secondary issue for resolution.

We suggest, therefore, that the primary objective of any acquisition is to improve the wealth-creating capacity of the organisation by adding to its present ability to control efficiently the environment.

This first question, then, 'Will the acquisition make us more efficient and/or more capable of controlling and exploiting the environment?' is fundamental and can be answered through reference to the following questions.

## Will the takeover afford synergistic opportunities?

Synergy is often explained as the concept of $2 \times 2 = 5$. The search for synergy requires the acquiring strategists to identify areas where particular strengths of the acquirer and/or acquiree can be applied to improve the other's performance. Synergistic benefits are in excess of those efficiency and/or control benefits which would have applied as the total benefits of separate activities. Hanson Trust and BTR, for example, are past masters at turning around ailing companies through implementing their management control programmes. Mothercare's alignment with Habitat enabled Conran to take the helm of a bigger success vehicle. Dixons' takeover of Currys, and the subsequently enhanced market presence for both organisations in both white and brown goods and in younger and middle-aged markets produced profits in excess of those which would have been generated prior to the amalgamation. Synergy thus improves performance internally and/or externally and generates greater total wealth than would otherwise have been the case.

## Case examples: searching for synergy

(a) Evode, an industrial adhesive group purchased (for £14.8 million) Supra, an automotive components group with a core business in car sound-deadening material, of which it held a 70 per cent UK market share. All the ingredients for a successful synergistic marriage were there:

- purchase of a large market share;
- shared technologies and manufacturing skills;
- common material sourcing.

(b) The industrial logic behind the acquisition merging Presto stores with more up-market Safeway stores for £681 million was quite clear to James Gulliver of Presto:

- An excellent geographic fit. Safeways are mainly located in the prosperous South East while Presto's strength is in the North and Scotland.
- The groups are operationally complementary. Presto brought buying power to its new partner. From a base of almost 300 stores it can squeeze suppliers more than a stand-alone Safeways ever could. In turn, Safeways brought in a proven expertise in managing high margin quality foods.
- The combined market share of the two (10 per cent) will more closely match its main rivals, Sainsbury (18 per cent), Tesco (14 per cent) and Dee Corporation (13 per cent).

## Will the takeover promote competitive advantage based on distinctive competence?

Many strategy theorists remind us that sustainable strategic success is born from competitive advantage. Thus, the acquiring strategists should be looking at potential acquisitions to find ways in which the acquisitions can assist in the attainment of *least-cost and/or differentiation advantages*. Elders, for example, has used acquisition to become the biggest operator in its market (and biggest usually infers a least-cost production position). A major GEC rationale for the acquisition of Creda was, again, improved market share. Research findings from the mid-1970s, such as those illustrated in Table 5.1, indicate that bigger acquisitions of market share promote a higher likelihood of subsequent success. These findings have been replicated more recently in the mid 1980s. If a high market share position is unlikely theory advises specialisation in smaller, more focused markets. Ideally, any acquisition should put you into a position where your organisation is more attractive and more profitable than competitors.

**Table 5.1  The significance of buying market share**

| Market share acquired | 1% | 1–5% | 5–10% | 10–25% | 25–50% | 50+% |
|---|---|---|---|---|---|---|
| Successful | 43 | 42 | 58 | 61 | 70 | 73 |
| Neutral | 22 | 23 | 24 | 20 | 12 | 24 |
| Failed | 35 | 35 | 18 | 19 | 18 | 3 |

## Is the market situation of the potential acquiree inherently attractive?

Particularly attractive market segments exhibit the following characteristics:

- the market segment is of sufficient current size;
- the market has the potential for further growth;
- the market segment is not 'owned' or over-occupied by existing competition;
- the market segment has some relative unsatisfied needs that the particular company can serve well.

Michael Porter's concept of structural analysis reminds us that the competitive structure of some industries is such that all competitors can do well, while in others strategic sophistication and effort are needed simply to earn acceptable returns. Acquisition is a means of acquiring competitive position in particular industries. These industries should be inherently attractive.

Imperial, despite a sophisticated search for the 'right' acquisition, made a fundamental market growth forecast mistake in its Howard Johnson buy. The BAT purchase of Eagle Star took BAT into insurance at the peak of a business cycle and when there was a strong question mark over the future growth potential of its own core products. The insurance company's results in 1984, the year after acquisition, were its worst since 1978.

Thus, the inherent attractiveness of the acquiree's markets and market positions should be well researched. Timing of the takeover bid, in this context, is crucial. Structural analysis of the acquiree's markets is essential prior to any takeover approach.

## Will the cost of the acquisition and of market entry provide us with the opportunity to earn acceptable returns?

It has been estimated that in 1986 overt fees of £500 million attached to the management/defence of £12 billion worth of contested bids. This says nothing of the 'opportunity costs' of in-house management time devoted to managing and fighting hostile bids. Neither does it take account of the costs of reorganising and re-equipping acquired enterprises or of the cost of fighting off newly alerted competitors hostile to the new entrant. Critics also argue that takeover battles often become personal power games rather than means to negotiate economically sensible investments. Top management, once into the game, often seem reluctant to get out – despite exorbitantly spiralling purchase prices.

BAT won Eagle Star, for example, against determined West German bidding. The £968 million purchase price represented about 20 times the then prospective earnings. Imperial not only paid too much for Courage, but paid it at exactly the wrong time – when the brewing industry was at a peak.

Of course, the higher the price paid, the less will be the returns on investment. Findings of researchers such as Bergman (26) which indicate that the higher the premium above market price, the less likely the acquisition is to succeed, seem to confirm our common sense expectations. Potential costs must be weighed against potential rewards in a cool, detached and professional manner if later recriminations are to be avoided.

## Do we have the resources and the commitment to acquire the potential acquisition and to achieve a successful integration?

Careful resource analysis of the acquirer's own organisation should resolve this issue. Minnows that bid for giants have need of adequate finance – not only to make the acquisition, but to continue to service adequately existing and acquired operations. Acquisition/break-up specialists such as Hanson have depths of expertise and experience in evaluating acquisition propositions and in 'turning round' operating subdivisions. Unless your organisation has these resource skills available for deployment it is probably best to leave the acquisition alone, unless existing acquiree management seems likely to possess the skills and motivation to work on successfully under your regime. This category of investigation should also be concerned to establish that the proposed acquisition fits with the emotional values of your stakeholders. Are shareholders, managers and existing customers, and so forth, likely to be in favour of – and committed to – the proposed acquisition?

### Case examples: resource problems

(a) When S & W Berisford eventually won control of British Sugar, its borrowings rose to over £400 million. British Sugar became both 'saint and sinner'. Faith in its potential profitability was justified to some extent, and it became the group's biggest profit generator. The money generated, however, was swallowed up by the group's financing costs.

(b) Hanson's 1986 'mega-bids' – SCM Inc (USA) for $930 million and the Imperial Group plc (UK) for £2.7 billion – increased net gearing from 44 per cent to 96 per cent. Divestment of periphery business units became a matter of urgency.

(c) In a 1984 *Fortune* magazine survey, four of the seven worst mergers found were of the 'know nothing about the nature of the acquired business type'. Managers successful in oil had 'burned their fingers badly', buying in copper, electrical equipment and retail stores.

(d) Howard Johnson's alien culture, American management and unfamiliar industrial operations, proved too much for the bureaucracy of Imperial to get to grips with.

Of course, synergistically orientated industrial logic, very much in vogue in the 1980s, prescribes acquisitions which stay within markets with which the organisation is familiar and so advocates takeovers which are amenable to easy transfer of managerial and other stakeholder inputs.

## What are the likely consequences of potential responses by new important stakeholders?

Before embarking on acquisition activity, it makes sense to check out the potential responses of interested parties. Once into the takeover situation heavy expenses will be incurred. Hostile reactions by 'prey' can lengthen the period of the battle and push up prices and costs. The need is for sophisticated intelligence gathering, communicating and evaluating systems. Such evaluations are not usually easy. BTR, for example, miscalculated the intensity of resistance from management, workforce and community in and around Pilkingtons. Guinness similarly misjudged the position of the Office of Fair Trading in the Distillers affair.

Stakeholder aspirations should be checked out before initial approaches are made. Longer term views are also necessary here. Assessments need to be made of the extent of any managerial, workforce and competitive resistance likely to be exerted after takeover has been achieved. For example, integration problems delayed Pan Am's merge of its schedules with those of the newly acquired National Airlines for two years. By this time terrible damage had been done to the 'combined' (or rather uncombined) airline's reputation and to Pan Am's finances.

## How does the acquisition proposition compare with other potential acquisitions and/or with other non-acquisition development proposals?

Some critics argue that, all too often, acquisition opportunities are taken as they arise, in isolation from mainstream strategic decision-making. Management strategy theory reminds us of the need to consider a range of alternative developments. After all, resources for investment in such important and expensive areas are limited. The need, then, is for a 'shopping around' expedition to establish whether better alternative acquisition opportunities are available. Strategies of joint development (agencies, franchises and co-operative ventures), and of internal developments, should also be considered as alternative methods for taking the organisation successfully into its future. There is a danger of jumping on to the takeover bandwagon in times of acquisition euphoria. Acquisition propositions need to be viewed in terms of total long-term organisational strategy.

# Corporate planning: strategic generation, evaluation and choice

The most important single decisions taken within the organisation are those which commit major resources and/or change the direction of the total organisation. Corporate planning theory attempts to help strategists improve these types of decision. Having developed useful insight from the strategic analysis process strategists should, according to the prescriptions contained in this chapter, undertake the following decision-making activities:

(a) Consider the theoretical range of generic product/market developments and methods of achieving them. Relate the theory to potential practice.

(b) Perform a similar exercise in the context of generic competitive strategies and implementation methods.

(c) Perform a similar exercise in the context of strategy formulation and implementation system changes.

(d) Perform a similar exercise in the context of political bargaining strategies.

(e) Brainstorm an extensive list of potential strategic developments for the organisation. Distil the list to one which contains only those worthy of detailed evaluation.

(f) Customise theoretical frameworks such as the suitability, feasibility, acceptability framework and/or the evaluatory checklist provided in this chapter. Apply the customised criteria to evaluate, rank and choose the way(s) forward.

## Case study: Dixons' success story

'Retailing is about buying rather than selling', according to Stanley Kalms the founder of Dixons. 'It is based on products and is about "competitive edge" and unique propositions.' Certainly the success of Dixons, the high street electrical and camera retailer, owes much to its professional purchasing operations.

Buyers at Dixons are seasoned veterans who know their industry inside out. Buying activities break down into three categories. First there are the deals with leading manufacturers of brown goods (e.g. TVs, videos, computers) and white goods (e.g. washers, cookers, fridges and freezers). Dixons has a successful record of working with leading manufacturers to develop new products, too. Second, and of growing importance are Dixons' own label products (labelled with Japanese type names such as Saisho). These are made for Dixons by foreign manufacturers and provide the organisation with the opportunity to beat famous brand prices and still make bigger margins. Finally, and most excitingly (according to some Dixons' buyers), are the 'one-off' bargain deals Dixons is able to strike with manufacturers. Such deals are forged with manufacturers who need to move stocks. Often the success of such transactions is down to Dixons better understanding of what will sell and how to sell in the market place. The financial capability of Dixons enables it to take massive stocks (the entrepreneurial spirit within the organisation makes acceptable the risks involved). This capability often means very low purchasing prices per unit. In the summer of 1985, for example, Dixons doubled its order of computer stock from the troubled Sinclair organisation. Ten thousand units represented an order of such magnitude that it might well have been beyond the scope of Dixons prior to their takeover of the family firm, Currys, the previous year. As it turned out an aggressively marketed package of a Spectrum computer together with software, disc drive and joystick, all at a lower price, made reordering possible.

The marketing operation is the mirror image of purchasing. Purchasing managers work closely with their marketing counterparts – even share the same office. They are jointly responsible for the selection of product ranges and for their margins. While according to the firm, 'good purchasing personnel ripen with age', marketing people are constantly moved to new product areas to maintain a continuous injection of new ideas.

The constant search is to find ways of making customers feel 'it is worth their while coming into Dixons, always worthwhile passing by someone else'. Exclusive merchandise, own label products, 'how to' books, better credit, better ranges, longer guarantees and an exciting, 'sexy' shop atmosphere have been hallmarks of the Dixons marketing approach.

Personnel in key positions are often recruited from famous name successful organisations such as Marks & Spencer. Commentators have agreed that the Dixons management team is one of the best. The company takes on over 100 graduates each year. Sales staff are encouraged to take an interest in Dixons' products and so acquire product expertise easily. On the job and off the job training programmes create the Dixons' school of retail management, though inevitably some high fliers leave to join other high street retailers.

Kalms, himself, provides the firm's major creative force. Chief Executive Mark Sonhams, described as an 'outstanding organiser', 'dynamic achiever' and 'charismatic leader' works very closely with Kalms, seeing his principal role as being 'to make sure what we've decided to do actually happens'. Strategic planning, introduced in the late 1970s gives 'continuity, direction and the resolve to continue to invest even in a down turn'. Periodically layers of management are eliminated. The aim is to work a very formal management structure informally.

Throughout the country Dixons' shops conform to a standard. Branch managers are given a store layout and instructed as to which goods to give prime space. The organisation is also extremely responsive. A decision to stock a new product can be taken on the Monday and the product, together with promotional material can be in all the stores by Wednesday. Electronic point of sale computerised systems and tight reporting systems enhance the responsiveness of the firm. Computerised stock control systems help improve stock efficiencies. The manual systems employed by Currys were described as antiquated.

Currys' five-pronged strategy of 'intercept shares' selling brown and white products; city centre superstores; specialist brown *or* white stores and Bridges' out of town stores, had been criticised for its diversity by Dixons during the takeover battle in 1984. The purchase of Currys in 1984 gave additional impetus to the Dixons move towards bigger stores and out of town shopping sites. Further, the takeover brought an additional 533 electrical shops to add to Dixons' 280. Following the acquisition Dixons had available a combined pool of 1.25 million square feet of selling space. The Currys acquisition also brought white goods into the Dixons portfolio. Previously it had only dealt in brown goods. The Currys customer, too – family-orientated, slightly older, slightly down-market and predominantly female – provided a new segment for the younger, higher spending, product fanatical, male-orientated Dixons. The move gave Dixons market leadership position in a number of product/markets.

(This case study has been adapted from *Management Today*, November 1986.)

## Think and discuss

1  So far as possible, use the eight question evaluatory check list given in this chapter to evaluate Dixons' takeover of Currys. Using the 'value chain' to illustrate your answer, discuss how the acquisition might improve Dixons' existing competitive advantage. Does Dixons employ a generic competitive strategy?

2    Consider an organisation of your choice. Trace its development and its directions and methods over the past decade or so. Discuss its competitive situation and evaluate its generic competitive approaches.

## For further study

1    Refer to the case study 'Silver Wheels Ltd' or 'HSE Ltd' in the accompanying case study volume. Undertake a strategic analysis, consider potential product/market developments and generic competitive strategies, and evaluate a selection of potential developments. Recommend the way(s) forward for your chosen organisation.
2    Refer to the 'What Next Case Study' in the accompanying volume. Use the value chain concept to discuss the resource factors behind Next's successful era of the 1980s.

# References

1    H I Ansoff, *Corporate Strategy*, Pelican, 1979, p 99
2    M E Porter, *Competitive Advantage*, New York, The Free Press, 1985, Ch 2
3    G Devlin and M Bleackley, 'Strategic Alliances – Guidelines for Success', *Long Range Planning*, 21, October 1988
4    R M Kanter, *When Giants Learn to Dance*, Unwin, 1990, p 118
5    C Clarke and K Brennan, 'Allied Forces', *Management Today*, November 1988 discuss the pricing problem of mergers and acquisitions at p 129.
6    C Lorenz, 'The trouble with takeovers', *Financial Times*, 8 December, 1986, discusses Porter's views on mergers and acquisitions.
7    G Foster, 'Europe's Merger Maze', *Management Today*, July 1990, pp 60–64
8    See for example, I I Mitroff and R H Kilmann, *Corporate Tragedies*, Praeger, 1984, Ch 2
9    See, for example, C E Schillaci, 'Designing Successful Joint Ventures', *The Journal of Business Strategy*, 8 (2), Fall, 1987, pp 57–63
10    G Hamel, Y L Doz and C K Prahalad, 'Collaborate with your Competitors and Win', *Harvard Business Review*, Jan–Feb 1989
11    B G James 'Alliance: The New Strategic Focus', *Long Range Planning*, 18, June 1985, p 131
12    J L Schaan, 'How to Control a Joint Venture even as a Minority Partner', *Journal of General Management*, 14 (1), 1988
13    R M Kanter, op. cit., 4 above, at p 167
14    T J Peters, *Thriving on Chaos*, Macmillan, 1988, p 128
15    M E Porter, *The Competitive Advantage of Nations*, Macmillan, 1990, p 67
16    Ibid
17    H I Ansoff, *Implementing Strategic Management*, New York, Prentice-Hall International, 1984, p 28
18    C Hill, 'The Pitfalls in Diversity', *Management Today*, December 1984, p 80
19    T Burns and G M Stalker, *The Management of Innovation*, Tavistock, 1961
20    P R Lawrence and J W Lorsch, *Organisation and Environment*, Cambridge, Mass., Harvard University Press, 1967
21    A H Chandler, *Strategy and Structure*, MIT Press, 1962
22    T J Peters and R H Waterman Jr, *In Search of Excellence*, New York, Harper & Row, 1982
23    J Argenti, *Practical Corporate Planning*, George Allen & Unwin, 1980, p 153
24    G Johnson and K Scholes, *Exploring Corporate Strategy*, 2nd edn, Prentice-Hall International, 1988, Ch 7
25    J Patterson and W Richardson, 'How to Acquire Success', *Sundridge Park Management Journal*, Spring, 1988

26   See A van de Vliet and D Isaac, 'The Mayhem in Mergers', *Management Today*, February
       1986, p 39

# Recommended reading

M E Porter, *Competitive Advantage*, New York, The Free Press, 1985
G Johnson and K Scholes, *Exploring Corporate Strategy*, 2nd edn, Prentice-Hall International,
       1988, Chs 6, 7 and 8

# 6 Contingency planning

Contingency planning is an increasingly vital means of *coping with plans that go wrong*. The complete business planning approach espoused by this book is a response to the uncertainty and risk created for business by today's environments. We might expect, therefore, that one of the planning subsystems of the complete planning framework will be concerned with the problem of how to cater for plans which do not work out. This is the task of contingency planning. In this short chapter we introduce readers to the need for and the nature of contingency planning. The aim is to help readers become more capable contingency planners. Thus, it should help to develop a more skilful approach to deciding when contingency planning is called for; how contingency problems might be resolved and whether the costs of contingency solutions are worthwhile. The discussion covers:

- What contingency planning is and why it is needed
- Assumptions, uncertainty and risk
- Strategies for contingency situations
- The costs of contingency planning
- The three steps of contingency planning

## What contingency planning is and why it is needed

'Planning is about examining the future and deciding on action', Fayol(1) and 'Planning is the commitment of resources to the future', Warren (2). Underlying plans however, are 'Assumptions [which] provide a foundation for plans. A sound plan based upon assumptions about the future will be valid for as long as the assumptions are valid', Hussey (3). The only assumption we can rely on about the future is that 'It will arrive and it will be different', Drucker (4).

The above quotations derived from the theory of management strategy help explain the need for contingency planning. An assumption is an opinion about the future. Often we have little or no control over the future. Nevertheless, plans have to be developed, decisions taken and activity implemented. Despite uncertainty, life has to go on. Contingency planning acknowledges the certainty of uncertainty and the likelihood that assumptions and the plans based on them will, in the event, prove to be unrealistic. Contingency planning seeks to establish in advance those things that might go wrong with mainstream plans, to decide how such adverse events might be dealt with and to prepare accordingly. Contingency planning goes on at all levels of the organisation. Corporate planners need to incorporate a contingency section into business plans for all major developments. This short chapter covers this important, but often neglected component of the complete planning framework.

# Assumptions, uncertainty and risk

Of course, it would be impractical for the people of the organisation to produce plans to meet every potential adverse eventuality. This is, if not impossible, over costly in time and resources. Fortunately, most plans and decisions made and implemented within the organisation can be relied on to work out according to the assumptions on which they are based. Further, the nature and significance of many organisation problems, compared to the associated costs in preparing and implementing contingency responses, is such that they can be more easily and cheaply dealt with as and when they occur. A temporary shortage of paper clips, as an example, is less damaging and more easily and quickly remedied than a 'stock out' of customer products. A contingency arrangement which raised the stock levels of paper clips might be non-cost effective, whereas one which raised the level of finished goods in stock might be considered worthwhile.

The organisation's capacity for dealing with adverse events will also depend upon its skills and motivations for spotting such events and responding to them as they arise. This aspect of 'organising for responsiveness' will be dealt with in Chapters 11, 12, 13 and 14. In this chapter, we view contingency planning as an advance warning/planning mechanism.

A useful model for generating and considering contingency planning applications is illustrated in Fig. 6.1. This model indicates three benchmarks for deciding whether contingency planning is called for in any particular situation. These are:

(a) uncertainty;

(b) risk;

(c) potential adverse effects.

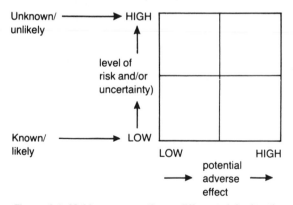

**Figure 6.1 Making assumptions: different risk situations**

## Uncertainty

Uncertainty is the state where, because knowledge is lacking, some estimate of the risks involved in a particular project is not possible. It might be the case that information which would stimulate understanding and risk assessment is simply not available to the decision-makers concerned. Alternatively, the information might be available but might not have yet been recognised or made sensible.

## Risk

Risk assessment is based on some perceived understanding of a potential situation. Here, the decision-maker is able to 'have a go' (no matter how subjectively) at assigning probabilities to the likelihood of events occurring. The greater the probability we assign to something not happening then the greater the risk we take through embarking on plans based on the assumption that it will happen. The more certain the planning environment, the more easy should be risk measurement. This is our customised definition of risk. Writers more commonly describe it as a measurement of probability times potential impact, i.e. as a function of placings on the vertical and horizontal axes in Fig. 6.1.

## Potential adverse effects

Some things can go wrong without harming the organisation (for example, the shortage of paper clips we mentioned above). Other adverse events can be disastrous. Projects which require the commitment of huge resources, say the building of a new factory in anticipation of growth in market demand, are extremely dangerous if only because of the massive losses which could be incurred if assumptions were significantly wrong. A decision to proceed with the factory building venture could perhaps destroy an organisation – should assumed demand not materialise – unless decision-makers had taken account of such a possibility in advance, and prepared accordingly. As a generalisation, extended future planning decisions committing high levels of resources and based on long-range forecasts of turbulent environments will tend towards the top right-hand corner of the model in Fig. 6.1. Daily operational decisions will tend to be located in the lower left-hand side of the model. *Low risk/low adverse effect* decisions should require little further attention. Routine control mechanisms can usually be applied to such problem areas. *Highly uncertain* or risky decisions which are of *low potential adverse effect* can be undertaken (or not) at the decision-makers' discretion. If things go wrong in such situations, they can be dealt with as they arise and, anyway, nothing too much will be lost. Highly certain but *high adverse situations* are perhaps best avoided – despite the certainty of the situation. If things do go wrong the consequences can be disastrous. Certainly, decisions to go ahead under such circumstances call for accompanying, carefully made, contingency plans. *High risk/high adverse effect* decisions should only be made if the decision-makers have no other choice. Again, decisions to implement such developments require careful contingency planning.

## Strategies for contingency situations

Faced with an uncertain, risky and/or potentially damaging course of action, decision-makers can respond in any number of specific ways. The following are some generic strategies for handling risky situations:

(a) *Do nothing*. Here the situation may be just too uncertain and/or important (in terms of getting it wrong). The decision-maker may simply opt out.

(b) *Search for further information*. Sometimes, if the decision is very important and not too urgent, then information seeking might make sense. Japanese business success is recognised as being due in part to the investment Japanese management makes in time spent collecting and sifting information before decisions are made. Of course, a trade off between the costs of collecting further information and the benefits expected to flow from using this additional information exists and should be assessed before instructions to 'find out more' are passed on. Managers should also avoid the trap of using a shortage of information as an excuse to avoid making a decision which could and/or should be made on the information already available.

(c) *Do something completely different.* Strategists caught up in the euphoria of a potential investment opportunity should remember that rarely must an organisation go down one route and one route only. Faced with a risky investment proposal a company can decide to direct its resources into some other non-related return generating venture.

(d) *Full steam ahead.* Exercising either foolhardiness or entrepreneurship, decision-makers often decide to go ahead despite the obvious risks. Massive investment in new technological developments is often necessary even in mature and declining market situations if competitive position is to be maintained. Conversely, in new market territories that are difficult to quantify, chancy investments might be taken to gain early market leadership in what may prove to be a major market. A spokesman for the Treasure Recovery Consortium said after an auction of sunken treasure in 1988: 'That's the way it goes. Next time could make us all fortunes.' The auction had raised £32,000, the expedition had cost £2 million.

(e) *Hedging.* This is the first of the generic risk strategies referred to so far which qualifies for a true contingency planning categorisation. 'Hedging bets' involves the modification of existing plans to make them more safe. Thus the fashion retailer might order fewer garments from a manufacturer to avoid being left with an out-of-date surplus, should expected demand not be realised. The power generating company might implement a dual power generating technology to avoid being over reliant on one supplier and/or one fuel.

(f) *Devise contingency plans.* Contingency plans are pre-prepared schedules of activities which are to be swung into action in the event of particular aspects of the 'blue print' going awry. Thus, bus company administrators have lists of relief drivers who are to be called out if scheduled drivers fail to turn up for work. Fire Authorities have pre-arranged plans which enable them to draw on the resources of neighbouring authorities in the unfortunate event of a major catastrophe.

# The costs of contingency strategies

Contingency planning seeks to reduce the costs that would otherwise occur if and when plans do not go as desired. However, decisions on contingency strategies should take account of the costs of the contingency strategies themselves. A labour reservoir to cover absenteeism; additional stock to ensure no 'stock out' situations; and dual sourcing, for example, all require additional expenditure to buy safety. Buying in less stock means, for the fashion retailer, that the price paid per unit will probably be higher and, of course, potential sales (and profits) will be lower. Choosing a less risky investment alternative implies the earning of smaller (if surer) returns. Sometimes it can make sense to chance potential adverse outcomes on the basis that effective contingency strategies cost more than the adverse outcomes themselves. A bus company administrator, for example, can simply cancel little used, early services if drivers do not report for the early shift. This, however, happens only rarely and most routes might be serviced regularly each hour anyway. Passengers simply have to wait a few minutes longer than they would normally wait. Such a situation is not ideal but the alternatives of paying for stand-by driver cover for these periods of the day is, on balance, not worthwhile. Look at the illustration which follows.

## Case example: arguing over the costs of contingency planning

Plans for Euro-express trains linking the north of England with Paris and Brussels were facing a crisis in late 1988. Instead of the continental system of mobile customs officers, the unions were demanding that all northern travellers should get off their trains at London and troop through a conventional customs hall carrying their baggage before scrambling back on board to complete their journey.

British Rail's plans to introduce airline-style anti-terrorist checks for every international passenger using the Channel Tunnel were greeted with dismay by transport experts and regional pressure groups. Rail chiefs admitted that any station which could not justify the cost of x-ray machines, metal detectors and other security equipment would not get a continental service.

Mr Richard Hope, editor of the authoritative *Railway Gazette International*, commented 'It is going to make the whole thing extremely costly and hopelessly uneconomic. All these precautions have to be paid for.'

The Chairman of the North of England Regional Council, Mr John Gunnell, said 'I think it will mean a very limited number of stations have international trains ... It will be too costly. The capital cost of the equipment alone will be high.'

(Adapted from A Whitehouse, 'Terror checks may hit Chunnel links', *Yorkshire Post*, 7 November 1988.)

### Think and discuss

In what ways might the Channel Tunnel planners prepare for the problem of terrorist activity? Identify the cost areas involved in your chosen strategies.

## The three steps of contingency planning

This brief chapter has considered the rationale for, and nature of contingency planning. This planning activity can be sub-divided into three interrelated activities as follows:

(a) *Decide which contingencies might prevail and evaluate their likelihoods and potential impacts.* Effective mainstream planning processes should already have uncovered and considered these contingency issues – contingency planning is not to be viewed as an activity which takes place after other plans have been devised. In the corporate planning process for example, consideration of events *which might arise* flows naturally from information analysis designed to predict what is most likely to happen. External and internal appraisals, sensitivity analysis and scenario planning activities will contribute to the reaching of assumptions from which to plan strategic developments *and* contingency strategies. Similarly, the significance of the proposed strategy in terms of likely resource expenditure and anticipated benefits will have been established, at least in broad terms, during the corporate planning process.

(b) *Decide whether, and if appropriate, how to reduce or negate the potential adverse effects identified.* At this very creative stage of the contingency planning exercise, decision-makers decide which, if any, of the generic risk handling strategies to take and then create specific plans for handling the perceived problem. The costs of proposed risk reducers need to be weighed at this stage also.

(c) *Monitor futures.* Finally, systems have to be implemented to ensure the speedy application of contingency plans as they become necessary. Feedback systems should also be utilised to provide information for the understanding of how, where and when planning assumptions failed to become reality. In this way the quality of future assumptions might be improved.

## Think and discuss
Place the following planning situations in appropriate places in the risk situation matrix (Fig. 6.1). Where appropriate, identify contingency strategies and/or other solutions which might be applied.

(a) 'You're asking us to commit £2 million to this project over the next 10 years but we actually have no idea of what the market will look like in ten years time.'

(b) '£2 million is a lot of resources but the government is guaranteeing our investments.'

(c) 'From what we know of this market, we reckon we have a 70 per cent chance of gaining the required market share. We have money available. Do we sanction the £100,000 development budget?'

(d) 'I know that 'just in time' stock systems are being employed in this industry and that we really need to join the bandwagon. Trouble is I'm worried about us getting it wrong. Missing customer delivery dates in this competitive environment could really damage us.'

(e) 'It's highly unlikely that he'll find a solution but the R & D manager says he is only asking for an extra £500 to conduct the necessary experiments. Do we give him the allowance?'

(f) 'Of course we need coffee in the office – you don't need to ask me when and where to buy it just so long as we don't run out.'

## For further study
Refer to the 'Scot-Plastic and Macdonald Ltd' case study in the accompanying case study volume. Place the proposed 'Full Steam Ahead' Strategy on the risk assessment matrix (Fig. 6.1). Identify your reasons for the placing chosen. Discuss potential contingency strategies for the situation described.

# References

1   H Fayol, *General and Industrial Management*, Pitman, 1949
2   E K Warren, *Long Range Planning: 'The Executive Viewpoint'*, Prentice-Hall, 1966
3   D E Hussey, *Corporate Planning Theory and Practice*, 2nd edn, Pergamon Press, 1982, p 55

4    P F Drucker, *Managing for Results*, Heinemann, 1964 (as quoted in D E Hussey, op. cit., p 43)

## Recommended reading

D E Hussey, *Corporate Planning Theory and Practice*, 2nd edn, Pergamon, 1982, Ch 5

# 7 Administration planning: marketing control and business functions

Plans are useless by themselves; they become effective only when they move into action.

Somebody in the organisation has to make things happen, to take plans and transform them into reality. This is the critical task of the administrator and the aim of administration planning. In this chapter and the next we seek to help readers consider how, through a *functional* approach to organising and through the system of *management by objectives*, effective methods of sequencing, scheduling, motivating and controlling activities are to be designed and implemented. In these two chapters we concentrate on the task of administrating corporate planning type strategic developments. This chapter examines the following issues:

- What is administration planning?
- Administration through functions planning
- The marketing function and the marketing controlled approach
- The production function
- The finance function
- The personnel function

## What is administration planning?

### Case example: the birth of a motor industry giant
In the early 1900s, Henry Ford dreamed his strategic dreams. In his dreams people and raw materials flowed into the Ford factory via its back gates. Out through the front gates rolled a continuous stream of shiny new Ford motor cars. The commencement of retooling for mass production began the transformation of strategic dream into operational reality. By 1914 Ford's newly equipped plant was producing, for an eager market, one new Ford every second minute of every day.

Administration planning, according to Mullins (1), is 'concerned with the design and implementation of systems and procedures to help meet stated objectives'. In the context of the Ford illustration above, administration planning 'fills in' the middle of the 'back gates to front gates' transformation. While *any* desired outcome requires administration to implement the activities for its achievement, here we are concerned with administration planning in its role as an implementer of those major organisational projects identified in Chapter 5 as 'strategic developments' on corporate planning. For our purposes administration planning is planning to take strategic objectives to operational reality. Administration planning, therefore, is concerned with designing and implementing systems which ensure that activities are:

(a) sequenced effectively: they occur in the right order (we lay the drains, for example, before we turf the lawn);

(b) synchronised/co-ordinated: they occur *together* in the right order (for example, publicity material, sales and sales support personnel and organisational systems are all in the right place at the right time to ensure a successful product launch);

(c) motivated: people are *activated* to perform their roles in the input/conversion/output process;

(d) controlled: control systems attempt to ensure that activities are undertaken in the required manner and that the planned for outcomes are actually achieved.

Administration planning, therefore, seeks to improve decision implementation through procedures designed to sequence, co-ordinate, motivate and control organisation activities better, as shown in Fig. 7.1.

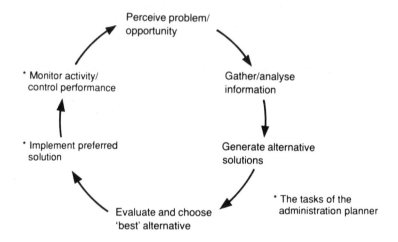

**Figure 7.1  Administration's role in the planning/decision-making process**

Two administration techniques for implementing strategic developments will be considered in this section. These are:

(a)  functions planning;

(b)  management by objectives (see also Chapter 8).

Successful 'today' organisations use versions of each of these techniques, interactively, to achieve greater administrative effectiveness.

## Case example: launching a new car

Key tasks and priorities for a new product development manager:

| Key dates | Field actions |
| --- | --- |
| 24 Sept | Attend training course 24–27 September |
| 11 Oct | All franchised dealers to be visited by this date; offers to be made |
| 14 Oct | Dealer approval forms submitted |
| 15 Oct | Dealer training 15–20 October |
| 20 Oct | Issue of dealer documents and marketing material |
| 1 Nov | ATTENDANCE AT MOTOR SHOW |
| 2 Nov | Dealer support activities |

# Administration through functions planning

Functions planning is based on the concept of the organisation comprising a series of related tasks which can be isolated and allocated to specialist departments and specialist personnel. Functions planning is necessary because of the nature of business. Any business transaction requires an exchange between buyer and seller and almost invariably these exchanges involve producing, organising, financing and marketing *functional* activities (see Fig. 7.2). Functions planning also offers a number of other benefits to the enterprise. Typically, for example, as organisations grow from very small beginnings, functions planning takes an important role as management strategists reorganise to gain the advantage of administrating through a departmental/functional organisation structure. In this context, the management strategist is primarily concerned with using functions planning to develop a system for *sequencing* and *controlling* the activities of his or her *growing* organisation. Continuing growth creates a sub-functionalisation – functional departments themselves adopt specialist functional section structures.

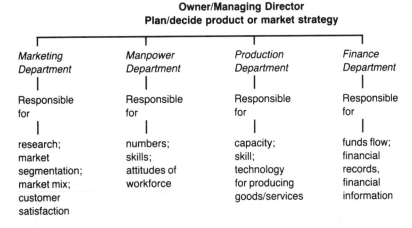

**Owner/Managing Director**
**Plan/decide product or market strategy**

| Marketing Department | Manpower Department | Production Department | Finance Department |
|---|---|---|---|
| Responsible for | Responsible for | Responsible for | Responsible for |
| research; market segmentation; market mix; customer satisfaction | numbers; skills; attitudes of workforce | capacity; skill; technology for producing goods/services | funds flow; financial records, financial information |

**Figure 7.2  Strategy to operators through a functional organisation structure**

In our hostile and efficiency conscious world, functions planning can also provide further major contributions more *clearly* related to those systems goals of *efficiency* and *control of the environment*. Some strategy 'gurus', for example, advocate formally undertaken, detailed breakdowns of the organisation's jobs and subsequent investigations into how component activities can be redesigned better to contribute to efficiency and control of the environment objectives. In essence, such modern day prescriptions (see for example, refs 3, 4 and 5) repackage and re-emphasise earlier prescriptions from theorists such as Drucker (6) and Taylor (7).

Briefly, efficiency improvements are seen to flow from a systematic weeding out of any 'slack' discovered in existing activities and/or from the learning curve advantages which accrue to specialisation of work activity. (The learning curve theory holds that the more we do something the more efficiently we do it.) Greater control of the environment is assumed to flow from the building of 'differentiators' into the functions/jobs of the firm. Differentiators are activities which enhance the attractiveness of the organisation and its products or services in the eyes of external stakeholders.

Theorists such as Burns and Stalker and Lawrence and Lorsch (see Chapter 5) have also indicated that functional planning lies at the heart of more successful organisational/environmental adaptations.

## Advantages and disadvantages of functions planning

In summary, therefore, potential advantages which can accrue from functional approaches to administration include:

(a) more effective control internally (monitoring of departmental performance is facilitated, for example) and externally (a uniform marketing image, for example, is easier to supervise);

(b) clear lines for the sequencing of work flows, for communications and for the allocation of areas of responsibility;

(c) reduced levels of complexity, hence, more easily managed units of activity;

(d) improved performance from more concentrated effort towards efficiency savings and/or differentiation building;

(e) improved skills and other economies from specialisation;

(f) economies of scale through standardisation (standard forms, corporate databases, high volume purchasing power, etc.);

(g) enhanced job satisfaction through expertise development and career progression in a chosen functional area;

(h) a more effective organisation/environment adaptation capability.

However, problems which can work against the realisation of these advantages are generated by the tendencies of many functionally organised organisations to exhibit:

(a) introversion (the organisation's personnel become more interested in the workings of their departments than in the workings of the environment). Civil servants, for example, have been accused of viewing the Minister rather than the general public, as their customer.

(b) bureaucracy, which can reduce organisational effectiveness through over-emphasis on the need to work within existing rules, regulations and managerial and communication hierarchies;

(c) concentrated attention on departmental matters at the expense of organisation-wide strategic matters;

(d) rich sources of specialists, a scarcity of potential management strategists;

(e) inter-departmental conflict rather than co-operation.

Key issues underlying successful functional planning, therefore, include:

(a) understanding the particular roles and contributions different functions make to the quest for system goal attainment;

(b) understanding the cumulative and interactive impact on systems goal performance created by the organisation's range of activities;

(c) understanding how the organisation should be administered in order to obtain the advantages of functional organisation without attracting the disadvantages.

A functional perspective underlies two administrative approaches currently gathering force as success generators in modern business environments. These approaches are the 'marketing led' approach and the 'management by objectives' approach. We will now take a brief look at the functions of marketing, production, personnel and finance within the context of an overall 'marketing led' approach to organising. The next chapter, on administration planning also will then offer a discussion on 'operationalising objectives' and on the philosophy and system known as management by objectives.

# The marketing function and the 'marketing' controlled approach

## Case example: modern banking environments

(Based on Ted Gardener, Paul Feeney and Phil Molyneux, 'Strategic Marketing', *Banking World*, October 1987)

The banking profession, traditionally, has been a bastion for those seeking employment opportunities within safe, secure, steady and bureaucratic organisations. Articles such as this, while profession specific (i.e. banking), serve as forceful warnings to remind organisation strategists, generally, that few industries/ organisations can now rely on safe and steady existences given the nature of modern environments. In this article, the authors describe how environments have changed for our bigger banks and how the banks are responding through applications of the strategic marketing concept. The authors advocate a further response progression – into a 'marketing controlled' era.

Although the 'retail banking revolution' began in Northern Europe during the late 1950s the retail and general banking environment in Britain really started to change rapidly during the early 1970s. Some factors identified as contributors to this new banking environment are:

(a) foreign banks 'pouring into London' in the early 1970s and penetrating the domestic corporate market and the top end of the retail market;

(b) a 'globalisation' of banking which has increased the volatility of interest rates and exchange rates;

(c) de-regulation of the banking industry which began with the Competition and Credit Control measures of 1971 and which has more recently opened up markets between the banks and the building societies;

(d) technology developments which continue to have impact on delivery systems product ranges and management information systems;

(e) consumers who, generally richer and more sophisticated, show increasing propensities to 'shop around';

(f) the advent of retailers offering 'in-house' store cards and credit facilities. This changing environment, with its attendant uncertainties, has stimulated a more demand-orientated approach from British banks. They have begun to emulate their counterparts in the consumer goods industry by moving towards greater 'market orientation'. This strategic marketing approach sets out the relevant courses of action in terms of objectives to be achieved by different parts of the organisation (product/service criteria, customer orientation, market to be served, marketing tactics to be employed, etc.). While this approach is a clear development away from the traditional supplier led approach (note the plethora of financial services now available for different customer segments) nevertheless, banks need to move forward again. The present era is one which emphasises marketing departments, selling and promotional effort. The banks now need to move into the 'marketing controlled' era. In essence, this means intensifying the marketing orientation concept. Operationally it means that the twin forces of marketing and associated profitability become the driving forces for the *whole* organisation - no function is absolved from responsibility for these twin objectives.

Winners of the future will be those who can best understand the environment in which they operate and who have the ability to exploit changing market conditions by anticipating correctly future trends and demands. They will be those organisations which 'anticipate the future by understanding the present' and which are adept at managing the process of change. A key function, here, will be management information. Information systems need to be developed to harness customer and financial information and to provide an effective reporting process. Recruitment, motivation, training and development programmes must support the need to develop staff who can support the drive for sales to targeted customers. Product innovators are required, not only to produce own brands but also to provide, in quick time, modified copies of new products emanating from competitors. Technology will also play an essential role and will itself change from a production tool to a marketing weapon. All these 'marketing control' organisational characteristics will be achieved only with clear direction and commitment from top managers.

## Comment

When banking strategists are warned 'there is no time like the present to emphasise the strategic importance of marketing – waiting until tomorrow may be just too late' then *all* British organisational strategists need to take note.

## Think and discuss

1   Which environmental factors have been important to banking situations?
2   Describe the environment facing banks today.
3   Which function(s) is/are important to the achievement of success in today's banking environments?
4   Model a bank as an open social system.
5   Compare and contrast two banks' organisational outputs.

Marketing has been defined as 'a human activity directed at satisfying needs and wants through exchange processes' (8). Marketing aims to attract customer contributions to the organisation's wealth-creating processes by ensuring that the enterprise offers well publicised, easily available, attractive product/service exchanges. While many firms still view marketing as a *departmental* activity, others are improving performance through the installation of marketing as an *organisation-wide* activity. For these 'marketing led' enterprises, caring about and providing for the needs of customers and society is a fundamental part of *everybody's* job (regardless of their departmental base). Of course, this growing emphasis on the importance of marketing is a reflection of how, in our dangerously competitive environment, external stakeholder contributions can no longer be automatically guaranteed – and of how, when particular organisational problems become critical, greater attention is usually (eventually) paid to their resolutions. Though the marketing led approach is only recently taking root in British industry the fundamental importance of marketing has long been advocated: 'Marketing is so basic that it cannot be considered a separate function ... It is the whole business seen from the point of view of its final result, that is, from the customer's point of view.' (9) Clearly, then, marketing is that organisation activity most concerned with the external interactions of the output stage of the system process. Those advocates who see marketing as *the* success generating function of our modern era also insist that *every* organisational function should be performed in the context of its impact on the organisation's marketing objectives.

## Progression to the marketing led approach

Theorists suggest that the current marketing led success recipe has, in fact, evolved over the course of this century in response to changing organisational/environmental circumstances. Concepts underlying this progression have been identified as follows:

(a) The *production*-orientated concept. This orientation is based on the belief that customers will buy almost anything that an organisation makes. The route to success, therefore, is to concentrate attention on achieving efficiency in terms of low cost production.

(b) The *product* concept. This approach is based on a belief that good products at reasonable prices will ensure, with only minimal marketing effort, satisfactory sales and profits.

(c) The *selling* concept. Here, management works on the basic assumption that while consumers will not buy without organisational stimulus, nevertheless the organisation can achieve successful sales levels through 'hard sell' and powerful promotional campaigns.

(d) The *marketing*-orientated organisation recognises success as flowing from:

- an understanding of the *needs* and *wants* of a selected *target* market;
- the planning and implementation of organisational activities which constantly seek to satisfy the changing needs of targeted customers more effectively than the competition.

Whereas selling focuses on the *needs of the seller*, marketing focuses on the *needs of the buyer*.

(e) The *societal marketing* concept. As society's 'publics' (governments, pressure groups, the media, etc.) become more influential, so too organisations are extending the marketing concept. The societal marketing concept recognises the need to look beyond today's customers and into the potential impacts of the organisation's activities on society generally. Social responsibility, for many theorists and practitioners, is not to be practised solely as an expression of organisational altruism. Rather it is an essential prerequisite to success in today's resource-short, equality-conscious, environmentally-aware business environments.

The movement, over time, from a production and product orientation to a marketing/societal marketing approach is neatly encapsulated via a comparison of the following quotations:

(a) 'The true aim of industry is to liberate minds and bodies from the drudgery of existence by filling the world with well made, low priced goods.' Henry Ford I (circa 1920)

(b) 'Social responsibility provides a way to steal a march on the competition. It is nothing more than another step in the evolutionary process of taking a more far sighted view of return on investment.' Henry Ford II (circa 1975).

## The marketing process

Before moving on to consider some of the other organisation functions we will now consider briefly a framework, prescribed by theory, for the systematic planning of successful marketing operations. This framework is built around the notion that a successful marketing process depends upon useful decisions and activities being made and implemented on:

(a)  market segmentation and targeting;

(b)  market entry strategy;

(c)  marketing mix variables;

(d)  timing.

### Market segmentation and choice of market

No organisation can be all things to all markets. Industries are made up of *market segments*, identifiable through a process of grouping together all those buyers with similar needs and/or similar propensities towards particular products/services and/or particular ways of promoting and distributing them. Segmentation is a creative planning activity. New ways of segmenting markets often provide the stimulus for organisations to go on and achieve competitive advantage. Some current methods of segmenting markets include:

(a) *Geographical segmentation.* European beer markets, for example, provide a segment different from British markets simply because of their different geographical location

(b) *Demographic segmentation.* This method of segmentation involves the sub-division of markets on the basis of variables such as age, sex, occupation and social class. Burton's Top Shop, as an example, has a leading position in the teenage/early 20s fashion market. Next has made significant progress aiming at the 25–40-year-old middle-class woman.

(c) *Customer size.* Organisations sometimes decide to cater only for customers who will place large orders or for customers who are too small to be served by the industry giants.

(d) *Lifestyle segmentation.* Over the past couple of decades a number of retailers have targeted their offers at classes of customers perceived to hold similar *self-identities*. Shops such as Laura Ashley, Next and Habitat provide goods, services and a *purchase experience* which satisfies not only more overt wants and needs but also provides an opportunity for the customer to express his or her self identity.

As noted in Chapter 4, an attractive market segment is one where:

(a)  the market segment is of sufficient current size;

(b)  the market segment has the potential for further growth (the concept of the product life cycle is useful here – see Fig. 7.3); theorists have described the progress shown as a typical sequence charting the birth to death of products and markets);

(c)  the market segment is not 'owned' or over-occupied by existing competition;

(d)  the market segment has some relative unsatisfied needs that the particular company can serve well.

**Figure 7.3 Product/market life cycle**

At the heart of effective segmentation, therefore, is an understanding of customer *needs* (the basic physical, psychological, and social needs which human beings seek to fulfil) and *wants* (those specific desires which focus on particular goods and services as satisfiers of the more basic needs). Effective segmentation also relies on forecasting skills and sophistication in resource and environmental analysis. Certainly, management strategy prescribes the development of these skills and the use of associated techniques, although, undoubtedly, success can still owe much to 'lucky' choices and/or 'being in the right place at the right time'. Strategic analysis issues have been covered more fully in Chapters 4 and 5 on corporate planning. We discuss the role of forecasting in business planning more fully in the next chapter.

## Market entry strategy

Decisions on how to achieve market entry have to be made once the target market has been identified. Here again we refer to the fuller discussion on development methods in Chapter 5 on corporate planning. Briefly, however, we can recap on the generic methods for achieving market entry:

(a) *Internal development* relies on the organisation's existing resources and capabilities to achieve initial penetration.

(b) *Joint Ventures* utilise the assistance of other organisations to make market inroads. Such collaborations might be, for example, via agencies or franchises. As an example, Elders, the Foster's lager brewing giant, entered Great Britain (Elders is Australian based) through an agreement with Watney Mann for Elders' products to be distributed through Watney Mann distribution channels.

(c) *Acquisitions* are the means to buy market share. The 1987 purchase of Courage from Hanson plc, for example, further developed Elders' foothold in the British brewing market into a major share position.

## The marketing mix

Following decisions on target markets and market entry strategies, marketing decision makers then need to determine the appropriate mix of:

(a) *P*roduct/service characteristics;

(b) *P*romotional channels and messages;

(c) *P*rices to be charged for products/services;

(d) *P*laces and methods of distribution of the products and services.

These four variables of the 'marketing mix' are often referred to as the 'four Ps'. Brief consideration of the marketing approaches of Lada and Jaguar should illustrate how same industry 'players' employ very different marketing mixes in order to be competitively attractive in their chosen market segments.

## Timing

The final decision in the development of a marketing campaign plan is that which decides when market entry activities will take place. These activities should, ideally, only be undertaken after organisational resources have been adequately prepared (trained salesmen, well tested goods, adequate production capacity, for example) and when market conditions are favourable.

# Case study: product launch problems

In 1985 the Spanish car giant SEAT became the first new entrant for many years into the UK car mass market. Its marketing campaign up to and including the motor show launch in the autumn of that year was acknowledged for its underlying expertise and its successful impact. Early impressions of the SEAT Ibiza and Malaga models were good and media and public interest was high. Despite the competitive and mature market conditions, therefore, optimism was high that successful market penetrations would be achieved. A number of problems emanating from functional activities outside the specific marketing campaign, however, detracted from the actual success achieved in the first year of market entry. For example:

(a) *Market research* had 'tipped' the more standard Ibiza model to be most popular. In fact, the higher range Malaga generated greater demand than had been expected or catered for.

(b) *Production* difficulties meant that Malagas were not made available in the UK until March 1986. Customers excited by the SEAT promotion campaign were advised they would have to wait. When cars did arrive quality problems created further delays.

(c) Not all models were widely available and many of the vehicles were red. Dealers were soon complaining over the *lack of variety* available to offer customers.

(d) *Inadequate integration* between purchasing and marketing had contributed to the importation of too many red cars.

(e) *Personnel* were in short supply. The 'dash' to launch SEAT at the motor show meant that insufficient time had been available to complete a comprehensive programme of dealer appointments and training.

(f) *Financial* problems continued to trouble SEAT's mother organisation and SEAT itself did not achieve its planned for early financial performance. Financial constraints meant that funds were not so quickly available to improve market take up.

## Think and discuss

Use the marketing process stages model to identify problem sources for the SEAT launch.

While the marketing function is currently taking a prominent role in management strategy, problems such as those experienced by SEAT reinforce the point that although advantages accrue to organising along specialist functional lines such activities cannot be undertaken in isolation. All functions in the organisation are interactive and interdependent. The most important measurement of functional activity is the *combined* effect of *all* activities on the *systems goals* performances of the enterprise.

# The production function

Production and operations management is concerned with designing the systems of the organisation that produce its products or services and with the planning and controlling of the day-to-day operations that take place within these systems.

While marketing is most clearly seen to relate to the tasks of researching, identifying, attracting and serving customers, the production function is concerned, primarily, to make available the goods or services required by customers – efficiently. Traditionally, marketing and production functions have existed at opposite ends of the organisation, pursuing different and often conflicting, objectives. Current management strategy recipes, however, emphasise the team nature of the organisation. All functions are interdependent and all have responsibility for achieving those twin system goals of quality of product/service and quality of productivity. (The quest for these twin 'qualities' is considered in greater detail in Chapter 11 on team culture planning.) Thus, while the production department might naturally incline towards 'production type' goals (see Table 7.1) and might be most concerned with the system tasks of input ordering and conversion, nevertheless, such tendencies need to be undertaken in the context of the team effort and within the constraints of having to satisfy customers.

**Table 7.1 Traditional perspectives of marketing and production goals**

| Production goals | Marketing goals |
| --- | --- |
| Efficiency of operation | Customer satisfaction |
| Standard products/services | Customised products/services |
| Long production runs | 'One-off' orders |
| Cost effective delivery | Quick delivery |
| Minimum stocks | High stock availability |
| Price based on costs | Manufacture within selling price constraint |

The production cycle illustrated in Fig. 7.4 illustrates how the production process starts and finishes in harmonious relationship (ideally) with the marketing department and the customer.

**Figure 7.4  Production process**

The production function, again, is one which can be sub-functionalised. Figure 7.5 provides an example of an organisation chart for a production department.

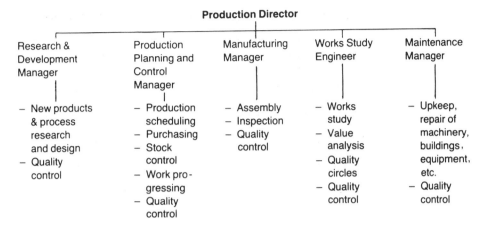

**Figure 7.5  A production department structure**

## Building in quality

Theorists such as Paul Mali (4) and Michael Porter (3) have recently advocated the analysis of all organisational activities so that they might be redesigned better to contribute on efficiency (reduced costs) and/or differentiation (enhanced customer value) fronts. Fig 7.5 has incorporated a 'quality control' function for each of the production department sub-functions in acknowledgement of the modern movement towards 'building in' (rather than 'inspecting out') quality. This movement assumes that *everybody* in the organisation has a duty to 'get it right first time' and that each function has potential for enhancing the efficiency and attractiveness of the organisation's processes and outputs. No longer is it good enough for defective products to be detected by quality control inspectors. Neither should the organisation rely on customer service to make good organisational mistakes through after-sales service and warranty schemes. Today's maxim is 'get it right first time'.

### Case examples: getting involved in quality

(a) 'One hospital clerical assistant suggested that instead of giving patients one questionnaire form on arrival and another on departure, we should utilise both sides of just one form. Over the years, we reckon this will save us thousands of pounds.'

(b) 'That receptionist is really good. Always knows my name, lets me know they value my custom. It's actually a pleasure coming here. I'd miss that if we switched accounts.'

(c) 'We deal with Croydon but we keep getting bills from their Newcastle Accounts Office. They even threatened court action over a bill we'd paid. Their products were OK but their admin lets them down. We're going to buy some place else.'

## Production methods

The production function itself can be modelled as an input/conversion/output process.

The transfiguration of any particular production system should be that which provides the most appropriate approach to efficiently serving the needs of the organisation's customers. Traditionally, three broad categories of production systems – *jobbing*, *batch*, and *mass* – have provided generic models upon which production system designers might base their own systems. Some of the characteristics of these generic methods are outlined below.

## Jobbing systems

(a)  'one-off' jobs/production runs

(b)  creativity above efficiency

(c)  general purposes machinery

(d)  greater value added/contribution from prices charged

(e)  skilled, versatile staff

Examples: shipbuilding, product prototype development, customised kitchens

## Batch systems

(a)  small or large quantities (batches) of products

(b)  systematic, standardised approach to one batch – move on to the next batch

(c)  short production runs

(d)  skilled production run scheduling

(e)  skilful planning of batch size (when not made to order) in order to minimise stock level inefficiencies

(f)  less skilful workforce (than for jobbing systems)

(g)  general purpose machinery often in groups of same type

Example: 70 per cent of British engineering output

## Mass production systems

(a)  flow line production, (e.g. *production line* (motor cars, confectionery, etc.); *continuous flow*, (liquids, glass, etc.) )

(b)  long production runs

(c)  specialist skills, repetitive activities

(d)  high investment in plant, equipment and machinery

(e)  standard products

Example: motor car manufacturing; glass making

Importantly, the traditional demarcations between batch and mass production systems are being eroded by the effect of new technology and competitive forces. Both types of producer are being forced to face up to the dilemma of markets which demand continuing supplies of *new* products, short production runs and customised and quick responses to orders. At the same time manufacturers cannot afford to forget the need to maintain price competitiveness. The illustration 'The engineering industry and batch production' (see below) highlights some of the problems being faced and identifies how new technology is, at one and the same time, a creator and a resolver of the problems being experienced.

## Case study: the engineering industry and batch production

British engineering manufacture has an important place in the national economy. About two and a half million people (over 10 per cent of the employed labour force) are employed in engineering. Although the contribution to the gross domestic product of the engineering and allied industries has gradually fallen over the past 20 years, the sector still contributes substantially (almost 40 per cent of the total) to Britain's visible exports. The more recent, and sharper, decline in engineering manufacturing has been mainly in three areas: motor vehicles, mechanical engineering and metal goods. Conversely, aerospace, marine, transport equipment and electrical and instrument engineering have shown some growth.

There are about 3,300 engineering manufacturing establishments (company sites) employing 100 or more people per site in the United Kingdom. The majority of these could benefit from upgrading their production techniques and procedures. Of these, about 2,500 are small- to medium-sized companies employing between 100 and 500 people. In British industry generally, as a NEDO analysis (British Industrial Performance, NEDO, 1983) showed, profitability remains inadequate to permit the long-term investment and expansion that is necessary.

Manufacturing covers a wide spectrum, from the mass production of a small number of different products at one end to the one-off manufacture of individual items at the other. The former can use purpose-built, dedicated and automated machinery in order to minimise costs of the high-volume production runs; the latter calls for general purpose machinery and traditionally has given little opportunity for automation.

In between these two extremes is a wide range of medium-volume, medium-variety batch production, which accounts for about 70 per cent of UK engineering output. Here the aim is to combine the low unit cost benefits of mass production plant with the flexibility of the small batch, general purpose machinery. In general terms the benefits of the advanced technology systems which meet these needs are:

(a)  better utilisation of capital equipment;

(b)  reduced levels of stocks and work in progress;

(c)  reduced lead times on new and modified designs;

(d)  shorter and more reliable deliveries;

(e)  more consistent product quality and reduced waste;

(f)  reduced unit costs.

Traditionally, batch engineering companies have responded to competitive pressures by trying to move towards higher volumes and reduced product variety, in order to be able to use mass production machinery. Although the possibility of a reduction in variety should always be investigated, options may be limited as customers demand a wider choice of products and a shortened timescale for product development and innovation.

The competitive environment today includes sound foreign companies ready to supply high quality products, and buyers willing to re-evaluate existing suppliers and to think internationally. In this situation, all batch manufacturers are finding that they have to respond more quickly to changes in the market. Not only is the market becoming more demanding in the type of product it requires, but manufacturers no longer have as much time as previously to decide whether they wish to compete in a particular product area. In addition, large customers now expect their component suppliers to respond as flexibly and quickly, and with the same high quality, as they have to do.

Batch manufacturing is already a vitally important part of the UK economy. The increasingly flexible requirements of markets and the resulting changes in products will, if anything, increase its importance. If this sector is to grow by reversing the penetration of foreign-made products in the UK and to export competitively, the manufacturing efficiency of batch processes must be increased and product costs minimised.

NEDO engineering sector committees agree that among the actions needed to improve their industries' performances, and so increase demand for their products, are better marketing and design (including design for manufacture and the use of new materials) and investment in advanced manufacturing technology. Such technology enables batch items of wide variety to be produced at costs approaching those of volume production, with sharply reduced manufacturing lead times, more consistent quality and reduced inventories. For component makers these techniques offer the only cost-effective way of responding to the demand for tight-tolerance components for automated assembly lines. For specialised machinery makers, the techniques will be needed to produce the new generation of flexible, multi-purpose production plants.

(Extracts from *Advanced Manufacturing Technology: the impact of new technology on engineering batch production*, NEDO, 1985)

## Think and discuss

1   What are the aims of:
    (a)  mass production;
    (b)  'one-off' manufacture;
    (c)  batch manufacture?
2   Describe the environment confronting British producers.
3   What is the dilemma facing batch manufacturers?
4   Outline the ways forward recommended by NEDO committees. Which systems goals are they addressing?

## The finance function

The argument that a co-ordinated, multifunctional approach is required for business succcess is supported by the ability of *each* generic function to put forward a strong case for being ranked as *the* most important. We have just indicated the fundamental roles of marketing and production and suggest that the personnel, research and development, and information functions could also lay claim to being the foremost functions. Certainly, the *finance* function can argue that, as chief planner of the organisation's most basic resource – money – it should occupy this position. Money underpins the organisation as an exchange mechanism, it buys inputs, pays for conversion processes and quantifies the value of organisational outputs. The ability to attract and utilise money is the key to organisational *survival* and *growth*. It keeps the systems cycle rolling – non-liquidity is a forerunner of insolvency and liquidation. The success of most organisations is judged mainly on how well money has been managed and/or how the money value of the organisation has been enhanced. The finance department has special responsibilities for over-seeing those critical organisation performance areas of *liquidity* and *profitability*. Also, organisations are required by law to record financial transactions and to prepare and present annual financial statements. Figure 7.6 shows the role of money in organisations.

Traditionally, the accountant has major responsibilities for, or inputs into, the following finance related sub-functions:

(a) *Financial policy planning.* Deciding (or assisting in decisions on) where and when to borrow, where and when to invest, the desired levels of profitability and liquidity to be aimed for and the associated efficiency/activity ratios which the organisation should achieve in its various resource utilisation activities.

(b) *Financial accounting.* Recording financial transactions, processing accounting information, preparing annual accounts (profit and loss account, balance sheet, etc.) and auditing the firm's financial systems and records.

(c) *Cost and managerial accounting.* Collecting and disseminating accounting information for management decision-making in areas such as pricing, forecasting, budgetary planning and control.

(d) *Taxation planning.* Advising management on the complexities of taxation, recording and managing the enterprise's PAYE, corporation tax and dividends transactions.

The accountant, therefore, is a central figure in decisions on how the organisation must act if it is to create *acceptable levels of wealth*, remain capable of *meeting its debts as they fall due* and in decisions on those organisational activities which provide opportunities for improving 'bottom line' (efficiency) and/or 'value-adding' (higher prices) performances.

# The personnel function

## Case example: the importance of staff at Sainsbury's

'The most important part of any Sainsbury's store is its team of staff. Although we pride ourselves on the range and quality of goods we sell, it is the people working at Sainsbury's who make us the leading UK food retailer and personnel management is therefore all-important. In Personnel you will be advising line management in all aspects of personnel: recruitment, induction, training and employee relations .... You'll also need to relish pressure and cope with constantly changing circumstances.' (Source: Job advert in the media)

When all is said and done, organisations are about people. They rely on people for

1. **The organisation as an exchange mechanism**

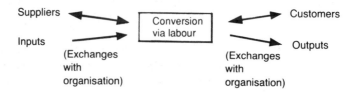

2. **Money as the exchange mechanism medium**

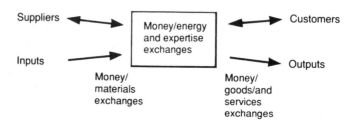

3. **Money and the systems cycles**

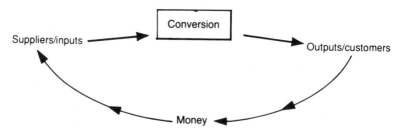

4. **The organisation money cycle**

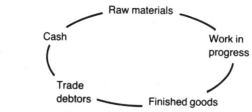

**Figure 7.6 Money in organisations**

their continued existence: 'Business is a human activity …. Although labour requirements change, clerical workers may be replaced by computers, factory workers by automation, there still remains a basic fact: no company can operate without people.' (10) Furthermore, regardless of which stakeholder perspective we adopt – be it customer, worker, manager/owner or whomever – the fundamental purpose of the organisation is to create benefits for people.

Inside the organisation, the personnel function is charged with achieving the enterprise's primary people needs, i.e. it has the responsibility to ensure that the organisation is always stocked with sufficient *numbers* of adequately *skilled* people, possessing the *appropriate attitudes* to propel and guide motivated commitment to the organisation's goals.

Some of the many activities which comprise the personnel function are identified in Figs 7.7 and 7.8 which illustrate the personnel (or manpower) flow cycle and a typical personnel department organisation chart, respectively. However, while the specialist personnel department has a major responsibility for ensuring a successful personnel function, the Institute of Personnel Management reminds us that 'Personnel management is a responsibility of *all those who manage people*, as well as being a description of those who are employed as specialists.' Thus, both personnel officers and line managers have crucial inputs into personnel activities. A major thrust of today's strategic success prescriptions is based on the belief that greater organisation effectiveness flows from the harnessing, by managers, of the efforts of 'free' workers. The call from management strategy is for organisations to create environmentally responsive, change flexible, efficient, market-orientated workforce teams. Chapters 11 and 12 on team culture planning, particularly, look at how successful enterprises have achieved this type of workforce.

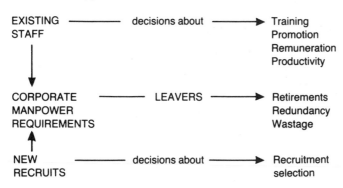

**Figure 7.7  Manpower flow cycle**

# Administration through functions planning: conclusion

Administration is that planning process which makes sure 'things get done'. It is required once desired outcomes and strategies have been worked out. It is the activity which plans and implements the sequencing, motivating, co-ordinating and controlling of work. The activities of the organisation can be dissected and analysed according to the functions they perform. Typically, in growing organisations, for example, the jobs of marketing, finance, personnel and production are separated and delegated to specialist personnel. How jobs are rearranged and reorganised is crucial to the effectiveness of the organisational/environmental adaptation process. Strategists need to think carefully, therefore, about beneficial changes. However, strategists should also take care to avoid the dangers inherent in functional differentiation. In particular, there is a need to ensure that integration mechanisms are employed to maintain an *effective whole*. A re-integrating concept which focuses the attention of the entire organisation – regardless of the particular locations and cultures of its

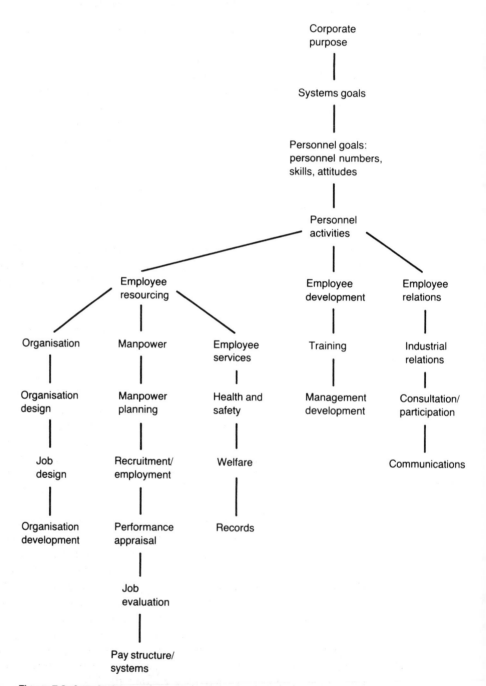

Figure 7.8 A typical personnel department structure (source: Armstrong, *A Handbook of Personnel Management,* 2nd edn, Kogan Page, 1984)

different parts – on the need to satisfy customers efficiently, is the marketing controlled concept. Today's business environment, generally, demands the adoption and installation of such an administrative approach.

# Case study: high flying Concorde heads for prosperity

(Source: H Robinson, 'High-Flying Concorde Heads for Prosperity', *Marketing Week*, 8 March 1985)

Nine years after its first commercial flight, Concorde can still turn heads. Its St Valentine's Day flight to Australia in the record-breaking time of 17 hours had the people of Sydney out in droves, not to see Clive James coming down the steps, but to catch a glimpse of the aeroplane with the unmistakable body and Roman nose.

That particular Concorde was on charter to Cunard, taking out and bringing back passengers from the *QE2* and the *Sagafjord*. Such trips are becoming increasingly important to British Airways (BA), which now operates six Concordes and is about to bring a seventh out of mothballs. Not just because they make money, but because they're one of the most effective flag-waving exercises for the pride of the fleet of British Airways.

A fresh burst of flag-waving will start next month when the airline unveils the new Concorde livery, which will be significantly different to that revealed last month for the rest of BA's aircraft. More importantly, a fresh marketing programme has been designed to put the spotlight firmly on Concorde and encourage more travellers to fly the world's favourite airline supersonically.

The man behind the new programme is Captain Brian Walpole, general manager of Concorde division at BA. He not only manages Concorde, he also flies it. Every week he takes Concorde on one of its twice-daily Heathrow/New York runs, which takes passengers at twice the speed of sound across the Atlantic in three and a half hours. Small, dapper and with the nervy alertness characteristic of pilots and others who live by their reflexes and concentration, Walpole spiritedly denies the suggestion that Concorde is now anything but an asset to BA: 'British Airways' policy is to redefine Concorde as its flagship, its market leader, its unique product. Last year Concorde generated more than £90 million revenue, and profits of £12 million. It's been in profit now for the past three years, and it will be in profit for the next 17; if it isn't, it won't continue ... The predictions for Concorde are highly favourable: we have a finite asset – only seven in the fleet – and an expanding demand. If that isn't a healthy recipe I don't know what is.'

Critics might say a healthier recipe would have been to never have built Concorde – reputedly dubbed 'the flying overdraft' by John Biffen when a mere Conservative MP – and to have saved the British and French governments and taxpayers the £1 billion development costs. They might also point to the £160 million cost to British Airways of buying Concorde, written off by the government in 1979, as further evidence of Concorde as a disaster. Not to mention the £30 million loss Concorde made in its first three years, from January 1976 to March 1979.

The critics have a point, but then the British government pretty quickly dropped any pretence that the Concorde project was a money-maker for it (a laughable position to maintain as orders dried up and project costs soared) and contented itself with calling Concorde a technological triumph for Britain.

But the money is spent, Concorde is flying (albeit only 11 of the 16 built) operated by BA and Air France, and BA at least is making some return on its most controversial aeroplane.

The fact that Concorde is at last operating in the black is largely attributable to the setting up, under BA chief Lord King, of a special Concorde Division in May 1982, at a time when much of BA's business was under ruthless and intense scrutiny. As a result Concorde got what it needed most – a team of specialists who understood Concorde's special problems.

The new division, which operates as a separate profit centre, had two aims: to reduce costs and improve revenue. General manager Walpole and his team tackled the first at a practical and balance sheet level. Costs which historically had been correctly attributed to Concorde – such as hangar space – but which were no longer valid, were weeded out. Then the division looked at external costs such as spare parts and maintenance, and rationalised these. The results were cost savings of 'many millions of pounds' according to Walpole, who has been in charge of the division since it was formed.

On the revenue side, Concorde was treated in textbook fashion. 'Our whole product range was taken apart then put back together again', explains Walpole, 'We looked at our schedule, our staff service, meals, in-flight giveaways – everything.'

The culmination of this reappraisal was a major promotional programme heavily centred on public relations and media exposure, including a lucky break with the BBC, which made a number of programmes about Concorde. Thus, phoenix-like, the new Concorde emerged.

Now Concorde needs a fresh injection of flair, a new coat of paint, and a brand new image. Walpole is pinning much of his marketing programme on the unveiling of the new livery, together with a sleek new interior design. This event, while of minimal news value in, say, a Jumbo or DC 10, acquires kudos when it involves the world's most talked about passenger plane. For this reason, Walpole will rely heavily on interest from the media to put across the new-look Concorde rather than paid-for advertising. 'I do question the value of advertising', he says, 'It's expensive and difficult to quantify. Only 15–20 per cent of our budget goes on advertising. There's mileage in selective advertising in the business press, but why should we pay to go on television when the BBC and ITV make lovely programmes about us when we fly to Sydney?'

Walpole's tactical weapons will include some advertising though, especially in the US business press, promotions and incentives for travel agents in markets spanning Europe, the UK and the US, and direct marketing targeted at top business travellers.

Walpole himself has just come back from South America, a region where he's anxious to drum up extra business for the Miami/Washington/London route launched a year ago. 'I've been talking to the top travel agents in eight South American countries, offering them incentives to sell Concorde on the Miami route, and I'm about to embark on a similar programme to the Caribbean.'

A new market research programme has revealed a key new area for Concorde to exploit – health. 'We think it's worth plugging the health benefits of Concorde', says Walpole, 'You get less jetlag flying supersonically because on, say, the New York run you're flying for only three and a half hours. People ask me why I can fly a plane, and creep in and out of my office: it's because I fly on Concorde.'

The research also picked up considerable interest in the new livery and refurbishment planned for Concorde next month: 'I think the old was becoming a little tired', comments Walpole.

New decor or not, most people fly and will continue to fly Concorde because it saves them time. Concorde is for a flying elite: the 100,000 passengers the 100-seat aeroplanes carry every year are a select coterie of top business people, sports and media stars, diluted with a few ordinary folk who have saved for years for the trip of a lifetime. 'About 80 per cent of our clientele are regular Concorde passengers', says Walpole, 'Typically about 85 per cent are business people, 10 per cent are the 'rich and famous' such as sports and entertainment stars, and the other 5 per cent are people on one-off trips (nine years ago the balance was more like 50 per cent).'

Walpole wants Concorde load factors to improve, although with an average load factor of around 60 per cent (80 per cent in peak seasons on the London/New York run, and 50 per cent in the off peak 'shoulder season') Concorde's performance is well up to the standard of the rest of BA, which has load factors typically of around 63 per cent. Concorde's break-even load factor is 40–50 per cent, so its seating equation looks cosy.

The people flying Concorde expect, and don't mind paying a premium for hours they save travelling supersonically. Passengers pay between 10 and 20 per cent more than for a first class ticket to the same destination; a one-way Concorde flight to New York is about £1,200 and £1,000 on the first class, subsonic seven-hour flight.

Market research shows people expect Concorde to cost far more: one reason Walpole would like to see the differential ended.'If we could compete directly on price with first class we'd get even more business. Typically people think Concorde is 50 per cent or double the first class fare.' But Concorde looks stuck with its unwanted premium – the other airlines insist on it, especially the American ones.

There is one consolation at the moment though: with the strong dollar Concorde is benefitting from the fact that most of its passengers are Americans paying for their tickets in dollars, which translate into more pounds for the Concorde coffers.

Apart from visiting the Caribbean to promote Concorde, Walpole, will also call in at Miami to try to crank up business for the London/Washington/Miami run which has a long way to go before it matches the New York route for profitability. 'There's huge potential for this run in the southern states. About a third of Concorde passengers are on connecting flights so there's clearly potential for a service such as ours.'

Europe will not escape Walpole and his team, who hope to convince the Continentals that a trip to Miami via London and Washington is preferable to a direct hop on a subsonic jet.

Alongside Concorde's schedule business is the rapidly growing charter operation, which first got off the ground four years ago when the Concorde fan club hired the plane for an hour and half trip around the Bay of Biscay. Today Concorde is chartered by a variety of tour operators and organisations for a wide range of destinations. But it is not quite the flying circus that business onlookers may fancy. It will only contribute 8 per cent of Concorde's revenue, and sooner or later a ceiling will be hit when 'the problem won't be finding work for Concorde but finding the Concordes to do the work', as Walpole puts it.

A big slice of Concorde's charter operation is with Cunard. This year the company expects to put £12m of business through Concorde, taking passengers to and from such destinations as Hong Kong, Cape Town and Rio. In addition there are 120 round trips scheduled where, for an astronomical fee, you can fly Concorde to New York, stay three nights in the Waldorf Astoria, and return on the *QE2*.

Bernard Crisp, UK director of Cunard, says 'QE2 plus Concorde is a highly attractive package because it offers two complementary but contrasting kinds of excellence in travelling.' He adds that Cunard has bought 6,000 seats to Miami on Concorde to fit in with Cunard's cruise programme, and envisages a growing amount of business with Concorde.

But the scheduled routes are the bread and butter of Concorde, and it is keenly eyeing the West African market, although as Walpole admits, 'these are the province of British Caledonian and Nigeria Airways.' Having tried and failed with several routes in the late 1970s and early 1980s – most notably Bahrain and Singapore – BA needs to get it right for Concorde if and when it gets a new destination. 'We're not interested in operating on any route that we're not absolutely certain will give us a good profit', stresses Walpole, 'The Middle East isn't particularly attractive. We've just come out of Saudia Arabia – there just wasn't the traffic. We have no particular plans to open up any more schedule services but there is a possibility of increasing our frequency on routes. I don't see us going to the Far East other than on charter.'

Quite apart from the problems of finding profitable schedule routes are those peculiar to Concorde, namely the din it makes taking off and landing, and the sonic boom when it hits Mach One. Fringe groups in the 1970s ascribed to the mysterious boom the causing of all evils, from destroying the ozone layer to frightening sheep. The scares were enough to get Concorde banned from flying supersonically through several tracts of important airspace and for a time it looked as if Concorde would be banned from New York, although reason prevailed and Concorde made its first landing there in November 1977. The more extreme objections to Concorde flying over any particular country have faded away, although there are still highly sensible restrictions on when it can land and take off in London and New York.

The next test for Concorde will come when BA goes public, which will probably be later this year. Our national carrier will probably go under the hammer with a £1 billion price tag, and the City, at least, seems to think Concorde will be a sweetener to the sale rather than a bitter pill. 'Concorde really is the flagship of British Airways. It is a profitable operation now, and it's suited very well to the North Atlantic runs', says Bill Seward, an analyst at one of BA's brokers, Phillips & Drew, 'It would have difficulties though on other routes, because of problems with its fuel consumption, load factors and noise levels. But Concorde, because it looks different, can bring something to BA that other airlines haven't got, and the halo effect it creates is important.'

## Think and discuss

1  Refer to the Concorde case study.
   (a) What market needs does Concorde satisfy? Consider customers, operators, manufacturers, governments.
   (b) What major changes in the marketing environment have affected the success of Concorde in the market place?
   (c) Describe Concorde's marketing mix.
   (d) Identify market segments for Concorde.

2  Refer to your own organisation or one of your choosing.
   (a) Draw its organisation structure.
   (b) Assess the effectiveness of the structure in motivating, co-ordinating, controlling and sequencing organisational activity. How would you change the structure to better achieve systems goals?

3  Model the Concorde operation as an open social system. Which functions are important to Concorde's success?

# References

1   L J Mullins, *Management and Organisational Behaviour*, Pitman, 1985, p 117
2   This classification of administration planning activities is derived from one provided by H Fayol, *General and Industrial Management*, Pitman, 1949.
3   M E Porter, *Competitive Advantage*, New York, The Free Press, 1985, introduces the concept of the 'value chain'.
4   P Mali, *MBO Updated*, Wiley Interscience, 1986
5   R McRobb, 'Industry's Lost Costs', *Management Today*, May 1984
6   P F Drucker, *The Practice of Management*, Pan Piper, 1968
7   F W Taylor, 'The Principles of Scientific Management', *Scientific Management*, New York, Harper, 1947
8   P Kotler, *Marketing Management Analysis, Planning and Control*, 4th edn, Prentice-Hall International, 1980, p 19
9   P F Drucker, op. cit., p 54
10  D E Hussey, *Corporate Planning Theory and Practice*, 2nd edn, Pergamon, 1982, Ch 16

# Recommended reading

G A Cole, *Management Theory and Practice*, D P Publications, 1983, pp 258–440
P Kotler, *Marketing Management Analysis, Planning and Control*, 5th edn, Prentice-Hall International, 1984
M Armstrong, *A Handbook of Personnel Management Practice*, 2nd edn, Kogan Page, 1984

# 8 Administration planning: putting objectives into operation

In this chapter we continue our exploration of administration planning by reference to the following topics:

- The organisation as a hierarchy of objectives
- Open or closed, stated or enacted objectives
- Gap analysis
- Management by objectives (MBO)
- Using theory to achieve successful MBO practice
- Implementing management by objectives
- Administration planning – the role of functions and objectives: conclusion
- Approaches to and techniques of forecasting

## The organisation as a hierarchy of objectives

### Case example: long- and short-term objectives

*Long-range objectives*

(a)  Health: more leisure

(b)  Money

(c)  Write book (play ?) – fame

(d)  Visit India

*Immediate objectives*

(a)  Pick up pattern at Hilda's

(b)  Change faucets – call plumber (who?)

(c)  Try yoghurt?

(From *The Diary of a Lady*; quoted in *The New Yorker*, Ansoff, *Corporate Strategy*, Penguin, 1979, p 47)

The concept of a hierarchy of objectives is helpful for linking organisational activity to the aspirations of important stakeholders. Planning an hierarchy of objectives requires the generation of an ends–means chain of increasingly specific and proximate performance objectives. (Ends–means chains refer to the relationship between objectives at linked levels. Lower objectives are the *means* for achieving the desired *ends* immediately above them.) The chain starts with objectives, often publicly stated within the company's accounts and other publications, which relate to the desired outcomes of important stakeholders. These objectives and associated statements can be classified as:

(a) *Organisation raison d'être statements/objectives* which identify the organisation's primary stakeholders and the organisation's obligations towards them.

(b) *Statements of intent towards particular categories of stakeholders* which indicate, in general terms, how the organisation will act for the benefit of specified 'secondary' stakeholders.

(c) *Ethos or mission statements/objectives* which describe the organisation's self identity – the way it sees itself and wants to be perceived.

These broad, enduring, stakeholder-related objectives are then translated into – and achieved by – a sequential chain of sub-objectives starting with:

(a) the corporate objective which in commercial organisations, is often a profit-related target; and on to

(b) tactical objectives which are often 'year on' objectives for departments' functions; and finally,

(c) operating objectives/activities which are specific, detailed and for more immediate implementation.

Table 8.1 and the illustration which follows provide examples of 'hierarchies of objectives'.

## Case example: the launch of a new car

In 1985 the Spanish car manufacturer SEAT was making plans for a successful launch of its Ibiza and Malaga models into the British market. The task ahead could not be easy. SEAT was the last major car manufacturer to enter the British market and its product/market strategy was one of gaining a viable base in an already highly competitive, small- to medium-size car sector.

The strategic plan called for the production and promotion of a high quality product to be distributed though a chain of small- to medium-sized franchises which could demonstrate ambition and a high reputation within their particular localities. Prices would be competitive with other manufacturers' models competing in the target market.

SEAT's strategic objectives included:

(a) to payback initial investment costs within three years;

(b) to take 1 per cent of the market within three years;

(c) to attain within three years a ratio of 65/35 between internal and external financing;

(d) to seek productivity improvements which would enable a break even point at 60

**Table 8.1  The organisation as a hierarchy of objectives**

| Type of objective | Objective setting area | Examples |
|---|---|---|
| Organisation *raison d'être* | Primary stake-holder satisfaction | To increase the wealth of share-holders at a rate faster than inflation (BTR) |
| | | To secure the fairest possible sharing by all the members of ownership, knowledge and power (John Lewis Partnership) |
| Statements of intent to stake-holders | Secondary stakeholder satisfaction | To provide staff with above industry norm working conditions |
| Mission or ethos | Organisational psychology or self identity | To maintain family status To be a caring and patriotic member of society |
| | | To continue as leader in high street fashion |
| Corporate objective | Overall profit/wealth generation | After tax profit of £1m by 1994 |
| | | 10 per cent return on shareholders capital |
| | | To regenerate economic and social wealth in the area |
| Strategic objective | Long-term product/market; financial and productivity development | To attain 3 per cent of the market within three years |
| | | To achieve payback within three years |
| | | To reduce man hours for present production levels by 33 per cent within five years |
| Tactical objectives | 'Year on', often departmental performance targets | Attain 1 per cent of market this year |
| | | Reduce labour turnover by 10 per cent this year |
| Operating objectives | Individual manager/ operator activities | Sign up 16 new dealers by end of month |
| | | Do weekly stock check |

per cent of forecasted sales and generally to tighten costs even further on top of the austerity plan introduced in 1983.

At a tactical level the company hoped, through the implementation of its planned marketing mix and the introduction of further models during the next year, to sell 8,000/9,000 cars in 1986.

More immediately and urgently, with only three months to go before the October 1985 motor show launch, newly appointed business development managers were working overtime to sign up targeted numbers of franchised dealers in time for the grand launch.

Success in the UK was part of the plan for a 'new era' for SEAT. Following the 'pull out' of Italian motor giant Fiat who, prior to 1980, had held substantial ownership and operating interests in the SEAT organisation, the Spanish government had stepped in to help out the ailing company. A new wealth generating era for SEAT was seen as vital to the achievement of the social and economic aspirations of the Spanish government and the people of its nation.

# Open or closed, stated or enacted objectives

Some of the objectives expressed in the above illustration are open objectives – statements of broad, unquantifiable aims. Many writers argue that objectives should be closed – in the form of specified targets, the achievement of which can thus be measured. Byars (1), for example, sums up a widespread belief that 'Management cannot be properly practised and organisations cannot be as successful as they should without pursuing specific objectives.' Later in this chapter, we shall discuss the motivational and control assisting properties of closed objectives in our look at an administrative planning technique known as 'management by objectives'. Closed objectives will also show up as being fundamental to resource utilisation and productivity drives when we consider the subject of efficiency planning. In these roles we shall see that closed, precisely defined objectives can be very useful. On the other hand, however, other writers remind us that open objectives, such as statements of mission, can also take useful roles in focusing strategy rather than as measurement devices. Further, highly specific objectives, once set, can become blueprints which the people of the organisation follow, even when they are no longer appropriate. Competitors, too, often have the opportunity to take advantage of published, detailed aims.

The need, of course, is to combine the advantages of the systematic approach to planning by objectives with mechanisms designed to monitor the situation and provide flexibility when necessary. Peter Drucker, perhaps the leading theorist in planning by objectives recognises the appropriateness of a combined systematic and flexible approach to planning objectives: 'Of course, objectives are not a railroad timetable. They can be compared to the compass bearing by which a ship navigates. The compass bearing itself is firm, pointing in a straight line toward the desired port. But in actual navigation the ship will veer off its course for many miles to avoid a storm. She will slow down to a walk in a fog and heave to altogether in a hurricane. She may even change destination in mid ocean and set a new compass bearing towards a new port – perhaps because war has broken out, perhaps only because her cargo has been sold in mid-passage. Still, four-fifths of all voyages end in the intended port at the originally scheduled time. And without a compass bearing, the ship would neither be able to find the port nor be able to estimate the time it will take to get there.'(2)

## Stated and enacted objectives

In the context of a discussion on aspirations to objectives, it is worth considering, briefly, the notion of *stated* and *enacted* objectives. This concept acts as a warning to those who might otherwise accept organisational statements of intention at face value. It reminds us that what is stated is not always the same as what is, in the event, enacted. Mental hospitals, for example, might publish intentions of care for and treatment of the mentally sick. The reality of organisational activity in such institutions, however, might be more directed towards custodial containment. Theorists have reminded us that interested parties should pay attention to 'what is done' as well as to 'what is said'. The concept also reminds management strategists themselves that the formal expression of enterprise objectives can provide vehicles for bargaining and public relations improvements.

## Gap analysis

If shareholders are to receive bigger dividends, managers bigger perks and workers bigger pay packets, then their enterprise has to have, or attract the wealth necessary to facilitate these distributions. The redistribution of *existing* stocks of wealth can be the means of benefiting certain groups at the expense of others. Short-term satisfactions can also be made available through 'selling the family's silver'. However, *growing* stocks of wealth are the prerequisites to continuing improvements in personal fulfilment. Gap analysis is a technique for helping strategists decide whether the organisation is, or will be, in a position to satisfy important stakeholder demands. It also helps in the quantification of any wealth shortfall which will have to be made good. This technique, favoured by corporate planning theorists such as John Argenti (3), requires that decisions be made on:

(a) *A suitable wealth growth performance indicator.* Many theorists emphasise the role of profits and profit-related indicators because of their predilections towards organisations as instruments of their owners. However, because of the residual nature of profits, practising management strategists have been seen to also use *sales* value indicators.

In terms of the growth indicator chosen, further decisions are required as follows:

(b) *'Where are we now?'* This requires agreement, often after reference to the organisation's financial statements, on the current position of the indicator chosen. Recently published accounts, for example, might form an agreed base point.

(c) *'Where do we want to be at an agreed point in time?'* Here the strategist and the management team have to set the target growth figure and the time to which it applies.

(d) *'Where are we likely to be at the agreed point in time?'* This decision necessitates prior *forecasting* of likely performance levels. (This chapter concludes with a resume of the role of, approaches to and techniques for forecasting in business planning.) The planning team has to forecast a likely performance figure in the context of the organisation *not taking* any new steps to influence future outcomes.

(e) '*What is the extent of any gap between (c) and (d)?*' This gap represents a stock of wealth shortfall which will have to be made good – the gap has to be filled through the successes of pertinent new organisational developments (gap analysis is, therefore, a useful technique for use in the process of corporate planning).

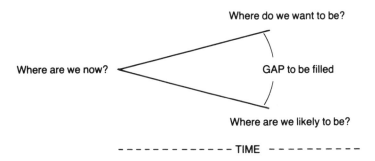

Figure 8.1  Filling the strategic gap with organisational developments

# Management by objectives (MBO)

## A layman's definition of the tasks of administration

Having decided corporate objectives and product/market and associated competitive strategies, the management strategist has to ensure that organisation systems successfully operationalise the strategic plans. In lay terms, the tasks of administration planning can, therefore, be expressed as:

(a) *Getting people to work.* This is the motivation role of administration. The enterprise has to attract personnel membership and has to motivate members, once present, to do jobs.

(b) *Getting people to work effectively.* It is not enough to motivate job performance only. Care needs to be taken to ensure that people *do things in the right order* – to achieve effective sequencing and co-ordination. Even more fundamentally, people need to *do the right things.* Despite the effort involved, for example, a hole dug in the wrong place provides no contribution to the drain laying process. In the systems goal context, people need to concentrate their efforts towards improving those job outcomes which contribute to the organisation's goals of efficiency and control of the environment.

(c) *Getting people to work together effectively.* Different jobs emphasise different tasks and outcomes, attract different types of personnel and utilise different ways of doing things. Environments which demand high levels of job differentiation also enhance the organisational need for *co-ordination* to maximise team effort. Too often, organisations are places of inter-departmental conflict and duplicated effort.

(d) *Ensuring that people are working together effectively.* Monitoring and controlling activities and systems are a necessary part of administration. Organisational life remains far too uncertain to allow credence to attach to the expectation that planned for motivational, sequencing and co-ordinating outcomes will automatically occur.

## What is management by objectives?

Management by objectives (MBO) is a system of administration which seeks to achieve strategic objectives through the setting and achieving of a hierarchy of linked objectives. Managers and subordinates, from top to bottom of the enterprise, together agree subordinates' key task targets, periodically review performances and reset new targets. Some definitions from some of the strategists working in this area are given below.

'MBO is directing each job towards the objectives of the whole business.' *Peter Drucker* (4)

'MBO is … management by results.' *Dale McConkey* (5)

'MBO is … a system that integrates the company goals of profit and growth with the manager's needs to contribute and develop himself personally.' *John Humble* (6)

The illustration in Fig. 8.2 provides an example of how a hierarchy of objectives, under a system of MBO, links back to the corporate and strategic objectives of the organisation.

*Corporate objective*

Increase return on capital employed
to 15 per cent within three years

↑    ↓

*Strategic objectives*

To attain an additional five
per cent of the market within
three years

To improve sales to employee
ratio by five per cent
within three years

↑    ↓

*Departmental managers' objectives*

To increase sales turnover
by seven per cent during first
six months

To reduce rejects by five
per cent per month within
six months

To increase production
output this year by five
per cent per month using existing
labour force only

↑    ↓

*Sales rep/shop floor objectives*

To sell to five new clients
each week

To achieve a production
output level of 100 units
per shift

**Figure 8.2 Linked targets in management by objectives**

For Peter Drucker, MBO is *the* means for stimulating a situation wherein the people of the organisation are working together effectively. Writing in 1954, Drucker said 'Any business enterprise must build a true team and weld individual efforts into a common effort. Each member of the enterprise contributes something different, but they must all contribute towards a common goal. Their efforts must all pull in the same direction, and their contributions must fit together to produce a whole – without gaps, without friction, without unnecessary duplication of effort.

'Business performance, therefore, requires that each job be directed towards the objectives of the whole business ... The performance that is expected of the manager must be derived from the performance goal of the business, his results must be measured by the contribution they make to the success of the enterprise. The manager must know and understand what the business goals demand of him in terms of performance, and his superior must know what contribution to demand and expect of him ... What the business needs is a principle of management that will give full scope to individual strength and responsibility, and at the same time give common direction of vision and effort, establish team work and harmonise the goals of the individual with the common weal.

'The only principle that can do this is management by objectives and self-control. It makes the common weal the goal of every manager. It substitutes for control from outside the stricter, more exacting and more effective control from the inside. It motivates the manager to action not because somebody tells him to do something ... but because the objective needs of his task demand it. He acts not because somebody wants him to but because he himself decides that he has to – he acts, in other words, as a free man.'(7)

Two principles of Drucker's MBO *philosophy* have formed fundamentals of other theorists' success paradigms. The notion of each job contributing to the organisation's overall position of competitive advantage is a major part of Michael Porter's success prescription, for example. Peters and Waterman Jr (8) too, see a crucial management task to be that of harnessing a 'free man, waiting for motivation' labour force (and the consequential achievement of productivity through people).

Using the previously offered 'layman definition' of the tasks of administration, we will now describe more fully the system that is MBO (according to the theorists). We will show why, if implemented in accord with theory, MBO is *the* administrative vehicle of our time.

## Getting people to work

Motivation theorists emphasise needs satisfaction as the key determinant of getting the workforce to increase commitment and effort in their jobs. In Chapter 3, we referred to Maslow's hierarchy of needs model. Illustrations following this section describe the works of Taylor, Mayo and Hertzberg. These are seminal works which have added to our understanding of people at work. They reveal a range of needs requiring satisfaction – from more basic physiological needs to socially-orientated aspirations and onto more introverted self-achievement needs.

A major attribute of MBO is its capacity to work at all motivational levels. For example, subordinates who, through the MBO process, develop an awareness of the important contributions they can make to the organisation's success also develop awareness of the importance of organisational success to their own security of tenure and work-related satisfactions. 'Pay for performance' – a regular feature of MBO systems – provides a further 'bottom line' motivator. The team orientation of MBO and the closer dialogue and interaction between manager and subordinate (as they debate, agree and reflect on performance targets) reinforces a person's inclination – given the appropriate environment – to work for the team. At higher needs levels, MBO provides motivation through greater status, responsibility and job satisfaction, emphasising, as it does, the need for subordinates to take part in the planning of their own work outcomes and activities. Those theorists who emphasise motivation as a process suggest that commitment is not simply about needs fulfilment but also about expectations by the job incumbent of whether he/she is capable of achieving the desired work outcomes and whether adequate performance will, in fact, produce the desired rewards (see Fig. 8.3). Again, MBO, in theory, provides a 'catch all' response. MBO targets are set, ideally, so that they are difficult enough to provide a challenge but not so optimistic as to be unrealistic. People do enjoy attaining targets – the mere process of setting clear, challenging and attainable goals is, in itself motivational. Further, the tasks of specifying job contents, targets to be achieved and types of activities to be undertaken, together with the review sessions which reflect on performance problems, together provide a major platform for training needs analysis and management development. Thus, staff are given, as an 'offshoot' of the MBO process, the facility for improving their actual and perceived abilities to meet some of those more difficult to attain targets. Regular attainment of targets creates a spiral to confirm that 'nothing succeeds like success'. Successful MBO systems stimulate the confidence to keep searching for continuing improvement.

## The work of Frederick Wilmslow Taylor (1856–1917)

Born in Boston, Massachusetts, Frederick Taylor spent the greater part of his life working on the problems of achieving greater efficiency on the shop floor. In Taylor's time, the most usual practice at the work operational level was to leave working methods to the initiative of the workers. This, observed Taylor, led to rule of thumb methods and gave full rein to man's tendencies towards 'soldiering', i.e. 'natural soldiering' (the innate desire to take things easy) and 'systematic soldiering' (the deliberate and organised restriction of work-rate by the employees).

Taylor's methods for generating greater efficiency involved the implementation of work study methods to determine the correct time and method for each job and the rewarding of employees in relation to the consequential productivity improvements. Taylor demonstrated the benefits of 'scientific management' in his work at the Bethlehem Steel Works. For example, by varying the size of shovels to maintain shovel loads weight at around 21 pounds, regardless of the type of material being shovelled, daily output increased dramatically. Over a three-year period his new methods reduced the workforce from around 500 men to 140, without the loss of any output. Handling costs were reduced by half. All this was achieved without any form of slave driving. Further, the 'first class shovellers' employed at the end of the three-year period now earned 60 per cent more in wages.

## Elton Mayo and the Hawthorne Studies (1924–36)

Elton Mayo (1880–1949) was Professor of Industrial Research at Harvard Graduate School of Business Administration and engaged in the study of issues such as fatigue, accident and labour turnover. Approached by the Western Electric Company in 1927 which was carrying out its own studies in these areas, Mayo and his Harvard colleagues responded to its request for help by setting up a closer and more detailed study of the effect of differing physical conditions on productivity.

Six women workers in the *relay assembly section* were segregated and housed in a room of their own. Over a period of time, numerous changes were made to their working conditions. Rest pauses were introduced and removed. The working week was changed – as was the length and timing of lunch breaks. The physical environment was altered too. At one point the women were working in semi-darkness. Before each change the ladies were consulted. Productivity increased whether conditions were made better or worse. These women were, in fact, the first acknowledged exhibitors of the 'Hawthorne effect' – responding not to environmental changes but to their perceptions of being a special group.

Later experiments in the *bank wiring room* aimed to observe a group of men working under more or less normal conditions for a period of six months or so. Here, the researchers found group actions which worked *against* productivity. The group of men developed its own rules and behaviour norms which included restricting production, ostracising 'rate busters' and largely ignoring, its official supervisors. Clearly, here was a case for the importance of *managing social needs* for the attainment of organisational goals.

## Hertzberg's motivation-hygiene theory

Frederick Hertzberg's studies concentrated on satisfaction at work. This initial research required some 200 engineers and accountants to recall when they had experienced satisfactory and unsatisfactory feelings about their jobs. Hertzberg's conclusions were that two types of motivators were operative in the work situation. The first type he labelled 'hygiene factors' and included:

(a)  company policy and administration;

(b)  supervision – the technical aspect;

(c)  salary;

(d)  interpersonal relations – supervision;

(e)  working conditions.

These were the factors mentioned most in the context of dissatisfaction. They related, Hertzberg noted, to the *context* or environment of work. They do not, in themselves, postulated Hertzberg, increase motivation or work satisfaction. Rather they act to cause dissatisfaction through their absences or inadequacies. In other words, hygiene factors act to prevent ill-health but do not promote higher levels of motivational fitness.

The second category of motivating factors, however, contained those items which were associated with satisfactory feelings – the *true* motivators, according to Hertzberg. These included:

(a)  achievement;

(b)  recognition;

(c)  work itself;

(d)  responsibility;

(e)  advancement.

The 'motivators' are intimately related to the *content* of work, Hertzberg pointed out. Hertzberg postulated, therefore, that it is attention to the design of *the job itself* which will reward managers most in terms of greater subordinate commitment and effort.

Hertzberg's works have, in fact, inspired many programmes of job enlargement/job enrichment (the inclusion in a job of a greater variety of tasks and of wider planning responsibility and more discretion over the methods of task performance). Hertzberg's motivation-hygiene theory has also helped foster the notion that *intrinsic* (self-actualisation) motivators are inherently preferable to *extrinsic*, more tangible, means such as pay.

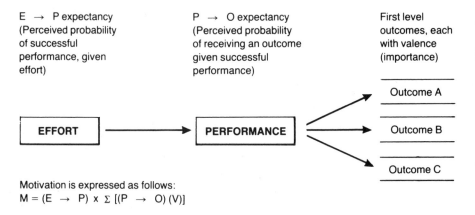

Motivation is expressed as follows:
$$M = (E \rightarrow P) \times \Sigma [(P \rightarrow O)(V)]$$

**Figure 8.3  Major components of expectancy theory (adapted from Nadler and Lawler, 'Motivation, a diagnostic approach' in Hackman, Lawler and Porter, *Perspectives on Behaviour in Organiaztions*, McGraw Hill, 1977)**

## Getting people to work effectively

Our earlier discussion has indicated the sequential nature of management by objectives. Tasks and job outcomes clearly relate to each other, the organisation becomes an ends–means chain of activities carried out in a logical sequence. MBO also emphasises *key tasks*. Drucker suggests that few of us have more than seven or eight really important activities to perform at work. These key tasks contribute significantly to organisational performance. Porter's concept of generic competitive strategies suggests that, in essence, individual work targets should relate to just two generic objectives – efficiency and differentiation. A primary objective of manager/subordinate deliberations on the setting of work objectives, therefore, is to isolate these really important functions. Under a MBO regime, therefore, it is no longer possible for people to spend all day doing nothing or devoting over much time to wasteful pet projects. Another key feature of MBO is its focus on *results* rather than *actions*. People are measured on performance against targets. No longer can the office manager spend time shuffling papers around and *looking* busy. The harassed executive who makes occasional forays around the corridors of head office giving an impression of overwork, has, under a MBO system, to prove the worthiness and effectiveness of his or her endeavours.

## Getting people to work together effectively

MBO is a great co-ordinator. It builds a *team* approach and employs *joint* target setting. Performance appraisal concentrates on future improvement rather than on present criticism. *Dual* roles means that many people involved in the process fill both managerial and subordinate roles. In total, MBO provides an integrated web of related objectives and activities.

## Ensuring that people are working together effectively

Regular monitoring of actual performances, joint appraisals and the ongoing concern of individuals to measure their own performances provide MBO's effective control mechanism. The common search to improve future organisational performance and subordinate job satisfaction rounds off the MBO cycle and propels a new round of targets and activities.

# Implementing management by objectives

Despite the administrative benefits to be had from the system of MBO many organisations in practice remain less than completely satisfied with the results of their attempts at MBO. Theory regards such failures to be the product of *inadequate implementations*. Management strategy remains convinced of the 'sure fire certainty' of MBO's potential. Further, research findings are available within the literature of management strategy (9) to indicate how successful MBO can be achieved in practice. The next section, is a research-based, practical guide, to the 'do's and don'ts' of MBO implementation. Designers of MBO programmes are advised to take into account the prescriptions which follow.

## Introducing MBO

(a) *Introduce MBO via top managers* themselves, rather than via the personnel department. This generates greater commitment to the new system and illustrates, to all personnel, top level support for the system.

(b) *Explain clearly, at all levels, the purpose(s) of the programme.* Personnel will usually show greater commitment to something they can understand and see the sense of. MBO is about success at organisational *and* personal levels. More formal and sophisticated approaches are necessary in our *hostile business environments* if these joint successes are to be attained. Make sure *everybody* affected by MBO is aware of the rationales behind its introduction.

(c) *Avoid excessive paperwork.* Develop a basic and simple form for recording objectives and performances. It is the results of MBO which are important. Do not make a 'bureaucratic god' of the system.

(d) *Introduce MBO in stages.* Start at top management levels and work down as successes are achieved. Consider making initial introductions in those departments which you feel will be most amenable to the system and most likely to be successful participants.

(e) *Check out the organisation climate and its readiness for MBO before you do anything.* Autocratic managers may need training. Communication campaigns might be necessary to alleviate the suspicions of a workforce not used to being taken into the planning stages of job design. The task of objectives setting is, itself, one which requires skills which might not be readily available, without prior training.

## Setting objectives

(a) *Subordinates should have major input into the setting of their key tasks and targets.* This input engenders that vital internalisation and commitment to the work objectives set. Periodical checks by top management are necessary to ensure that objectives at lower levels are not being *imposed from above*. Different managers will have different styles in, and different propensities towards participative objectives setting. Greater attention in this area is likely to be required for lower levels of the managerial chain where the opportunities for, and traditions in, discretionary decision making are smallest.

(b) *Aim for difficult but achievable objectives which are customised to take account of the subordinates' personal strengths, weaknesses and environmental situation.*

(c) *So far as possible quantify objectives.* Exhortations to 'do your best' are not nearly so useful as stated, formal agreements to achieve, say, 5 per cent increase on last month's sales turnover. Agree clear and specific targets.

(d) *Set time constraint targets.* Make clear the date by which targets should be attained.

(e) *Prioritise objectives.* Agree and record (for future reference) the order of importance of the goals set.

## Reviewing performance

(a) *Ensure that each participant receives ongoing feedback on performance.* This facilitates rapid adjustments to correct performance deviations or to re-set objectives. It also helps to maintain the presence and momentum of the MBO programme. Information technology assisted systems can now help overcome this traditional problem area of MBO systems by providing more accurate, timely information.

(b) *Make review sessions forums for constructive analysis of performance problem areas and for the setting of future improvement-orientated objectives and activities.* Subordinates who receive too much criticism in MBO review sessions perform less well in the future than those who experience realistic but *constructive, collaborative* appraisal sessions. Similarly, review sessions which do not produce *new* performance goals are less useful than those which do.

## Organising support for the MBO system

(a) *Make sure that the very top managers of the firm are seen to provide time, effort and commitment to the MBO process.*

(b) *Arrange the organisation's systems to provide a barrage of ongoing support for MBO.* Use memos, notices, videos, etc. to reinforce the importance of MBO. Back up the system with appropriate training programmes. Incorporate regular performance feedback systems and review sessions. Use MBO as a major input into the organisation's reward systems and into its management development programmes.

## Monitoring the MBO programme

Periodically (say, annually) check:

(a) *Attitudes.* Do personnel feel that the programme is worthwhile organisationally and/or personally?

(b) *Relationships.* Are boss/subordinate relationships conducive to effective MBO? Is MBO improving relationships and building organisational team spirit?

(c) *Performance.* Is MBO improving the efficiency and effectiveness of the organisation in its totality? Is it improving systems goals attainment? Do any component parts of the enterprise seem to be underperforming and failing to achieve suitable performance improvements?

# Administration planning – the role of functions and objectives: conclusion

Administration planning is that planning activity which is responsible for the effectiveness with which the organisation's major objectives are actually achieved. In this section we have emphasised the strategy to operations, sequential nature of administration. Administration, here, has been about the taking of major strategic developments into operational reality through processes which guide the necessary sequence of key tasks, and which motivate, co-ordinate and control the activities taking place on the strategy to operations route.

Two administrative planning approaches considered in this chapter and the previous one, have been the *marketing led functional organisation* approach and the system of *management by objectives*.

In conclusion to this first section on administration planning, we would advise that management strategists, having decided their organisation's strategic development directions, should:

(a) decide which are the generic functions most important to the successful implementation of strategy;

(b) decide, and draw up an organisation chart which seems most pertinent for the sequencing, co-ordinating, motivating and controlling of strategic implementation;

(c) design a model of the organisation as a series of ends–means, linked objectives;

(d) embark upon a management by objectives programme which aims to stimulate *everyone* in the organisation to work towards improving efficiency and differentiation contributions for their own jobs. The programme should be based on theoretical prescriptions, of how to implement MBO.

A strategy remains a dream until it is administrated into reality. The concepts of functionally based organisation structures and management by objectives, considered in this chapter and the previous one, provide powerful forces for successfully converting strategy to operation. Chapter 9, which follows, seeks to provide help to the administrator working in particularly diverse organisational situations. That chapter will make reference to another helpful concept for the administrator – that of *vision management*. Meanwhile this chapter concludes with a brief look at some forecasting techniques which are helpful to the process of establishing performance gaps and setting performance objectives.

## Approaches to and techniques of forecasting

Forecasting is an essential part of the planning process. Since planning is about anticipating the future, it is about making assumptions about what that future is likely to be. This is the task of forecasting. Forecasts seek to predict likely future scenarios and outcomes. We then use these assumptions of potential outcomes to decide on and plan how to get our own preferred outcomes. Thus, we could redefine our definition of planning from 'the design of a desired future and effective ways of bringing it about' to one which more clearly takes account of the important role of forecasting in planning, i.e. '*the forecasting of potential outcomes* and the design of desired futures and effective ways of bringing them about'. Thus, forecasting is an inherent part of any and all of the planning activities which take place continuously within the organisation. As environments become more dynamic and dangerous, forecasting reliable assumptions becomes at one and the same time more important and more difficult. A range of forecasting techniques/approaches is, however, available to those who wish to take more sophisticated 'looks' at the future.

(a)  Extrapolation of past trends is based on the assumption that future situations will simply be reflections of how things have occurred, over time, in the past. So, if sales have achieved levels of £20,000, £25,000 and £30,000 units for each of the previous three years, an extrapolation of the past trend would produce forecasts of £35,000, £40,000 and £45,000 units for each of the next three years. Of course, in real life results rarely, if ever, occur in such a neat, linear fashion. *Moving averages, semi-average* and *least squares regression* are techniques which produce a straight line trend from non-linear data and which thus allow straight line projections to be extrapolated into the future.

(b)  Causal methods seek to establish which factors have caused particular outcomes. These causal factors are referred to as independent variables. Statisticians, often with the help of computers, attempt to produce a mathematical relationship between such variables and the dependent variable which might be, for example, sales levels. The most commonly used method here, *multiple regression*, seeks to make sense – in the form of a mathematical equation – of the relationship between outcomes and a range of independent causal variables. If the state of future independent variables can then be forecasted (a difficult job in itself, of course) then the dependent outcome can also be predicted.

(c) Softer approaches to forecasting accede to the need for more subjectively based expressions of what the future is likely to bring. The current emphasis on business planning is, of course, due to the lack of reliability of time based and causal factor predictions. Softer approaches call for the gathering of *informed opinion*; of *scenario planning* (the generation and consideration of a range of potential outcomes to create insight into potential impacts and likely situations); and of *sensitivity analysis*. (Sensitivity analysis asks 'what if?' questions, changing some of the forecasted assumptions to note the effects of wrong assumptions and, in the process, to question more intensely the validity of assumptions.)

(d) In important and ambiguous forecasting situations, it is advisable to interweave the full range of forecasting approaches wherever possible. A process which uses an extrapolatory approach as a base point but which also takes account of causal and softer forecasting methods is likely to generate (ultimately) more realistic forecasts. In such circumstances, too, theorists argue against the adoption of a 'one outcome' forecast but suggest, instead, the generation of *'pessimistic'*, *'most likely'* and *'optimistic'* predictions.

(e) Organisational flexibility deserves to be mentioned in the context of organisational attempts to handle uncertain futures. This approach requires the building into the organisation of characteristics of responsiveness and speedy flexibility. The emphasis, here, is more on reacting usefully to events as they happen rather than on anticipating them effectively well in advance. This approach is fundamental to team culture planning systems and shock event planning systems (see Chapters 11, 12 and 14).

## Forecasting annual growth using semi-averages and least squares regression

Fairly simple techniques which can be performed manually, without the assistance of computers, include those of semi-averages and least squares regression. Their purposes and procedures are as follows.

### The method of semi-averages
*Purpose*: to find a trend line which can be used for prediction.

*Procedure*:
(a) List in sequence a range of consecutive annual totals for the variable to be predicted (say, for example, sales value). The sequence should end with the most recently available annual figure.

(b) Divide the series of figures into two halves (the most recent and the most historic). Each half should contain an equal number of years. If the series contains an odd number of years, omit the middle year.

(c) Compute the mean value of each half.

(d) Plot the two mean values on a graph at the mid-points of their respective periods and join the points. This gives the trend line.

(e) Project the trend line to the right and read off future (forecasted) annual totals at the *mid*-point of the year chosen for prediction.

Basic data: 1984   50,000 (annual sales value)
                1985   55,000 (annual sales value)
                1986   72,000 (annual sales value)
                1987   80,000 (annual sales value)

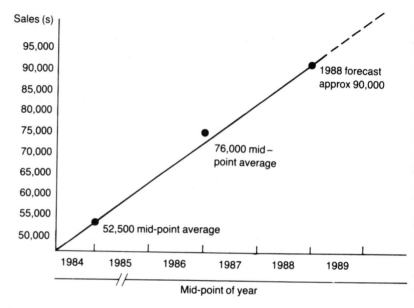

**Figure 8.4 Semi-averages: a simple example**

## The method of least squares regression

*Purpose*: to find a trend line mathematically (that line which produces the smallest figure in terms of the total of the squared deviations of the actual variable values from the line).

*Procedure*: use the formula: $y = a + bd$

$y$ = value of variable concerned (e.g. sales)

$a$ = arithmetic mean of the series of variables

$b$ is found through the formula: $b = \text{total of } \dfrac{\sum yd}{\sum d^2}$

$d$ is the deviation of the required point of time from the mid-point of the series

(a) Compute $a$ by adding together the values of the variables and dividing the total obtained by the number of variables, i.e. $y/n$.

(b) Compute $b$ in the following way:

- Set down the annual figures in a vertical column.
- Find the time mid-point of the series.
- Against each year, insert the deviation of the mid-point of that year from the

mid-point of the series (with an odd number of years in the series these deviations will be whole years, but with an even number they will involve half years).

- Multiply the variable value for each year by its deviation and add the totals obtained to give $\Sigma yd$.
- Square the deviations and add the totals obtained to give $\Sigma d^2$.
- Apply the formula $b = \dfrac{\Sigma yd}{\Sigma d^2}$

to determine the value of b.

- Take the year for which a forecast is required and find its deviation – d – from the mid-point of the original series.
- Insert this value into the formula: $y = a + bd$, to calculate y (the forecast result).

---

| Basic data: | 1984 | 50,000 | (annual sales value) |
|---|---|---|---|
| | 1985 | 55,000 | (annual sales value) |
| | 1986 | 72,000 | (annual sales value) |
| | 1987 | 80,000 | (annual sales value) |

| Year | y (sales) | d | yd | $d^2$ |
|---|---|---|---|---|
| 1984 | 50,000 | −1.5 | −75,000 | 2.25 |
| 1985 | 55,000 | −0.5 | −27,500 | 0.25 |
| Mid point | | | | |
| 1986 | 72,000 | +0.5 | +36,000 | 0.25 |
| 1987 | 80,000 | +1.5 | +120,000 | 2.25 |
| | $\Sigma y = 257,000$ | | $\Sigma yd = 53,000$ | $\Sigma d^2 = 5.0$ |

$$a = \frac{y}{n} = \frac{257,000}{4} = 64,250$$

$$b = \frac{\Sigma yd}{\Sigma d^2} = \frac{53,500}{5} = 10,700$$

Applying formula $y = a + bd$, then

$y = 64,250 + 10,700 \times d$

In 1988 (for example) deviation of d from the mid-point of the original series is 2.5

So sales forecast for 1988 is $64,250 + (10,700 \times 2.5)$

$= 64,250 + 26,750 = 91,000$

---

**Figure 8.5  Least squares regression: a simple example**

## Case study: the finance houses and growth of credit

'A continuation of strong consumer demand can be expected ... although the market for business credit in both the leasing and non leasing sectors will undergo a period of change due to the phased abolition of First Year Allowances', concluded the first section of the Finance Houses Association's Annual Report for 1986.

The basic optimism underlying the report certainly seemed to be supported by some of the statistics contained therein and illustrated in Fig. 8.6. A breakdown of new credit growth showed the following.

| Growth of new credit | | | | | 1980–1985 |
|---|---|---|---|---|---|
| | | | | | 11,695 |
| | | | | 9,835 | |
| | | | 8,101 | | |
| | | 7,207 | | | |
| | 6,078 | | | | |
| 5,244 | | | | | |
| 1980 | 1981 | 1982 | 1983 | 1984 | 1985 |

1985
Consumer lending                          = 43%
Leasing                                   = 30%
Business lending (excluding leasing)      = 27%

*New credit* 1980 – 5,224m
              1985 – 11,695m

**Figure 8.6  New credit (Finance Houses Association)**

Under the heading of consumer credit, hire purchase (HP) credit makes up 68 per cent of credit extended. The HP form of credit had been given a boost some years earlier with the relaxation of minimum deposit legislative requirements. Credit card lending was growing as finance houses introduced their own schemes or underwrote the schemes being introduced by high street retailers. This type of lending now took a 15 per cent share of consumer credit activity. Mortgage-based lending made a 9 per cent contribution to the total of consumer credit extended. Lending of this type in connection with home improvements had declined since 1984 (when changes in the VAT laws had made it expedient for home improvers to get their jobs done before such work became 'vatable'). However, lending for home improvements and the property market had showed a marked increase over the previous year. Consumer credit in connection with the purchase of new and used cars took 40 per cent of total consumer lending and remained the dominant source of credit transactions (by value). However, the most significant growth in consumer lending had been in the domestic goods area – up 31 per cent since 1984 to take a 24 per cent share of total consumer lending (although some of this increase had been created by Finance Houses Association membership changes).

Under the heading of business lending, a similar breakdown revealed the dominance of instalment type credit and, by product category, new and used car lending (accounting for around 50 per cent of business type lending). Property purchase-based lending was growing while finance for computer, office and farm equipment showed only modest increases. Ships- and aircraft-based lending had been clearly stimulated by tax changes and had risen 120 per cent over the 1984 value. Oil was down at £70 million. Overall, the report noted a variety of factors and trends underlying the finance industry. For example:

(a) A general steady growth in economic performance and affluence was reported, although the distribution of this wealth was not even. Geographical pockets of less affluence and falling house prices had been noted.

(b) The finance houses would need 'to meet the inevitable challenge of a more competitive market in which the number and range of participants is all the time increasing'. In particular the Building Societies Act would, in the course of the next year, open up the personal, unsecured lending market to these powerful institutions. Many large high street retailers were also entering the lending market on their own account.

(c) In other legislative areas, the Association had noted that the Consumer Credit Act, through its application to Association members but not to the building societies, would create an unfair competitive situation. The EC directive on doorstep selling (and the granting of 'cooling off'/cancellation periods to customers signing agreements at home) also held implications for major sources of finance house business.

(d) Generally, levels of debt were rising and commercial sense plus the expressed concern of bodies such as the Office of Fair Trading and Consumers' Association seemed to demand a more selective and caring approach to lending. Many sections of society were expressing a belief that too many consumers found borrowing too easy, that many disadvantaged customers were being 'screwed' by the members of the finance industry and that for many of these people information on the terms of debt contracts was still inadequate.

## Think and discuss

1   Refer to the case study above.
    (a) Extrapolate the growth of new credit for 1986.
    (b) Does your answer provide a pessimistic, optimistic or likely forecast?
    (c) What factors might you wish to research further in order to obtain a more certain forecast?
    (d) How might you go about obtaining this information?
    (e) What 'real growth' does your likely forecast represent?
2   Refer to your own organisation (or one of your choosing). Explain why you might introduce a system of management by objectives therein. How would you implement such a system?
    Why and how might you amend the present system of management by objectives employed by an organisation of your choosing?

## For further study

1   Refer to the 'Credit Grantors plc' case study in the accompanying case study book. Use theoretical prescriptions to evaluate whether the system of MBO being

used in Credit Grantors is likely to be totally effective. How might you change the present system?

2   Motivation as a process problem: which of the following situations is likely to lead to John embarking on a BA in Business Studies course?

Rank each situation according to its comparative strength of probability (1 is highest). Explain your choice.

(a) John was ambitious but not academically clever. His boss promised him promotion if John obtained a BABS degree.

(b) John was ambitious and bright. His boss offered to do the best he could 'promotion wise' if John obtained a BABS degree.

(c) John was bright and generally happy with his lot. His boss promised him promotion if John obtained a BABS degree.

(d) John was not academically clever but generally was happy with his lot. His boss promised to do the best he could 'promotion wise' if John obtained a BABS degree.

(e) John was ambitious and bright. His boss promised him promotion if John obtained a BABS degree.

(f) John was ambitious but not academically clever. His boss promised to do the best he could 'promotion wise' if John obtained a BABS degree.

(g) John was not academically clever but generally was happy with his lot. His boss promised him promotion if John obtained a BABS degree.

(h) John was bright and generally happy with his lot. His boss promised to do the best he could 'promotion wise' if John obtained a BABS degree.

3   Refer to the 'Palin' case study in the companion volume (10).

(a) Prepare the sales forecast required by the Managing Director, using the data provided.

(b) Explain why Palin's sales were well below your forecast.

(c) Tell the Managing Director what you intend to do to prevent future forecasting disasters.

(d) Refer to branches of organisation theory as appropriate to discuss motivational and structural problems which Palin should anticipate in its future quest for survival and/or growth.

4   Refer to the 'Silver Wheels Ltd' case study in the accompanying case study book. Assuming that Silver Wheels' directors would like net profits for 1984 to be at least £15,000, advise them of the potential profit gap which is likely to apply if no new strategic developments are undertaken.

5   Refer to the 'Dave Stocks and Strong Seals Bearings Ltd' case study in the accompanying volume.

(a) Identify strengths and weaknesses of Strong Seals Bearings Ltd.

(b) Prepare a list of key tasks for the organisation. Put the tasks in chronological order.

(c) Discuss the factors which are likely to influence Dave's human resource development function aims.

(d) Do Dave's views challenge the generic pertinence of much management strategy theory? Discuss.

# References

1  L L Byars, *Strategic Management, Planning and Implementation Concepts and Cases*, New York, Harper & Row, 1984, p 50
2  P F Drucker, *The Practice of Management*, Pan Piper, 1968, pp 80–81
3  J Argenti, *Practical Corporate Planning*, George Allen & Unwin, 1980, Ch 4
4  Drucker, op. cit., p 150
5  D D McConkey, *How to Manage by Results*, New York, American Management Association, 1975
6  J W Humble, *Management By Objectives in Action*, New York, McGraw-Hill, 1970, p 21
7  Drucker, op. cit., pp 167–8
8  T J Peters and R H Waterman Jr, *In Search of Excellence*, Harper & Row, 1982, Ch 3
9  R W Holman, 'Applying MBO Research to Practice', *Human Resource Management*, 15 (4), Winter, 1976, pp 28–36 provides a useful review of research in this area.
10  W Richardson, J Patterson, A Gregory and S Leeson, *Case Studies in Business Planning*, 2nd edn, Pitman, 1992

# Recommended reading

P F Drucker, *The Practice of Management*, Pan Piper, 1968
R W Holman, 'Applying MBO Research to Practice', *Human Resource Management*, 15 (4), Winter 1976, pp 28–36
P Mali, *MBO Updated*, Wiley Interscience, 1986

# 9 Administration planning: administrating the diverse organisation – practising vision management

The modern management strategist needs the qualities of a skilful administrator to turn strategic dreams into successful reality. Henri Fayol defined administration in terms of five primary elements: planning, organisation, command, co-ordination and control (1). Fayol's contribution earned him the title of 'father of the classical school of management'. However, the classical school has been criticised (2) for being too rigid in its approach, not sufficiently descriptive of what managers actually do and better suited to the more stable business conditions of the first half of the twentieth century.

This chapter reinforces and develops business environment themes raised in Chapter 2 and describes the pressures which lead today's organisations into increasingly diverse situations. It provides a ten point checklist which incorporates a discussion on the increasingly popular concept of vision management to help chief executives more effectively administrate their diverse businesses. Finally, it asks these executives to reflect on the nature of their jobs by reference to Fayol's own checklist of administrative principles. This additional view of the administrative planning task is offered via the following topics:

- The pressures creating diverse business situations
- Prescriptions for the successful administration of diverse organisations
- Administrating the diverse organisation: conclusion

## The pressures creating diverse business situations

A diverse situation is one where there are *many, different* things to do. Today's organisations face much more diversity than their predecessors. Looking into the medium-term future we can say that tomorrow will be more diverse than today. Diversity is increasing due to a number of related factors including:

(a) *The growth aspirations of organisation decision makers.* When questioned about his motives for pursuing acquisitions Lord King of British Airways responded 'It's simple. Like all businesses we want to grow.' (3) *Growth* is implicitly accepted as a fundamental modern business goal. The government's economic policies aim to assist the regeneration and growth of British business. Modern management theory exhorts that 'to stand still is to go backwards'. At a personal level successful business growth also equates with bigger personal reward packages. Thus, the environment in and around business insists on growth. Few people enter business these days with 'small shopkeeper' aims and philosophies. Business people, generally, search for growth. However, the benefits of growth incur the penalties of increased administrative difficulty due to the impacts of greater diversity. Growth is often based on *new* and *additional* product and market operations. Often, too, these developments are undertaken by acquisition or joint venture strategies which are organisationally more complex then the self-development alternative, requiring *new* and *additional* operating linkages and relationships.

Also, 'scattershot', undifferentiated marketing approaches are out of favour as means for creating productive growth. The trend of the past decades, has been towards 'rifle shot', market targeting involving the creation of *newly perceived* segments from the bigger, traditionally perceived segment and the design and implementation of *differentiated* marketing campaigns.

Growth, therefore, is based on *innovation* – the ability to design and implement new products, services and processes and to enter new markets. A generally significant management maxim for today is 'innovate or die' (4). Rather than acting as replacements for traditional activities, innovations are often 'tack ons'.

(b) *The growth aspirations of other environmental players.* The growth activities of individual institutions contribute to the macro situation. Modern markets, therefore, are arenas of diverse and quickly occurring change. Globally, governmental activity is *breaking down barriers between markets* and assisting the trend towards the achievement of a 'global village'. Innovations in communications, new product developments and the global strategies of big corporations contribute to the same outcomes. The nature of the ecosystem within which modern business operates is now such that, regardless of the organisation's own strategic activities, the environment can be expected to bring *more, new, and wider drawn* variables, *regularly* to the organisation.

(c) *Competition.* The firm that doesn't take part in the diversity generating race is in danger of losing out to more proactive and capable rival managers of diversity. Business, generally, is in a 'Catch 22' situation. Individually, firms dare not drop out of the competitively inspired race to achieve productivity through change and growth.

Collectively, this produces a situation of spiralling change and increasingly difficult to handle diversity. One response might be to instigate mutually beneficial, collective, attempts to slow down the spiral. A trend towards business collaborations has been identified (5), and has been discussed in Chapter 5, but this is based, still, on a perceived need to innovate more quickly and effectively and to gain greater competitive power. The trend towards strategic alliances described in Chapter 5 is a trend towards collaboration for the sake of improved competitive prowess. Recently, too, a clear call to perpetuate and intensify the diversity trends – through creating organisational capability for 'thriving' on change – has also been made (6).

## Prescriptions for the successful administration of diverse organisations

The tasks of administration, therefore, become more difficult as we approach the century's end. The theory of management strategy is, however, a vibrant source of help. It continues to provide models designed to help management strategists in their new situations. The next section of this chapter synthesises some contributions from the management literature which address the problem of how to administrate, successfully, in modern day, diverse business situations. It provides a ten point checklist of administrative 'dos'. Dogmatically prescriptive checklists are not appropriate in the management strategist context – individual situations demand customised responses. This list, therefore, is presented to facilitate comparisons with readers' own organisation systems and to stimulate thought about the appropriateness of any changes which might be made to them. This checklist of prescriptions is presented in Table 9.1.

**Table 9.1 Ten steps towards the succesful administration of a diverse situation**

| | |
|---|---|
| 1' | Choose the strategy |
| 2 | Decide the skeleton structure |
| 3 | Allocate the finance |
| 4 | Implement a business planning system |
| 5 | Practise vision management |
| 6 | Measure performance, control the detail |
| 7 | Be involved in key player recruitment |
| 8 | Develop general management skills and an 'enthused' culture |
| 9 | Employ a 'catch all' motivation system |
| 10 | Be a supermanager |

## Choose the strategy

Perhaps the single most important way in which control can be exercised by the corporate centre is for it to control decisions on where it will earn its living. Sub-unit managers might be best placed to make decisions on *how* to compete. *'Where'* decisions on new product/market developments, however, are ultimately the concern of central strategists. In this way the level of diversity which might otherwise be attracted can be reduced through decisions which 'stick to the knitting' (7). New market moves which take advantage of existing technologies or skills, for example, build on to existing strengths and so require less learning and fewer new operations. Moves which increase market share, too, can attract 'experience' benefits arising from 'learning efficiencies' (through doing more of the same thing) and economies of scale. Through controlling product/market developments central strategists can thus shape their multi-operations organisation into greater cohesion and productivity. The illustration below, demonstrates how some successful big business strategists have clear focii over where they will compete.

### Case examples: central choices over where to compete
- The Group will concentrate on its principal business areas .... Our objective is to maximise the use of existing assets rather than to diversify into unrelated areas.

  In confectionery we at present hold a 5 per cent share of the world chocolate market and are ranked as the fifth largest company in it. We intend to increase that share and to climb the league of international chocolate companies.

In soft drinks we are currently number three in the market outside the USA but fifth in the world overall. Our aim is to become the world's leading non-cola carbonated soft drinks company. (Cadbury Schweppes)

- Our objectives are to invest in good quality basic businesses providing essential goods and services for the consumer and industry and to obtain an improving return for shareholders by maximising earnings per share and dividend growth. ...Those in the operating companies have clear responsibility for running their businesses. (Lord Hanson, Hanson Trust Ltd)
- Lord Rayner forecast the spread of M & S across the globe like a religious visionary talking of the spread of peace .... We do better than most. We rely on value and quality .... We must never forget that we are a retailer .... I must take the lead in caring for people – customers, suppliers and especially the personnel. (Extracts from an interview with Lord Rayner)

Clarification and communication of a focused corporate strategy also helps co-ordinate the disparate parts of the firm by developing a shared identity and commitment to the overall strategic vision. Pure conglomerate corporations which simply tack on new business units without any concern for the achievement of synergy (the new whole contributes something over and beyond the value of the parts (8)) are out of fashion. These business forms are recipes for poor performance, takeover raids (because the parts are worth more than the whole), and eventual divestments.

## Decide the skeleton structure

Rather than simply allowing the organisation structure to evolve as the firm diversifies, central strategists should, according to theory, take an active role in its design and implementation. A market-based sub-unit structure is prescribed to ensure rapid, market sensitive and responsive decisions from market-close, dedicated to success, sub-unit managers. If divisional headquarters which link the corporate centre with product/market sub-units are necessary they should be kept as small as possible – in terms of staff employed and decision-making influence (9). General functions such as finance, accounting, personnel, public relations and *corporate strategy*, should be maintained as centrally based support and *influence* mechanisms.

The successful multi-unit business is most likely to operate a *centralised/ centralised* system. The corporate strategists dictate, to some large extent, the parameters within which business units must operate and they indoctrinate the middle level managers to internalise the broader goals of the corporation. Thereafter, the middle managers run their own operations in their own centralised manner (10).

## Allocate the finance

The diverse organisation will be more likely to act in ways required by the centre if the centre controls the corporation 'purse-strings'. Major investments should depend upon centrally decided allocations of budget. In this way, the top strategists can use their overview of the organisation to create a *balanced* portfolio of activities. 'Cash cow' activities (net cash generators) can be used as the source of funds for the development of 'stars' (activities which have the potential to become 'cash cows' given further investment) and 'question marks' (activities which have still to demonstrate clearly wealth-producing potential but which are, nevertheless, considered to be worth additional funding). 'Dogs' (activities which are deemed to have little or no wealth-creating potential) can be divested. Figure 9.1 (introduced previously in Chapter 5) is adapted from the Boston Consulting Group's growth/share matrix to illustrate the directions along which portfolio balancing investments should flow. In emphasising the importance of future returns on investment rather than current sizes of unit activities this cash control mechanism conveys clear messages *throughout* the enterprise about the prime importance of *productivity* as both a corporate and a unit goal. It thus motivates personnel to seek out and achieve productive developments. This mechanism, too, provides a further means for the centre to control where the organisation will locate its product/market activities.

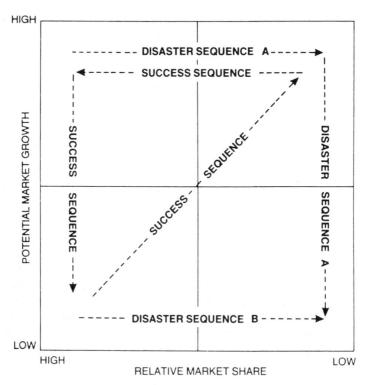

**Figure 9.1 Prescribed investment sequences for a balanced portfolio of organisation activities**

## Implement a business planning system

Despite the exhortations of corporate planning advocates, many small- and medium-sized businesses manage to grow without ever using formal business planning procedures. In bigger, more diverse organisation settings, however, the requirement that product/market units should submit business plans and be judged on performance against plan makes much sense. Goold and Campbell (11) recommend a formal planning system which is in harmony with the core business philosophy adopted by the corporate centre. The natures of these philosophies and their associated planning systems are described in Fig. 9.2.

| * Core business philosophy | * Diverse businesses philosophy | * Manageable businesses philosophy |
|---|---|---|
| * Strategic planning | * Strategic control | * Financial control |
| * Centre participates in, and influences business unit strategies. Requires demanding planning processes. Flexible targets set and reviewed in context of long-term progress. | * Requires demanding planning processes, but focuses on reviews and critiques of proposals rather than influencing, initially. Tight control of strategic and financial objectives. | * Primarily control organisations. Centre sanctions expenditure and monitors financial performance against annual targets. |

**Figure 9.2 Fits between business planning systems and business philosophies**

Cadbury Schweppes, BP and BOC, are *core business/strategic planning* type organisations. These corporations concentrate on core product/market-*related* developments and seek growth through organic self-development. Courtaulds, Plessey, ICI and Vickers utilise a *strategic control* planning system which fits their *diverse business* philosophy. This type of organisation divides its activities into homogeneous product/market groups and proceeds on this more diverse front via organic and acquisitory developments. *Financial control* system adopters include BTR, Hanson, GEC and Tarmac. These corporations look for '*acquisition with divestment*' opportunities. They emphasise managerial reorganisations, two- to four-year payback periods, and short-term, ratio-based, performance measures.

## Practice vision management

The first four checklist steps have emphasised the harder, control aspect of the administrator's job. Diversity, according to theory, also calls for 'softer' approaches. 'Vision management' is a concept gaining popularity in the 1990s. It is based upon the articulation and communication of what and where the organisation is to be in terms of its present and future market place positions.

The case example, 'Central choices over where to compete', shown previously, describes the positions of big corporation leaders who have clearly articulated such 'visions'. Effective visionaries are able to anticipate lucrative markets of the future and the needs of future stakeholders (particularly customers). Consequently they are able to discern how their organisations might become *special* and *profitable* providers of needs satisfactions. Articulations of vision are usually concise and easily internalised by rank and file personnel. They develop and support a strong belief that the corporation is the best performer, in the market place, on some important criterion. In the literature on vision management concepts of productivity, growth, leading market positions, quality of customer interaction, innovation, employee care, and team work, re-occur. Such aspects of the organisation's *chosen* self-identity, set out in published mission statements, stand as charters to guide all organisational activity. More 'stand alone' branches of the organisation should be encouraged to create their own expressions of mission which are related to the corporate trunk culture.

Visionary managers make *meanings* for people as well as money. When the vision is communicated effectively, and supported by organisational activities (its reward and training programmes, the actions of its top managers, and its customer care activities, for example) then it becomes part of the social fabric of the entire organisation. It is known, understood and *lived* by its employees *and* by its customers. Vision management, therefore, controls through employee internalisation of core corporate values. While there is always likely to be some conflict between the aspirations of the individual and the objectives of the organisation nevertheless, to quote Kast and Rosenzweig, 'To the extent that individuals do internalise organisation values ... it is a key factor in providing integration' (12). Ultimately, the aim of the visionary strategist is to emulate St Augustine who expressed only one rule of control: 'Love God and do what you like.' People who are committed to the goals of the organisation will act freely and creatively *for the organisation's benefit*.

## Case examples: expressions of vision and mission in big business

- 'The Best Get Better' – Delta Airlines
- Some visions are idealistic – Steve Jobs of Apple wanted to democratise technology and take computers into the American home.
- Some visions are achievement oriented – Peter Magown wants Safeway to be the best-run food retailer in the United States. Jack Welch of GE wants to make his company worth more than any other company (13).
- Ray Kroc has only one message for the people at McDonalds – 'Quality, service, cleanliness and value' and he never tires of repeating it.
- Ford says simply, 'Quality is Job 1.'
- Lord Rayner forecast the spread of M & S across the globe like a religious visionary. 'We do better than most. We rely on value and quality.'
- 'The focusing has to be done ... by a shared vision ... the differentiation between successful and unsuccessful companies is a clear sense of mission.' (Sir John Harvey-Jones)

## Measure performance, control the detail

'What gets measured gets done' is a modern management maxim. Concepts such as vision, mission and zeal need to be operationalised through attention to detail. Otherwise people do not really understand what 'quality', or 'customer satisfaction' or 'productivity' mean and they don't know what the corporation expects of them. Tom Peters says of the USA's 'excellent' corporations, 'But there is a value set ... it is executed by attention to mundane, nitty-gritty details. Every minute, every hour, every day is an opportunity to act in support of overarching themes.' (14) Performance standards help ensure that people are striving in the right directions. McDonalds' emphasis on quality, value and service is operationalised throughout its network through the use of very detailed operating manuals which must be followed to the letter.

Key divisional performance ratios including return on capital employed, return on sales, liquidity and debtor and creditor payment ratios feature in many successful diverse situation control systems. BTR, for example, reputedly works to the maxim 'if it doesn't produce 10 per cent return on sales either sell it or shut it'. Creativity in setting management by objective type quantified targets is called for in the 'softer' harder to define, standards areas. Nevertheless, targets and measures in these areas are vital if the entire organisation is to work productively in the centrally defined way. Of course, target-based control systems also demand the presence of sophisticated information systems.

## Be involved in key player recruitment

The managers in the middle rungs of the diverse organisation occupy especially important positions. They are, at one and the same time, the culture carriers for the corporate strategists and the leaders of their own sections and divisions. These 'linchpins', therefore, must have excellent communication and general management skills to supplement any functional expertise they bring to their jobs. Further, they need to 'buy in' to the overall culture. Once in place these talented culture carriers will create their own momentum for co-ordinative and productive effort (15). Central strategists, therefore, should be involved in the selection of these people not only to make sure that the right calibre people are chosen but also to use the selection occasion as a cogent vehicle for communicating the corporate vision and the associated characteristics and activities *demanded* of middle managers.

## Develop general management skills and the desired 'enthused' culture

Training and development programmes are exceptionally cogent vehicles for conveying cultural expectations to, and instilling them in key subordinates (16). Corporate strategists, therefore, should insist that key subordinates receive *general* management training. These development programmes should be set in the context of the enterprise's objectives and its overall business situation. Training events, too, are important instruments for corporate team building. Spending time together is an essential pre-requisite to building bridges and developing common identities (17). Top corporate managers should make personal contributions to these development programmes. People need to be told – and reminded – why they are being developed. The rationale for training should be one of personal *and* organisational development. An important outcome of these sessions, as part of a total indoctrination programme involving *all* aspects of the organisation system, is individual and collective enthusiasm for the corporate vision.

## Employ a 'catch all' motivation system

Many firms still employ an old fashioned approach to rewarding employees. Over time, industry average basic wages and industry average bonus systems form the basis of personnel rewards. Length of service dictates positions occupied on the pay scale and idiosyncratic perks negotiated with individual employees become institutionalised in particular job reward packages. The result of this old fashioned approach is an industry average package of rewards and disintegrative feelings over the inequity of the system. People rewarded in this way tend to see pay as the price which the top people begrudgingly pay as a prerequisite to getting people to 'turn up' for work. This promotes 'just enough effort' attitudes. Irrational differences between reward packages promote divisiveness rather than collective commitment. Also such packages do not relate rewards (and so channel efforts) towards important performance areas.

In contrast, modern administrators are designing reward packages which i) give a growing role to rewards for performance and declining roles to basic pay and length of service awards; and ii) pay bonuses for individual achievements *and* group *and* organisation performances. Such schemes utilise tangible and intangible rewards. People at Pedigree Petfoods, for example, are all 'associates' and all receive weekly pay packets in an effort to remove divisive status differentials. At IBM successful performance can lead to the valued perk of choosing a 'pet project' for the next work activity. IBM also pays cash awards for 'Outstanding Innovation'. Harvey's of Bristol pays bonuses for money saving suggestions. Profit-sharing, too, is growing. GM's chairman Roger Smith is confident that, 'Profit sharing puts entrepreneurship back in the free enterprise system.' (18) Traditional 'rewards related to hierarchies' systems are changing, too. Many top performing managers are beginning to earn more than their chief executives. Involvement as a reward in itself is becoming commonplace. Rank and file staff are being asked to contribute to business problem solving, quality circle/suggestion scheme type activities. As job satisfaction improves so too does rank and file commitment to the organisation's goals.

A varied, customised and changing reward package which continues to clearly emphasise fairness, teamwork and individual effort and which guides activity towards the achievement of key targets will continue to motivate desired performances. In highly competitive market places superior performance is required. In diverse situations the central strategists simply cannot be everywhere at the same time, ensuring that superior performance is the norm. Superior performance has to be delegated. Reward systems should make sure that superior performance is worthwhile. Self-motivation is the best controller of all, commitment to the team is the most effective co-ordinator.

## Be a supermanager

Administrating the diverse organisation demands the abilities of a supermanager. Despite the truism that productivity takes place through people – all the organisation's people – theory saves a special place for the top manager as an instrument of success. The top strategists are the people who must plan the administrative campaign prescribed by this chapter. Also, they are the ones who will have the biggest personal impact on its success. Modern strategists at the top of diverse corporations have to play demanding *contrasting roles, often simultaneously.* Some (only) of these include:

(a) *Employing broad helicopter vision and attending to detail*. The supermanager must be able to rise above the organisation situation to develop a picture of its internal and external situation in order to anticipate and, thereafter, to design and administrate appropriate organisation/environment 'fits'. At the same time he/she must lead, *by example*, an organisation which attends *in detail* to the important issues of quality control, personnel motivation, innovation and productivity.

(b) *Being the 'biggest softie' and the 'toughest cookie'*. Today's successful leaders are capable of moving rapidly between two interpersonal styles. The supportive, open door style manager encourages openness and team spirit. The ruthless autocrat swings into action whenever organisational core values are being breached (see the illustration below for some big business examples). Modern administrators should be the *cheerleaders* (the loudest applauders of effective performances) and the *choppers* (who punish to the point of dismissal and legal action those personnel who buck the system and its values).

## Case examples: some 'soft/hard' management style examples

- 'Normally I think it is discourteous not to say that I shall be coming.' (Lord Rayner on his approach to store visiting) 'He is not a man you lightly cross', a colleague once said (of Lord Rayner).
- 'They lived by their values, these men, Marriott, Ray Kroc, Bill Hewlett and Dave Packard, Levi Strauss, James Cash Penney, Robert Wood Johnson. And they meticulously applied them within their organisations. They *believed* in the customer. They *believed* in granting autonomy, room to perform. They *believed* in open doors, in quality. But they were strict disciplinarians, every one.' In T J Peters and R H Waterman Jr, *In Search of Excellence*, Harper & Row, 1982, p 319.
- IBM's job security policy and its exceptional approach to personnel is a major source of competitive advantage. Violate the lofty phrase, 'IBM Means Service', and you are out of a job.

(c) *Being externally active and internally omnipresent*. Strategists are spending an increasing amount of time in important relationships with parties outside the firm. At the same time they are being extolled to MBWA (Manage By Wandering Around) and to enthuse their entire organisation *personally*. These conflicting roles demand a timetabled approach to managing, the motivation to work long hours, and physical strength.

(d) *Being involved without interfering*. This is a balancing act which treads a fine line between allowing too much discretion to subordinates (who might thus act 'out of line') and exercising too much (time consuming and demotivational) influence.

(e) *Being controlling and innovative*. An emphasis on control and co-ordination can support and reinforce, *inappropriately*, presently successful recipes. Successful visions and their associated operating recipes can become dated and ineffective. Steve Job's phenomenally successful vision eventually underpinned Apple's temporary decline. A new, harder edged, more marketing-orientated vision (inspired by a *new* leader) has replaced the more youthful exuberance, creativity at any cost, social mission elements of the early Apple vision.

The diversity administrating executive must concentrate on control but must, at the same time, build into the organisation a capacity for constantly reviewing and challenging existing ways of doing things. In particular, he/she needs to ensure an environment where middle level innovation champions are encouraged to work on new products and processes and to challenge existing recipes *without* creating corporate disharmony. He/she also needs to ensure that control mechanisms are not stifling motivation and commitment. The aim, according to Chris Hogg, Chairman of Courtaulds, is 'control to get things done, not to stop getting things done'.

(f) *Being the 'vision in practice' model.* One unambiguous role which the corporate strategist must play is that of the most passionate and committed member of the team. If the leader extols frugality and yet sports an extravagantly expensive limousine and a super, plush office; if he/she espouses customer responsiveness but is personally discourteous in dealing with clients; if he/she exhorts subordinates to work harder and longer but spends much of the working week on the golf course or takes numerous holidays, the people of the organisation will take note and amend their own philosophies and actions accordingly. Conversely, the leader who constantly, consistently and passionately behaves according to the articulated ideal, takes the rest of the organisation with him/her. Peter Wolff, chairman of S R Gent *half jokes*, 'If someone turns up to an interview in lace-up shoes we don't take him, because it shows he is prepared to waste time doing them up.'

Wolff regularly turns up at his factories at 7.30 am and so conveys a clear message about the hours his managers should be prepared to work. Middle management members do not expect an easy ride at Gents but they do respect the fact that the hardest workers in the organisation are the chief executives.

## Administrating the diverse organisation: conclusion

Decisions on how to administrate are ultimately personal ones which are customised to particular situations. Fayol (20) himself advocates flexibility in the use of his principles: 'Principles are flexible and capable of adaptation to every need: it is a matter of knowing how to make use of them, which is a difficult art requiring intelligence, experience, decision and proportion.' As organisational situations become more diverse they become more difficult to administrate. This chapter has sought to build on Chapters 7 and 8 to provide a reminder of the diverse situations facing many management strategists and to indicate some of the theoretically espoused steps which might be taken in an attempt to ensure more effective sequencing, scheduling, motivating and controlling. The remaining chapters of this book will seek to develop further, readers' knowledge and skills for the task of harnessing the entire organisation to the quest for improved synergy. Meanwhile, strategists can use the ten steps identified in this chapter as 'thinking platforms' to consider whether and how their existing approaches to administrating diversity might be improved.

### For further study

At the beginning of this chapter the question was inferred 'Do Fayol's elements and associated principles of administration provide a relevant framework for the job of the modern management strategist?' His elements, as a reminder, are those of planning, organisation, command, co-ordination and control. His principles are described in Table 9.2. Readers might now answer and discuss this question.

**Table 9.2 Henri Fayol's principles of administration**

1    Division of work. The principle of specialisation of labour in order to concentrate activities for more efficiency.

2    Authority and responsibility. Authority is the right to give orders and the power to exact obedience.

3    Discipline. Discipline is absolutely essential for the smooth running of business, and without discipline no enterprise could prosper.

4    Unit of command. An employee should receive orders from one superior only.

5    Unity of direction. One head and one plan for a group of activities having the same objectives.

6    Subordination of individual interests to general interests. The interest of one employee or a group should not prevail over that of the organisation.

7    Remuneration of personnel. Compensation should be fair and, as far as possible, afford satisfaction to both personnel and the firm.

8    Centralisation. Centralisation is essential to the organisation and is a natural consequence of organising.

9    Scaler chain. The scaler chain is the chain of superiors ranging from the ultimate authority to the lowest rank.

10    Order. The organisation should provide an orderly place for every individual. A place for everyone and everyone in their place.

11    Equity. Equity and a sense of justice pervade the organisation.

12    Stability of tenure of personnel. Time is needed for the employees to adapt to their work and to perform it effectively.

13    Initiative. At all levels of the organisational ladder, zeal and energy are augmented by initiative.

14    Esprit de corps. This principle emphasises the need for teamwork and the maintenance of interpersonal relationships.

# References

1    H Fayol, *General and Industrial Management*, trans. by C Storrs, Pitman, 1949
2    H Mintzberg, for example, says 'Thus we can find little of use in the writings of the classical school ... (which has) for too long served to block our search for a deeper understanding of the work of the manager', *The Nature of Managerial Work* , Harper & Row, 1973, p 11
3    Lord King being interviewed in *Airline: King's Way*, video, BBC 2, 1988
4    A Johne and P Snelson, 'Innovate or Die', *Management Today*,  November 1987
5    See, for example, R M Kanter, *When Giants Learn to Dance*, Unwin, 1990
6    T J Peters, *Thriving on Chaos* , Macmillan, 1988
7    This is a prescription from T J Peters and R H Waterman Jr, *In Search of Excellence*, New York, Harper & Row, 1982, based on their research into successful, growing, USA corporations of the previous 25 years.
8    R M Kanter, *When Giants Learn to Dance,* Unwin, 1990, p 91
9    C Hill, 'The Pitfalls in Diversity', *Management Today*, December 1984

10  J B Quinn, H Mintzberg and R M James, *The Strategy Process*, Prentice-Hall International, 1988, pp 578–9

11  M Goold and A Campbell, 'Managing Diversity, Strategy and Control in Diversified British Companies', *Long Range Planning*, 20 (5), 1987, pp 42–52

12  F E Kast and J E Rosenzweig, *Organisations and Management, A Systems and Contingency Approach*, 2nd edn, McGraw-Hill, 1986, p 192

13  E Morris, 'Vision and Strategy: A Focus for the Future', *The Journal of Business Strategy*, 8 (2), Fall, 1987, pp 51–8

14  T J Peters and R H Waterman Jr, op. cit., p 324

15  M Daniell, 'Webs they Weave', *Management Today*, February 1990, pp 81–6 provides a discussion around the need for 'networked' organisation structures and the qualities demanded of their middle managers.

16  E H Schein, *Organisation Culture and Leadership*, San Francisco, Jossey-Bass, 1987, Ch 10

17  R M Kanter, op. cit., p 113

18  Ibid, p 241

19  A van de Vliet, 'A Saint in Gents Clothing', *Management Today*, May 1990, pp 93–7

20  H Fayol, op. cit., p 19

# 10 Productivity planning

The organisation is a wealth breeder. Strategy is about achieving 'more for less' over time. If the organisation is to survive and grow its complete business planning system must achieve this productive end result. Today's environments demand that the search for productivity is given formal, specific attention.

In this chapter we discuss how a productivity planning subsystem might be utilised to achieve improving productivity returns. Our discussion explores the differences between efficiency, effectiveness and productivity and goes on to consider how productivity ratios and attention to 'both sides' of the productivity equation (costs and contributions) can enhance productivity performance. The roles of quantitative techniques, people and information in productivity campaigns are also discussed. The chapter, therefore, covers:

- Effectiveness, efficiency and productivity
- Rationales for productivity planning
- Reasons for and signs of productivity decline
- Generic strategies for improving the productivity ratio
- Planning productivity improvements
- Cutting costs
- Creating contribution
- Productivity and quantitative techniques
- Productivity and information
- Productivity and people

## Effectiveness, efficiency and productivity

'The era of the casual manager who uses trial and error methods until the work is completed began disappearing about a decade ago. Casual performance results in a waste of resources, heavy expenditure of time, and low levels of performance. To compete in the 1980s and on into the future, efficiency processes that accomplish productivity gains are needed .... We've moved into an era in which productivity must clearly and deliberately define the results wanted, allocate carefully the resources needed, set up effective and efficient work processes, and provide the day-to-day surveillance and control needed for accomplishment of the intended results. We've moved into an era in which productivity must be managed.'(1)

In the 1988 FA Cup Final the consistently productive Liverpool FC faced football league newcomers, Wimbledon FC. In the context of that one competition both clubs had, at the start of the match, achieved the pinnacle of *effectiveness*. (This comparison is a one year, one competition comparison of productivities. It ignores Liverpool's magnificient productivity record.) Effectiveness is a measure of performance outcomes. However, in terms of *efficiency* – the measurement of inputs or costs expended – then Wimbledon, the 'minnow' in terms of its organisational resources including the value of its players, was a clear winner. In terms of *productivity*, too, Wimbledon could claim to have been the more productive FA Cup competitor. Productivity is a measurement of the *ratio* between outputs and inputs, between benefits and costs, between effectiveness and efficiency.

$$\text{Productivity} = \frac{\text{output obtained;}}{\text{input expended}} \quad \frac{\text{benefits;}}{\text{costs}} \quad \frac{\text{effectiveness;}}{\text{efficiency}}$$

Productivity, therefore, is not just about producing and selling more. The most productive organisations are not always the market share leaders. Neither is productivity solely about reducing costs. The most productive workforces are not always the lowest paid. Productivity, rather, is the achievement of a positive effectiveness/efficiency ratio. A productivity improvement is an improvement in this ratio. *Productivity planning* is a systematic attempt to improve both sides of the organisation's productivity ratio(s). It is a planned approach to 'getting more for less'. These days the productivity planning component of the 'complete' planning framework is gaining massive importance.

## Rationales for productivity planning

Productivity and the organisation's systems goals are intertwined. Productivity is a measurement of the organisation's wealth breeding performance. Wealth is generated by efficiency of operation and by control of the environment. Productivity planning seeks to improve the wealth breeding capability of the organisation by planning those changes which improve its efficiency and control of the environment performances. The major rationale for productivity planning, therefore, is its ability to improve systems goal performance. More specific productivity benefits, however, include the following:

(a)  competitive advantage;

(b)  better jobs;

(c)  contributions to society;

(d)  innovation and continuing development;

(e)  enhanced shareholder satisfaction;

(f)  the way forward, particularly in low domain choice situations.

## Competitive advantage

Competitive advantage enables the achievement of a higher return on investment than that achieved by competitors. In accord with the 'value chain' (2) and associated prescriptions (see Chapter 5), comprehensive productivity planning seeks to improve the contributions of all organising activities. Least-cost producing positions, price competitiveness and value-adding differentiation capabilities are all developed, maintained and improved continuously in the productivity conscious enterprise.

## Better jobs

When increased costs can no longer be passed on to the consumer the inefficient organisation struggles to survive. The productive organisation, on the other hand, continues to be competitive and so ensures *job security*. Productivity reduces costs and improves sales levels. The resulting increases to the organisation's wealth can then be made available to improve the rewards packages of all personnel. *Improved working conditions* can be generated by the installation of safer, more modern machinery and by improvements to welfare facilities. *Job satisfaction* is enhanced as workers begin to take credit for improvements in productivity and as they develop a liking for involvement in the productivity planning activity and a pride in contributing to a successful organisation.

## Contributions to society

Higher profits mean higher taxes and a greater ability to make other societal contributions (via socially responsible acts such as donations to charitable causes, for example). In an era when resources are seen to be dwindling, their efficient use is a socially responsible act, in itself. Bigger outcomes are usually, in competitive situations, the product of more environmentally attractive goods and services.

## Innovation and continuing development

Productivity pays for the costly experimentation that accompanies research and development. It thus pays for those new products, services and processes which underpin the continuing viability of the organisation. It also provides the 'slack' which bolsters the enterprise in cases of emergency and shock events.

## Enhanced shareholder satisfaction

In the commercial setting productivity improvements provide the wealth which enables the important owners/shareholders to take their satisfactions and so induces them to maintain their contributions.

## The way forward particularly in low domain choice situations

As market development through growth opportunities begins to wane and as new injections of growth capital seem, for many institutions, more difficult to obtain then productivity improvements take on greater importance. Improving productivity is the most feasible of all development directions. Some organisations, such as local authorities, have very little domain choice flexibility and are being offered reducing supplies of central support. For such institutions productivity planning is the lifeline to survival.

# Reasons for and signs of productivity decline

Of the top 100 British organisations in 1966 (ranked by market capitalisation) 41 had disappeared from the list by 1987. During the same period 'midgets' such as BTR and

Hanson Trust became top ten entrants as they acquired falling giants such as Tilling, Dunlop, and London Brick and Imperial and Every Ready (3). An important paradox discernible within business history is that which reveals success to be a breeder of failure. Productivity has to be constantly worked at if the process of organisational decline is to be avoided. Lorange and Nelson (4) provide some of the reasons why decline sets in.

(a) *Complacency born from competitive success.* Success recipes most suitable for expansionist growth eras become ingrained as *generally* applicable formulas for success. When environmental conditions change no corresponding change in organisational activity occurs and decline sets in.

(b) *Top management blindness* to new and different business natures. Managers often filter out evidence which suggests the need for new approaches. They sometimes overemphasise the importance of any signals which tend to still confirm their largely outdated views. Self-deception is a major cause of decline.

(c) *A hierarchy orientation* which directs organisation decisions towards the perceived desires of the enterprise hierarchy rather than towards those market-orientated type goals which preoccupied the enterprise founders.

(d) *Cultural rigidity.* The entrenchment of bureaucracy to the detriment of innovation.

(e) *Entrenchment of the existing status quo.* A strong desire for acceptance or conformity which works against change.

(f) *The search for consensus and compromise solutions.* Large, diverse, organisations develop 'meetings cultures' wherein responsibility for specific projects is often shared and diluted. These cultures work against urgency and resolve.

(g) *The push for organisational growth rather than productivity growth.* Costs soar as the organisation recruits new staff in response to management's desire for size (rather than wealth) growth.

(h) *Benefits awarded without equivalent increases in productivity.* Real growth gives rise to demands for improved benefits. Over time regular reward improvements become the norm, regardless of whether the enterprise is improving its stock of wealth (5).

(i) *Rising 'white collar' costs.* White collar workers make up the bulk of a growing employment force in the service industries, knowledge jobs and government services. White collar workers have no tradition of having their work examined for productivity. The tendency is for existing workloads to be expanded to fill working time.

(j) *Low motivation among employees.* As workers become more affluent traditional motivators no longer seem adequate. Further, specialised jobs so designed to achieve greater efficiency often breed boredom, dissatisfaction and a productivity 'kickback' in the form of high labour absenteeism, increased labour turnover and poor quality workmanship.

If industrial history identifies clearly a tendency for decline to follow success, why then does the sequence continue to occur with regularity? Organisations, unlike the humans that comprise them do not have to decline. Some do seem to have developed the capability of maintaining – even improving – success over long periods. In those many cases where decline does set in, however, its cause is often one of apathy. Failure to recognise the existence of a productivity issue creates a situation, in many cases, where decision-makers remain blissfully unaware of worsening performance. What is needed for the 'today' organisation is an awareness that without formal productivity planning eventual decline is almost certain. A first step and, thereafter, an ongoing feature of productivity planning should thus involve the systematic monitoring of business situations for early signals of worsening performance. Regular monitoring can ensure that decline is checked before the need for remedial action becomes critical and before the remedies, themselves, become painful. The theory of management strategy (see, for example, 6 and 7) recommends the following checklist of early warning indicators of productivity decline.

(a) *Excess personnel.* Have workforces and workforce costs been rising at a rate greater than output? Are managers creating small kingdoms? Over-sized staff bases are not only over costly in salary terms they are also less effective communication media.

(b) *Tolerance of incompetence.* Have, for example, many key executives reached their 'levels of incompetence' and yet, because of loyalty for past services or reluctance to weed them out, such personnel remain entrenched and ineffective? Meanwhile more capable subordinates become disgruntled with this inequitable and inefficient blockage to promotion and leave.

(c) *Cumbersome administration procedures.* Is the enterprise bogged down with excessive paperwork, slow approval systems and endless alternative evaluations in decision-making?

(d) *Disproportionate staff power.* Have staff groups, originally introduced to supplement the line with specialist knowledge, increased their sizes (in relation to line) and their influence, perhaps to the extent that they have started to manage the company?

(e) *Replacement of substance with form.* Is the organisation characterised by formal, rehearsed meetings? Are plans and procedures created and followed for their own sakes rather than as facilitators of effective actions?

(f) *Scarcity of goals and decision benchmarks.* Has the business lost its day-to-day focus on basic business issues? Has the organisation common visions on what are the fundamental causes of organisational success? Do staff at all levels have clearly defined objectives to guide their decisions and activities?

(g) *Fear of embarrassment and conflict.* Do personnel feel they have more to lose from making mistakes and 'rocking the boat' than they have to gain from pursuing issue-orientated, positive (but potentially controversial) accomplishments?

(h) *Loss of effective communication.* Do meeting agendas concentrate on items of good news and gloss over less optimistic items? Is morale such that people are not really listening to each other? Does important information tend to arrive too late? Is relevant information not available from present systems?

(i) *Outdated jobs.* Do many of the organisation's jobs continue to concentrate on old, now less important, problem areas? Are newly important problems deserving of greater attention? Do tight job descriptions prevail where broader duties and flexible responsibilities would be more pertinent?

(j) *Poor morale.* Do people work 'for a wage' only or 'for a wage *and* the company'? Would greater commitment produce greater productivity? Is conflict and non-cooperation damaging the organisation's performance?

The above checklist provides the basis for an early warning system to spot productivity decline. Those strategists who have not thought extensively about productivity would do well to take time to consider whether any of the questions above are relevant to their organisations.

## Generic strategies for improving the productivity ratio

If we agree that effectiveness is 'doing the right things' and efficiency is 'doing things right' (8) then we might agree that productivity is about 'doing the right things right'. An important test when considering productivity issues, according to Johnson and Scholes (9) is one which assesses whether resources could be expended in more productive areas. In other words, productivity planning is not simply about improving present areas of activity but also about assessing whether existing operations should be replaced by new, more productive activities. Economists refer to the opportunity costs of undertaking particular activities rather than others. The marginally profitable public house, for example, might be more productively employed (with some alterations, of course) as a residential home for elderly people. Thus there is a need to ask 'Are we doing the right things?'

Once the strategist is satisfied that the right activity is being performed he or she can turn to the work of Paul Mali (10) who has provided a useful categorisation of *five generic strategies* for achieving more successfully the productivity objective of doing the right things right. Mali points out that productivity improvements are to be achieved through one or more of the following activities.

(a) *Managing effectively*, i.e. increase performance while holding resource use (costs) the same, for example:

$$\frac{\text{Sales (up)}}{\text{Employees (static)}} \qquad \frac{\pounds700,000}{10} = \pounds70,000 \text{ per employee}$$

(b) *Managing efficiently*, i.e. hold performance the same while reducing resources (costs), for example:

$$\frac{\text{Sales (static)}}{\text{Employees (down)}} \qquad \frac{\pounds600,000}{8} = \pounds75,000 \text{ per employee}$$

(c) *Managing effectively and efficiently,* i.e. increase performance while at the same time reducing resource input (costs), for example:

$$\frac{\text{Sales (up)}}{\text{Employees (down)}} \qquad \frac{\pounds630,000}{9} = \pounds70,000 \text{ per employee}$$

(d) *Managing real growth*, i.e. increase both performance and resource use (costs) but increase performance more than costs, for example:

$$\frac{\text{Sales (up)}}{\text{Employees (up)}} \qquad \frac{£900,000}{12} = £75,000 \text{ per employee}$$

(e) *Managing economic slow up*, i.e. decrease both performance and resource use (costs) but decrease performance less than costs, for example:

$$\frac{\text{Sales (down)}}{\text{Employees (down)}} \qquad \frac{£525,000}{7} = £75,000 \text{ per employee}$$

Management strategists, looking for ways in which to improve organisational productivity, will find the basic means for such improvement within the above list.

# Planning productivity improvements

## The productivity improvement process

Many productivity theorists/practitioners share similar views over the nature of the productivity improvement process (see, for example, 11, 12 and 13). Whether the process is one which is orientated towards organisation-wide issues and conducted by top management or one which seeks to improve individual job contributions the same main steps are advocated. These are as follows:

(a) Identify all the potentially significant cost and contribution areas.

(b) Measure existing performances in these areas with appropriate productivity ratios (see Fig. 10.1 for some ratio examples).

(c) Determine through comparisons (see below) the desired productivity ratio for each improvement area (these ratios will be the productivity targets).

(d) Rank the productivity improvement areas in order of monetary importance to ensure that the areas of maximum return are dealt with first (computerised models which simulate the financial consequences of each strategy can be useful at this stage).

(e) Choose the top six (say) from the list for immediate action.

(f) Develop a plan for attaining the productivity improvement targets including a detailed description of individual tasks, a timetable for implementing these tasks and the names of individuals to be responsible for their achievement. Include also the forecasted financial effects of the plan.

(g) Monitor progress regularly.

(h) Evaluate and communicate the actual productivity performances achieved.

Note that many of these steps might already have been undertaken if the productivity planning exercise is following any of the processes of corporate planning, functions planning or management by objectives.

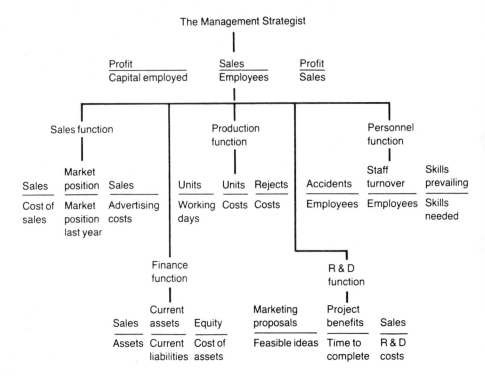

**Figure 10.1  Some organisation productivity ratios**

## Comparing and assessing present performance and choosing productivity targets

The following criteria can be used:

(a)  To do better than we do now. This criterion infers that present performances exist to be measured and improved on. Improvement targets (say 5 per cent ratio improvement) are applied simply because the organisation wants – and expects – to do better.

(b)  To meet internal and external personnel's opinions and expectations. The bank manager may have expressed a hope that the firm will do better, shareholders might be asking for improved performance, the corporate head office might have issued a target achievement directive. Here, the management strategist is testing present performance against important stakeholders' opinions and is setting targets in the context of them.

(c)  To more closely compete with or to beat the competition. Industry norm productivity ratios are calculated and made available through institutions such as Dunn & Bradstreet. Individual competitor ratios are available from published accounts and media reports. These indicators provide a source of comparison which can stimulate and guide the choice of new productivity targets. Michael Porter, of course, suggests that the quest to beat competitive productivity performance is *the* stimulator of competitive advantage and organisational success.

(d) To improve the organisation's performance trend and its target setting/attaining record. Comparison of previous performances over time (perhaps against targets) provides an assessment of the organisation's performance trend and target attainment capability and can help decision-makers think about whether targets are being set too high or too low. This should then lead to the implementation of more pertinent future productivity targets.

# Case study: productivity success at Sainsbury

In the year to March 1988, the high street retailer Sainsbury became the first British retailing group to top £5 billion sales turnover. In his Chairman's statement, Sir John Sainsbury said that the £308 million profit recorded (after profit sharing) compared with £200 million two years ago and £100 million five years earlier. Net margins moved up to 6.62 per cent from 6.19 per cent in 1987. Earnings per share increased by 20 per cent and since 1983 had grown by 126 per cent in real terms. In the Management Today Growth League (based on return on shareholders capital measurements) Sainsbury cruised up from a 1987 position of 32nd to occupy 18th place. Most stakeholders and commentators, understandably, expressed favourable opinions on the Sainsbury performance. Nevertheless, Sainsbury continued to plan further productivity improvements. Growth targets had been set for 'own label' product sales. Own label products, at 55 per cent of total sales, already provided the highest own label proportion of any supermarket group. These products enable a supermarket group to retail at below the price of manufacturers' branded products and yet increase their own profit margin. Expansion was also targeted for the home improvement and garden subsidiary, Homebase, from the present 38 store operation to one of 50 stores by Spring 1989.

## Think and discuss
Assess Sainsbury's productivity performance. Consider and suggest targets for the future.

## Case example: productivity planning in the pig industry
Increased competition from pig producers in other EC countries will mean greater pressure on UK pig producers to become technically more efficient. Speaking at the 1991 Pig Fair, at the National Agricultural Centre, Mr Tim Brigstocke, BOCM Silcock's Chief Agricultural Adviser said 'With one sow producing around 1.66 tonnes of pig meat annually in Holland, compared to 1.26 tonnes in the UK, the threat to our industry is not difficult to evaluate.' The most social area for research and development activity was in the development of alternative production systems. There was a need to develop new systems which enhanced productivity *and* animal welfare. Mr Brigstocke noted that British producers could be at considerable disadvantage as they move towards greater welfare-orientated methods while such systems as sow-stalls and tethes are allowed on the continent.

In effort to improve productivity many pig farmers were already working to a best practice ratio checklist. In 1989 some of the best practice targets had included:

• Sows should be capable of producing 24 piglets per annum on one tonne of sow feed.

- Growing pigs should convert food between weaning and bacon weight at no more than 2.3:1.
- Conception should be 90 per cent to first service.
- Mortality should never be more than 10 per cent before weaning.

## Productivity planning at the corporate level

Productivity campaigns should start in the offices of the top management. An early step in the productivity planning process, therefore, should be the setting up of a 'productivity campaign meeting' between the top officers of the organisation (perhaps, for example, the chief executive and the functions directors). A number of benefits should flow from such a step.

(a) Commitment of those important people who are to lead the productivity implementations is secured immediately.

(b) Top level support for the concept of productivity improvement is recognised throughout the organisation.

(c) The ensuing productivity improvement programme immediately takes the role of an organisation-wide activity (it should never become the responsibility and province of 'productivity specialist' personnel or departments).

(d) Potential productivity improvement strategies can be considered in the context of their organisation-wide impacts. For example, the top team is best placed to consider productivity strategies in the context of chosen generic competitive strategies. It is also best placed, via its access to corporate information, to determine where the most signficant areas for productivity improvement are. This meeting of minds can also examine strategies from different perspectives. The production director's suggestion for an efficiency saving move, for example, can be considered in relation to the marketing director's views on how such a move might affect customer satisfaction and sales. Discussions on departmental savings estimated to flow from the installation of a computer system can incorporate the data processing manager's views on how such a development might increase the costs in his or her department.

(e) The exercise can act as a unifying, team building process which creates long-term benefits over and above the specific productivity improvement effort.

(f) The top officials can bring their experience and expertise together to 'spark off' ideas and to generate effective productivity solutions.

As a start to the productivity programme, Rohlwink (14) suggests a one or two day brainstorming session involving functional managers undertaking our previously considered 'steps in the productivity improvement process'. The task of this top team is to generate and prioritise a list of productivity improvement strategies, to formulate detailed plans for their implementations and, thereafter, to monitor, evaluate and communicate their outcomes. The early task of this team, therefore, is to decide where and how the most significant savings (cost cuttings) and/or the most significant value-addings (contribution creators) can be made. We will consider these activities in greater detail shortly. For the time being, however, we will simply note that useful thought around these two sides of the productivity equation can be stimulated by the introduction of a checklist of generic marketing, manufacturing, R & D, etc. strategies (see for example the productivity improvement strategies listed below). The managers concerned should use these checklist strategies to generate their own customised improvement strategy suggestions.

- Put prices up/down
- Charge what *each* customer will pay
- Customer rationalisation
- Product rationalisation
- Competitive sourcing
- Backward integration
- Contract out production processes
- Rationalise production amongst plants
- Centralise purchasing
- Make or buy
- Just in time stock procedures
- Cost engineering products and processes
- Automate existing processes

The financial effect of potential productivity strategies should be estimated before decisions on which ones to implement are made (the effect of price reductions needs to be considered, for example, in the context of anticipated increases in sales volume bearing in mind the consequences of competitive reactions). Figure 10.2 provides an example of the sort of information which computers can help generate on the effect that different productivity strategies have on total profits. This type of modelling is very useful to the task of deciding on, and prioritising productivity activities.

## Productivity planning at the individual job level

A massive force for productivity is created when everybody in the organisation becomes personally involved and committed to the productivity effort. We have already considered how a system of management by objectives can be introduced to improve productivity in all the jobs of the firm. In Chapter 11 we will emphasise the point that the harnessing of a *total* productivity effort requires attention to all those structures, systems and other components which create organisational culture. Here, therefore, we will restrict the text to an illustration of how productivity improvement at operational level might be planned. Steps toward improvements are illustrated below through an extended example of planning productivity gains in refuse collection.

### Step 1: Identify productivity area
(a) *Responsibility*: empty household dustbins

(b) *Performance*: empty 5,000 dustbins every week

(c) *Resources*: five workers, one wagon, 40 hours per person, per week.

### Step 2: Measure existing performance
5,000 dustbins in 200 hours (5 x 40)

| | BASE CASE (MILLION) | | | | EFFECT OF PRICING STRATEGY | | | |
|---|---|---|---|---|---|---|---|---|
| | Product line 1 | Product line 2 | Product line 3 | Total | Product line 1 | Product line 2 | Product line 3 | Total |
| Average price | 20.0 | 23.0 | 27.0 | 23.3 | 21.0 | 23.0 | 27.0 | 23.68 |
| Volume (millions of units) | | | | | | | | |
| Total revenue | 100.0 | 92.0 | 108.0 | 300.0 | 94.5 | 92.0 | 108.0 | 294.5 |
| Direct materials | 30.0 | 27.0 | 32.0 | 89.0 | 27.0 | 27.0 | 32.0 | 86.0 |
| Direct labour | 20.0 | 13.0 | 14.0 | 47.0 | 18.0 | 13.0 | 14.0 | 45.0 |
| Direct production | 15.0 | 16.0 | 15.0 | 46.0 | 13.5 | 16.0 | 15.0 | 44.5 |
| Total variable | 65.0 | 56.0 | 61.0 | 182.0 | 58.5 | 56.0 | 61.0 | 175.5 |
| Indirect labour | 10.0 | 12.0 | 15.0 | 37.0 | 10.0 | 12.0 | 15.0 | 37.0 |
| Depreciation | 10.0 | 8.0 | 14.0 | 32.0 | 10.0 | 8.0 | 14.0 | 32.0 |
| Marketing | 3.0 | 4.0 | 3.0 | 10.0 | 3.0 | 4.0 | 3.0 | 10.0 |
| R & D | 1.0 | 2.0 | 2.0 | 5.0 | 1.0 | 2.0 | 2.0 | 5.0 |
| Administration | 1.0 | 1.0 | 1.0 | 3.0 | 1.0 | 1.0 | 1.0 | 3.0 |
| Total fixed | 25.0 | 27.0 | 35.0 | 87.0 | 25.0 | 27.0 | 35.0 | 87.0 |
| NPBIT | 10.0 | 9.0 | 12.0 | 31.0 | 11.0 | 9.0 | 12.0 | 32.0 |
| Fixed assets | 50.0 | 40.0 | 70.0 | 160.0 | 50.0 | 40.0 | 70.0 | 160.0 |
| Stocks | 20.0 | 20.0 | 20.0 | 60.0 | 18.0 | 20.0 | 20.0 | 58.0 |
| Debtors | 10.0 | 10.0 | 15.0 | 35.0 | 9.0 | l0.0 | l5.0 | 34.0 |
| Creditors | 5.0 | 7.0 | 10.0 | 22.0 | 4.5 | 7.0 | 10.0 | 21.5 |
| Net assets | 75.0 | 63.0 | 95.0 | 233.0 | 72.5 | 63.0 | 95.0 | 230.5 |
| Return on net assets (%) | 13.3 | 14.3 | 12.6 | 13.3 | 15.2 | 14.3 | 12.6 | 13.8 |

| | EFFECT OF BACKWARD INTEGRATION | | | | EFFECT OF COST ENGINEERING | | | |
|---|---|---|---|---|---|---|---|---|
| Average price | 20.0 | 23.0 | 27.0 | 23.3 | 20.0 | 23.0 | 27.0 | 23.3 |
| Volume (millions of units) | 5.0 | 4.0 | 4.0 | 13.0 | 5.0 | 4.0 | 4.0 | 13.0 |
| Total revenue | 100.0 | 92.0 | 108.0 | 300.0 | 100.0 | 92.0 | 108.0 | 300.0 |
| Direct materials | 30.0 | 19.0 | 32.0 | 81.0 | 30.0 | 27.0 | 25.0 | 82.0 |
| Direct labour | 20.0 | 14.0 | 14.0 | 48.0 | 20.0 | 13.0 | 15.0 | 48.0 |
| Direct production | 15.0 | 18.0 | 15.0 | 48.0 | 15.0 | 16.0 | 16.0 | 47.0 |
| Total variable | 65.0 | 51.0 | 61.0 | 177.0 | 65.0 | 56.0 | 56.0 | 177.0 |
| Indirect labour | 10.0 | 12.0 | 15.0 | 37.0 | 10.0 | 12.0 | 15.0 | 37.0 |
| Depreciation | 10.0 | 9.0 | 14.0 | 33.0 | 10.0 | 8.0 | 14.0 | 32.0 |
| Marketing | 3.0 | 4.0 | 3.0 | 10.0 | 3.0 | 4.0 | 3.0 | 10.0 |
| R & D | 1.0 | 2.0 | 2.0 | 5.0 | 1.0 | 2.0 | 2.0 | 5.0 |
| Administration | 1.0 | 1.0 | 1.0 | 3.0 | 1.0 | 1.0 | 1.0 | 3.0 |
| Total fixed | 25.0 | 28.0 | 35.0 | 88.0 | 25.0 | 27.0 | 35.0 | 87.0 |
| NPBIT | 10.0 | 13.0 | 12.0 | 35.0 | 10.0 | 9.0 | 17.0 | 36.0 |
| Fixed assets | 50.0 | 45.0 | 70.0 | 165.0 | 50.0 | 40.0 | 70.0 | 160.0 |
| Stocks | 20.0 | 18.0 | 20.0 | 58.0 | 20.0 | 20.0 | 19.0 | 59.0 |
| Debtors | 10.0 | 10.0 | 15.0 | 35.0 | 10.0 | 10.0 | 15.0 | 35.0 |
| Creditors | 5.0 | 7.0 | 10.0 | 22.0 | 5.0 | 7.0 | 10.0 | 22.0 |
| Net assets | 75.0 | 66.0 | 95.0 | 236.0 | 75.0 | 63.0 | 94.0 | 232.0 |
| Return on net assets (%) | 13.3 | 19.7 | 12.6 | 14.8 | 13.3 | 14.3 | 18.0 | 15.5 |

Figure 10.2 Modelling the financial effects of alternative productivity strategies

## Step 3: Determine productivity target
New productivity target is 30 dustbins per hour. This target has been agreed as necessary (given the nature of the newly competitive public service sector) and as feasible (in the context of the plans identified below) by the departmental manager and the refuse collection team. It has been noted that some neighbouring local authorities are already achieving this level of productivity.

## Step 4: Develop a plan
(a) The team will be reorganised so that the drivers 'mate' job will no longer exist. Instead this personnel will work on the collection of bins.

(b) One team member will take early retirement and will not be replaced.

(c) The hydraulic lift section of the wagon will be modified to increase its speed of operation.

## Step 5: Monitor progress
June: 26 dustbins per hour
July: 25 dustbins per hour (staff holidays taken this month)
Aug: 28 dustbins per hour
Sept: 32 dustbins per hour
Oct: 31 dustbins per hour

Note: Productivity improvements have been achieved without any increase in levels of customer complaints.

## Step 6: Evaluate and communicate productivity performance
Memo to: Refuse collection team (copy to Chief Officer)
During the first five months of the refuse collection productivity improvement programme average refuse collection has been at the rate of 28.4 bins per hour. This represents a productivity improvement of around 15 per cent on last year's performance. While I am sure you will agree there is no room for complacency (particularly as our target for this year is an average of 30 bins per hour) this progress at this early stage of our campaign is most encouraging and congratulations and thanks are in order.

# Cutting costs

'A firm has a cost advantage if its cumulative cost of performing its value activities is lower than competitor costs. Cost advantage leads to superior performance if the firm provides an acceptable level of value to the buyer so that its cost advantage is not nullified by the need to charge a lower price than competitors.' (15)

Cost improvement campaigns should seek to reduce costs – without damaging, to a greater extent, contributions – throughout the organisation. Again, we will refer to the role played by cultural arrangements in supporting cost cutting campaigns. More often than not cost leader organisations have a culture emanating from senior management that reinforces cost cutting behaviour. It is often reflected in spartan facilities and limited executive perks.

Once again Paul Mali (16) provides us with a framework for thinking out the range of activities which might be adopted to improve productivity in our own organisational settings, and, at the same time, to contribute to the installation of a 'cost cutting culture'. The six cost cutting approaches together with their accompanying techniques are described briefly below. Cost improvement is, according to Mali, most successful when attention is given to all six approaches.

(a) Cost attitude improvement: the development of employee commitment to the cost improvement effort.

- *By example*. Supervisors set the tone and provide a model for emulation.
- *Coaching and training*. On-the-job and off-the-job training activities instil and reinforce the skills and attitudes necessary for effective cost improvement.
- *Incentives*. Benefits are shared with those who help produce them.

(b) Cost planning and budgeting (the development of short range plans which target the cost performance desired and needed).

- *Zero base budgeting*. Managers have to justify, each year, the projects and activities to be continued or undertaken and, consequently, the funds requested.
- *Responsibility centre organisation*. Parts of the organisation are designated *cost* or *profit* or *productivity* or *investment centres* and are measured for productivity results.
- *Productivity targeting*. Awareness of the need for productivity is developed, generally, and productivity objectives are set throughout the organisation.

(c) Cost avoidance: the removal of anticipated costs before they are incurred.

- *Methods improvement*. Based on the philosophy 'there must be a better way', activities are analysed to ascertain whether materials and/or processes can be eliminated, combined, simplified, or rearranged to avoid or lower costs.
- *Value analysis*. Analysis in great depth is undertaken to achieve functions at the lowest overall cost while maintaining the necessary standards of performance, reliability, maintainability, etc.
- *Waste prevention*. Plans are devised to eradicate organisational wastes of time, materials, equipment and labour.

(d) Cost reduction: the performance of work so efficiently that costs incurred remain below allowable limits.

- *Expense reduction*. Make those responsible for incurring expenditure responsible for reducing it by 'laying off' mediocre employees, natural wastage, elimination of non-essential budgetary items, reducing departmental telephone calls, etc.
- *Increased productivity*. Reduce unit costs through improving cost performance and output performance through job re-design and training.
- *Procurement cost improvement*. Implement a planned approach to create clear purchasing guidelines and to undertake competitive bidding, value analysis and quality buying.
- *Standardisation*. Reduce a wide variety of unique items to a few basic models

(e) Cost control: systems to ensure that costs are held within pre-determined limits.

- *Cost standards.* Set standards to control costs in activities, for example wage costs per unit of product value, quality failure costs as a percentage of value produced.
- *Budgetary control.* This requires plans for different parts of the organisation which project the receipts and/or expenditures to be obtained and incurred. Performance is then monitored against budget.
- *Pilferage control.* Introduce precautionary procedures including audits and stock control systems to minimise theft and pilferage of goods, materials, tools, company time, telephone calls and money – by external parties or by white and blue collar workers.

(f) Cost effectiveness: the spending of money to save money.

- *Capital investment.* This involves the formal consideration of potential applications of significant sums of money to generate positive effects on the longer term economic health of the organisation.
- *Cost–benefit analysis.* Evaluate potential investment opportunities in order to prioritise between them.
- *Equipment aids and mechanisation.* Introduce labour saving mechanisation.

## Some cost cutting pitfalls

Strategists anxious to introduce cost improvement campaigns should be aware of common pitfalls associated with many previous cost improvement programmes (17). These pitfalls reduce the effectiveness of cost cutting campaigns. They include:

(a) *Too much emphasis on specialists.* Cost accountants, economists and statisticians are often delegated the task of designing the cost improvement campaign. The result, often, is a technically elegant system which the implementing manager never really understands, has little commitment to, and so does not implement.

(b) *Too much emphasis placed on direct labour costs.* Productivity is a measure of input to output. Too often cost cutting exercises concentrate on direct labour costs per hour and ignore the need to measure such costs against the value they create. Highly productive workers can be paid much more than ineffective counterparts. Also, direct labour, for many organisations is a *minor* cost element. Other overhead cost areas provide greater performance improvement potential but remain neglected as attention focuses on direct labour costs.

(c) *Too much emphasis placed on individual cost areas.* A firm achieves competitive advantage through creating more output value for a given level of *total* resource inputs than its competitors. Intense effort to produce cost savings in specific areas produces negative side effects if:

- the cost reduction reduces output value more than proportionately – savings in production costs, for example, through the use of cheaper, inferior materials might be more than offset by customers who find the newly constituted product unattractive, and so stop buying;
- cost cutting exercises in one area produce even greater costs in another –

making a quality control inspector redundant can create bigger warranty and after sales service costs.

(d) *Too much emphasis on statistics in performance appraisal.* Cost cutting is basically an economic, objective exercise. It relies heavily on performance statistics. Cost cutting appraisal sessions can be demotivating if appraising managers forget that what really happens at the company depends upon what really happened at the plant and in the market place rather than what happened in the numbers.

(e) *Too little emphasis on people.* While the economic reality for many British organisations in the 1980s was one which necessitated wholesale job shedding many of those organisations which have successfully emerged from this era are now paying much attention to the political, psychological and social aspects of work, people and productivity. Our chapters on aspirations planning, team culture planning and management by objectives provide assistance to those strategists who are planning on the basis that workforce motivation is a major aspect of productivity planning success. These chapters counterbalance the very objective, rational and economic perspective which efficiency planning attracts so easily.

(f) *Preconceptions.* Cost improvements are best created by those managers most prepared to question the traditional and 'hallowed' ways of doing things.

## Creating contribution

Cost cutting addresses the bottom line of the productivity equation. It is primarily a function of *efficiency planning*. However, *productivity planning* demands that a formal and sophisticated attempt to improve 'top lines' should also be undertaken. Significant wealth generations are to be had when the enterprise gears itself up to manage customers for profits (and not just for sales) (18). Many of today's organisations neglect this strategy for increasing productivity. They give insufficient attention to issues of customer account profitability, customer selection and customer account management. Many managers are unaware of the *profit dispersion* over their range of accounts. Because of this they do not make productive decisions over which customers to serve and which generic competitive strategies to pursue. While different customers usually create different combined levels of pre-sale, production, distribution and post-sale service costs, evidence suggests that prices seldom reflect the actual costs incurred in serving the customer. Shapiro et al., for example, claim 'In a wide variety of situations, we have consistently observed a lack of correlation between price and cost to serve' (19). This lack of understanding of account profitability results in carrying unprofitable accounts and in embarking into unsuitable product/market areas. Figure 10.3 is a useful device for identifying the profitability status of an organisation's customers.

In the low price/low cost to serve quadrant are those 'bargain basement' customers who are price sensitive but not so concerned about service and quality. Low cost/high price segments are comprised of 'passive' customers who, perhaps because of high switching costs or a monopoly supply position, or perhaps simply because of apathy, are prepared to stay with their existing supplier, paying high prices and creating, for the supplying organisation, high profits. 'Carriage trade' customers cost much to serve (small 'one-off' type clients, for example). However, they are prepared to pay top price for what they get. The 'aggressive' customer is the high cost/low price searcher who demands (and often receives) the highest product quality at 'knock down' prices. Procter and Gamble, for example, through their procurement cost improvement expertise have a reputation for paying the least and getting the most.

**Net price**

**Cost to serve**

**Figure 10.3 Customer profitability classification matrix**

Marketing managers often assume a strong correlation between net price and cost to serve, reasoning that price sensitive customers will accept lower quality and service and that demanding customers will pay more for better quality and service. The matrix in Fig. 10.3 can help decision-makers identify the reality of their particular situation. Its use might produce some surprises for those holding the above assumption. In our productivity conscious, customer powerful, strategically sophisticated 1990s we might expect more and more customers to progress towards the 'aggressive' quadrant.

Clearly, then, it is becoming increasingly important for strategists to develop sophistication as *contribution creators. Weak cost accounting practices* (which average costs over products and customers) need to be improved so that an analysis of the firm's customer profile can place customers into the appropriate quadrants of Fig. 10.3. Shapiro and colleagues (18) suggest a five step action programme for the benefit of those strategists charged with the task of enhancing customer contribution. The five steps are:

(a) *Pinpoint your costs*. It seems likely that customer profitability varies more widely in business where a large percentage of the total expenditure is incurred outside the factory doors. Without a good cost accounting system 'it is management by anecdote'.

(b) *Know your profitability dispersion*. Once costs are known the company can plot them against realised prices to show the dispersion of account profitability. Sales management might then find it easier to develop accounts in the 'passive' sector where biggest value is to be earned.

(c) *Focus your strategy*. In Michael Porter fashion, Shapiro et al. advise the choice of a generic account management stragegy. Companies which reside in a particular quadrant will tend to generate orders in that quadrant. Do not (again in the Porter mould) get 'stuck in the middle', attempting to serve all quadrants. Decide which type of customer best suits your strengths and objectives, get to know that customer and set prices on the basis of product value to customers rather than on costs to serve.

(d) *Provide support systems*. Having chosen the quadrant of business activity the organisation will seek to develop, the systems, structures and activities of the organisation should be developed, to provide an organisation-wide approach to the chosen account segment. Here, interestingly, Shapiro et al. advocate a separation of strategy development and customer negotiation functions. Those negotiating with customers need only to have a clear remit of the terms acceptable as a minimum. Knowledge of account profitability, it is argued, leads to giving too much away in the negotiation situation.

(e) *Repeat the analysis regularly.* Profit dispersion patterns experience 'drift' as 'carriage trade' customers move, with time, to a position in the 'aggressive' or 'bargain basement' categories. Repeat analyses are necessary to monitor changing profit dispersion situations.

## Productivity and quantitative techniques

Generally speaking, quantitative techniques take little account of political and psychological values and assume perfect information inputs. By themselves, therefore, they are unreliable decision-making aids. However, these techniques, drawn from the disciplines of economics, accounting, mathematics and statistics are vital parts of the complete strategist's armoury. Quantitative techniques provide formulas which direct us towards finding pertinent information and which, when the information is worked in the associated formula, project the financial and/or economic effects of a decision. Quantitative techniques, typically have been created for the purpose of helping decision-makers make the best (i.e. most economically productive) decision. Used as part of more comprehensive decision making processes, therefore, such techniques are invaluable insight generators in the solving of productivity problems. This section is not intended as an in depth treatment of quantitative techniques. Other works are available for this purpose (see, for example, 20 and 21). However, in order to indicate how such techniques can be useful to productivity planners we will spend some time looking at the role of one quantitative technique for the solving of problems on how to make productive investments.

### What is an investment?

Individuals at work invest effort, time, expertise and resources in doing their daily jobs. At the other extreme, the organisation itself is an investment – a combination of resources which has been, and continues to be deployed in the expectation that, over time, a 'more from less' outcome will be achieved. There is no hard and fast rule on what should or should not be described as an investment. In this section, however, we are defining an investment as 'a significant allocation of resources to a project in the expectation that the project will, over the medium to longer term, produce net beneficial results for the enterprise'. In this section we are talking about capital expenditures rather than operating expenditures.

### The time value of money and the net present value technique for investment appraisal

Suppose a friend borrowed £1.00 from you today and promised to repay it in exactly one year's time. Does this proposition sound like a beneficial economic deal from your point of view? The investment appraisal technique of *net present value discounting* would indicate not. The assumption underlying this method is that, in the absence of a loan to your friend, you would have been making that £1.00 work at creating wealth, perhaps through its deposit in an interest earning building society account. Because 91p invested in the building society today would produce a balance of £1.00 in one year's time (assuming 10 per cent interest rates) then, in *discounted cash flow* terms, your friend's promise of £1.00 in one year's time is worth only 91p today. Its *net present value* (npv) is only 91p. Thus, the net present value method of investment appraisal seeks to take account of the *time value* of money and discounts anticipated future inflows of cash back to their 'today' value. If the net present value of the sum of the anticipated cash flows is greater than the value of the resources invested then the investment is economically attractive. If your friend promised you £1.20 in a year's time, this would discount back to a net present value of £1.09 (again, at 10 per cent interest rates). This would yield 9p in excess of the £1.00 you loaned. Thus, in this instance, the proposition appears to be economically attractive. Discount rate factor tables are available to help in working out the net present value of each £ of income expected to flow from a given investment. (Such a table is appended to the 'Medway Menswear' case study in the accompanying case study book (22).)

A step-by-step checklist is provided below to help readers better understand the net present value technique.

(a) *Identify the values of all the project related cash flows* (not *profit* flows), *in* and *out*, for each of the years of the project's anticipated life. This is a critical part of the process and, often, a highly uncertain one. Information is required on revenue and cost related items such as forecast demand, prices, initial costs and their phasings into the project, fixed and variable costs, life expectancy of facilities and of the project itself, tax liabilities, depreciation allowances and the residual value of assets. It is not difficult to see why this aspect of net present value discounting is both critical and uncertain.

(b) *Decide the rate* which is to be used as the discount rate. This 'hurdle rate' is expressed in percentage terms. It is that minimum rate which the company expects its investments to earn. It might be ascertained, for example, by reference to those stakeholders such as bankers and shareholders who provide it with funds at a charge. Figure 10.4 provides an example of how an *average cost of capital* might be worked out. Alternatively, the discount rate might be determined by reference to some fairly safe alternative interest earning opportunity (in our personal example, provided earlier, this was the building society's offer of 10 per cent per annum). Additional per cents can be added to take some account of any perceived extra riskiness which attaches to the investment under review.

(c) *Discount back to today's net values*, using tables provided, all the cash inflows and outflows identified in (a) above.

(d) *Add together the discounted outflows and the initial investment expenditure, add together the discounted inflows*. Take one total from the other. If the inflows total is greater than the outflows total then the investment is worthwhile.

(e) *Perform steps (a) to (d) with any alternative investment proposals.*

(f) *Prioritise the list of alternatives* in terms of each project's attractiveness for implementation. Attractiveness criteria might include:

| Source of finance | Amount used | Weight | Individual Cost % | Weighted av. cost % |
|---|---|---|---|---|
| Ordinary shares | 500,000 | .25 | 10 | 2.5 |
| Retained profit | 500,000 | .25 | 10 | 2.5 |
| Preference shares | 200,000 | .1 | 8 | .8 |
| Debentures | 250,000 | .125 | 7 | .875 |
| Bank overdraft | 250,000 | .125 | 8 | 1.0 |
| Bank credit | 300,000 | .15 | 8 | 1.2 |
| | 2,000,000 | 1.0 | | 8.875 |

**Figure 10.4 Calculating the average cost of capital**

- the comparative size of positive cash flows for individual investments and for alternative packages of investments;
- the resource cost of the investment (or range of investments if more than one alternative can be chosen) – can the company afford the investment(s)?
- the productivity returns (benefits compared to costs) which each project (or range of projects) is expected to earn. This is the true test of productivity but should be used in the context of the need to create greater *total* wealth. The choice of a highly productive small project, for example, might leave other investment monies idle and unproductive;
- the anticipated *payback* period. This is the period of time within which investment earnings (not discounted) are expected to equal (and hence, payback) the initial investment cost;
- the risk involved with each project, although this might have been taken account of to some extent in step (b);
- the decision-makers' personal preferences and their perceptions of other important stakeholders' personal preferences and power positions. (A lucrative investment proposition in South Africa, for example, might be unattractive for other than economic reasons);
- the fit of the investment with other organisational activities and strategies.

(g) *Choose the most appropriate investment(s)*. The net present value technique for investment appraisal is a most useful information generator and investment evaluator. In using it, however, decision-makers should bear in mind the highly uncertain nature of much of the information which goes into the npv model – a model which produces, ultimately, a very objective, one answer specific, numerical result. Further, investment evaluations need to take account of emotional (as well as economic) values and of the need to treat investment decisions within the context of their being part of organisation-wide strategy.

## Think and discuss

1 Calculate the present value of future cash flows at the given rates of interest (r). (Discount factor tables are available in the companion volume (22).)

    (a) £550     1 year away,    r = 10%
    (b) £1728    3 years away,   r = 20%
    (c) £251     2 years away,   r = 12%
    (d) £2000   9 years away,   r = 8%

2 A project requires initial investment funds of £6,000 and will produce cash receipts of £1,000 per year for ten years. Required rate of return is 15 per cent. Should you undertake the project?

3 You have £10,000 in the building society currently earning you 10 per cent per annum. Your friend Harry wants to borrow £8,000 of this to start up an estate agency. He says things will be difficult initially but that he will split the profits equally with you for the first five years and will repay the loan at the end of the sixth year. He reckons that total profits will be around:

| Year | Profits |
|------|---------|
| 1 | £  500 |
| 2 | £1,000 |
| 3 | £1,500 |
| 4 | £3,000 |
| 5 | £5,000 |

Jim, another friend, wants to borrow £8,000 as well. This time the money is for an 'up and running' newsagency. He says he can guarantee £1,000 per year repayment for each of the next five years and the return of the £8,000 at the end of the sixth year.

    Which friend, if any, should you support?

# Productivity and information

Information and the need for information is integral to the planning process. At the heart of successful productivity planning are pertinent information systems. Information is necessary to enable measurement of productivity ratios – decision-makers need to know what has happened and what is happening in productivity terms. In particular, costs and benefits have to be allocated to particular productivity areas. Information is also necessary to facilitate comparisons – with the competition, for example. It underpins decisions on productivity targets and on the strategies for attaining targets. How far will customers and/or the competition allow the firm to go in changing prices, for example? How soon will a particular employee be capable of achieving a 10 per cent increase in his or her productivity (and what training, etc. inputs will be necessary)? Monitoring systems are needed to provide information for the assessment of productivity performances including any countervailing (or synergistic) impacts across organisational linkages. Have price increases reduced customer loyalty? Have savings in one department produced additional expense in another?

Many organisations, approaching formal productivity planning for the first time, find their information systems woefully inadequate. Without the appropriate information productivity planning is a non-starter. In such circumstances there is no course of action available other than first to improve the enterprise's information systems. Having said this, however, we will emphasise the danger of putting off productivity planning pending the search for *perfect* information. We have already referred to the imperfect information nature of many planning situations. In the productivity planning area, for example, the apportionment of overhead costs to specific products and/or customers is a notoriously difficult and subjective task. Productivity planning, however, needs to be undertaken sooner rather than later. Strategists should use information, therefore, as soon as it becomes meaningful. Information systems can then be refined as time and the productivity planning process develop.

## Productivity and people

If productivity is much about information it is equally as much about *people*, that resource which uses information and which designs, leads and implements the productivity plans. Another danger created by the very economic and numerical approach to improving productivity lies in the failure of management strategists to pay sufficient regard to the need to motivate productivity performance from people. We shall see in the next chapter how British 'winners' of the past decade paid a great deal of attention to the achievement of productivity through people.

## Productivity planning: conclusion

Productivity planning is the systematic attempt to get more for less. Its major aim is to improve the ratio between the organisation's resource input costs and its outcome values – to improve its wealth breeding function. Improving productivity in existing areas of operation is a development option available at all times to every organisation. As society and customers grow more powerful and more ecologically aware, as resources become more scarce and as competition becomes more strategically sophisticated so it becomes more unlikely that *in*effective productivity planners will survive. Getting more for less requires *formal* planning in today's business situations. Steps in a formal approach to productivity planning include:

(a) Rearrange, where necessary, the organisation information systems to ensure that pertinent information is available to the productivity planners.

(b) Monitor the organisation for signs of – and reasons for – productivity decline. Make this a periodic activity.

(c) Bring top planners together to commence the productivity campaign.

(d) Establish major cost cutting, contribution creating plans (take account of the potential pitfalls in efficiency planning and in particular remember that productivity is achieved through people).

(e) Introduce related productivity plans at lower levels of the organisation (perhaps via a system of management by objectives).

(f) Monitor the productivity effort and communicate results.

# Case study: productivity in the high street grocery industry

Tesco, the supermarket giant, demonstrated the resilience of the food retailing sector in the recession when it announced full-year pre-tax profits, excluding property, up 28 per cent from £326.6m to £417.1m for the year ended 1990. The group, which in January asked shareholders for an extra £572 million to pay for continuing expansion, said that after property profits of £19 million (£35 million in 1989) pre-tax profits rose 21 per cent to £436 million. The Tesco Chairman, Sir Ian MacLaurin, who now heads a British retailing empire of 384 trading stores, said 'We are fortunate that food retailing is very resilient.'

The profits were just ahead of the forecast given at the time of the rights issue. Sales, excluding VAT, leapt 17.5 per cent to £6.3 billion and the margins have also beaten the recession blues, moving up from 6 per cent to 6.6 per cent. The cash call strengthened the Tesco balance sheet so that at the year end it had a cash pile of £177 million compared with borrowings of £317 million 12 months earlier. That helped boost interest received from £9.8 million to £19.1 million.

During the year Tesco's staff received a 13 per cent pay rise as the competition for recruitment hotted up between the supermarket heavyweights. But Sir Ian said that productivity improvements meant that was possible without increasing retail wage costs as a percentage of sales. After splashing out £2.8 billion on investment in the past five years Tesco has 9.2 per cent of the market compared with 8.7 per cent a year ago. Sir Ian said the four-year-old profit-sharing scheme continued apace and this year 38,000 staff would share £22 million.

During the year 20 new stores and two extensions, totalling 866,500 sq. ft were opened. Another 1,100,000 sq. ft are on the blocks to be opened this year. Four-fifths of Tesco's sales are now electronically scanned and all stores should be converted by October 1992, Sir Ian said. He added 'With regard to current trade, despite the economic climate and lower food price inflation, our food sales are holding up well and we are maintaining our real volume growth.' The total dividend goes up to 5.25p with a 3.60p final payment – up 26 per cent.

## Think and discuss

1  Compare and contrast the productivity performances of Sainsbury and Tesco over the years covered in the case study (see Table 10.1).
2  In the context of a firm of your choice evaluate its present approach to productivity planning and draw up a plan for its productivitiy improvement.

## For further study

Refer to the 'Medway Menswear' case study in the accompanying case study book.

'What I really need is some advice on how to tackle the future, how to become more efficient, tougher', Derek Armitage, MD Medway Menswear.

(a)  What general advice have you to offer Armitage on the running of his business?

(b)  Identify the major causes of any deficiencies in Medway's present approach to productivity planning.

(c)  Should Medway buy the jacket line machinery it needs from Honers or from Iztal?

Table 10.1 Tesco plc and J Sainsbury plc – financial analysis (source: media extracts, audited accounts and student BABS (Hons) assignment)

|  | No. Employees | Full-time equivalent | No. Stores | Sales Area (mn sq.ft) | Market Share (%) | Capital employed (m) | Capital expenditure (m) | Fixed assets (m) | Long-term debt (m) | Current assets (m) | Stock (m) | Current liability (m) | Overdraft/ loan (m) | Gearing ratio (%) | Sales Inc. (inc VAT) (m) |
|---|---|---|---|---|---|---|---|---|---|---|---|---|---|---|---|
| **Tesco** | | | | | | | | | | | | | | | |
| 1986 | 60,781 | 43,447 | 395 | 7.51 | 6.7 | 588.6 | 225 | 772.2 | 61.2 | 351.1 | 191.1 | 456.3 | 21.8 | 8.10% | 3556.3 |
| 1987 | 62,652 | 45,260 | 337 | 6.99 | 7.1 | 690.1 | 310 | 999.9 | 120.4 | 256.8 | 182.5 | 440.4 | 10 | 17.45% | 3808.6 |
| 1988 | 71,262 | 50,192 | 379 | 8.22 | 7.6 | 870.7 | 400 | 1415.7 | 230.1 | 254 | 179.1 | 508.7 | 58.5 | 13.15% | 4366.2 |
| 1989 | 75,658 | 54,345 | 374 | 8.54 | 8.2 | 1031.3 | 475 | 1716.3 | 293 | 317 | 192.2 | 625.2 | 2.1 | 18.61% | 5000.8 |
| 1990 | 83,224 | 52,742 | 379 | 9.07 | 8.7 | 1254.1 | 651 | 2159.4 | 327.6 | 275.4 | 212.8 | 749.4 | 2.1 | 16.29% | 5726.1 |
| **Sainsbury** | | | | | | | | | | | | | | | |
| 1986 | 64,007 | 42,244 | 281 | 4.69 | 9.7 | 653.5 | 247 | 1124.9 | 73.1 | 266.2 | 174.4 | 643.5 | 115.2 | 21.81% | 3575.2 |
| 1987 | 67,620 | 44,629 | 290 | 5.03 | 10.2 | 781.3 | 291 | 1330.6 | 135.6 | 285.3 | 178.6 | 683.7 | 30.5 | 21.26% | 4043.5 |
| 1988 | 82,607 | 55,346 | 316 | 5.47 | 10.7 | 1024.4 | 435 | 1810.2 | 212.4 | 354.9 | 239.6 | 913.1 | 109.2 | 11.39% | 5009.5 |
| 1989 | 88,283 | 59,678 | 347 | 5.96 | 10.9 | 1167.6 | 503 | 2369.6 | 136.1 | 498.6 | 286.1 | 1314.1 | 322.8 | 19.30% | 5915.1 |
| 1990 | 100,001 | 65,309 | 374 | 6.43 | 11.6 | 1465.5 | 693 | 2755.5 | 431.8 | 599.3 | 308.4 | 1352.3 | 386.7 | 15.85% | 7257.1 |

**Table 10.1 continued**

| | Margin (%) | Interest payable (m) | Net profit before int. (m) | Wages (m) | Net profit before tax (m) (kpa) | Sales per employee | Wkly Sales per sq ft (No. of wk) | Stock turnover | Return on equity (%) | Return on s/hld fund (%) | EPS | Dividend per share | Interest cover | Wages per employee |
|---|---|---|---|---|---|---|---|---|---|---|---|---|---|---|
| **Tesco** | | | | | | | | | | | | | | |
| 1986 | 3.7 | 18.8 | 150.1 | | 131.2 | 81.85 | 9.14 | 2.79 | 22.1 | 22.3 | 7.03 | 1.93 | 7.98 | |
| 1987 | 4.7 | 27.4 | 203.3 | | 175.9 | 84.15 | 10.23 | 2.49 | 23.4 | 25.9 | 9.51 | 2.43 | 7.42 | |
| 1988 | 5.6 | 42.2 | 267.8 | | 225.6 | 86.99 | 11.01 | 2.13 | 24.2 | 27.2 | 10.69 | 2.85 | 6.35 | |
| 1989 | 5.9 | 97.7 | 373.7 | 458.6 | 276 | 92.02 | 11.51 | 2.00 | 24.4 | 28.0 | 12.35 | 3.5 | 3.82 | 8,439 |
| 1990 | 6.4 | 137.1 | 498.7 | 543.9 | 361.6 | 108.57 | 12.69 | 1.93 | 25.6 | 30.2 | 6.36 | 4.3 | 3.64 | 10,312 |
| **Sainsbury** | | | | | | | | | | | | | | |
| 1986 | 5.3 | 22 | 214.7 | | 192.7 | 84.63 | 14.87 | 2.54 | 24.9 | 31.9 | 8.96 | 2.75 | 9.76 | |
| 1987 | 5.75 | 39.4 | 286.3 | | 246.9 | 90.60 | 15.43 | 2.30 | 26.3 | 34.4 | 11.34 | 3.5 | 7.27 | |
| 1988 | 6.16 | 25.8 | 334.2 | | 308.4 | 90.51 | 16.31 | 2.49 | 25.4 | 34.2 | 13.63 | 4.2 | 12.95 | |
| 1989 | 6.89 | 86.8 | 384.6 | 606.1 | 375.1 | 99.12 | 16.50 | 2.52 | 24.4 | 34.2 | 16.25 | 5.05 | 4.43 | 10,156 |
| 1990 | 7.04 | 152.1 | 603.5 | 751.4 | 451.4 | 111.12 | 17.26 | 2.21 | 22.5 | 35.1 | 9.64 | 6.1 | 3.97 | 11,505 |

(d)  How satisfactory do you consider Medway's pricing policies to be? Refer in your answer to mail order pricing.

Refer to the British Telecom case study in the case study volume. Evaluate BT's productivity performances over the last few years.

# References

1   P Mali, *MBO Updated*, Wiley Interscience, 1986, p 255
2   M E Porter, *Competitive Advantage*, New York, The Free Press, 1985, Ch 2
3   R Heller, '21 Years of Success and Failure', *Management Today*, May 1987, p 42
4   P Lorange and R T Nelson, 'How to Recognise – and Avoid – Organisational Decline', *Sloan Management Review*, Spring, 1987, pp 41–8
5   R M Cyert and S G March, in *A Behavioural Theory of the Firm*, Englewood Cliffs, NJ, Prentice-Hall, 1963 discuss how 'slack' builds up in a successful firm.
6   P Lorange and R T Nelson, op. cit.
7   J Child, *Organisation: A Guide to Problems and Practice*, 2nd edn, Harper & Row, 1984, pp 5–7
8   P F Drucker, *The Practice of Management*, Pan Piper, 1968
9   G Johnson and K Scholes, *Exploring Corporate Strategy*, 2nd edn, Prentice-Hall International, 1988, Ch 4
10  P Mali, op. cit., Ch 8
11  R McRobb, 'Industry's Lost Costs', *Management Today*, May 1984
12  P Mali, op. cit., p 283, for example
13  A Rohlwink, 'The Mature Strategist', *Management Today*, February 1988, p 110
14  Ibid
15  M E Porter, op. cit., p 97
16  P Mali, op. cit., p 97
17  W B Chew, 'No-Nonsense Guide to Measuring Productivity', *Harvard Business Review*, Jan–Feb 1988, pp 110–18
18  B P Shapiro, Y K Rangan, R T Moriarty and E B Ross, 'Manage Customers for Profit (not just sales)', *Harvard Business Review*, Sept–Oct 1987, pp 101–8
19  Ibid
20  B Lowes and J R Sparkes, *Modern Managerial Economics*, Heinemann, 1983
21  T Lucey, *Management Accounting*, D P Publications, 1983
22  W Richardson, J Patterson, A Gregory and S Leeson, *Case Studies in Business Planning*, 2nd edn, Pitman 1992

# Recommended reading

P Mali, *MBO Updated*, Wiley Interscience, 1986, Chs 7, 8 and 9
T Lucey, *Management Accounting*, D P Publications, 1983

# 11 Team culture planning: creating the quality organisation

In highly competitive and homogeneous markets competitive moves are quickly copied. In such conditions the skill and commitment of personnel provide the ultimate source of differentiation and competitive advantage. How can the management strategist create a responsive team culture within which collective effort gets the organisation ahead through improving performance incrementally across all organisation areas? This chapter and the next consider a subsystem of the 'complete' planning system which addresses this critical modern day business problem.

Britain's declining industrial performance is well monitored and many UK companies are 'desperately in need of a recovery strategy'(1). At the heart of the problem is the inability to come to terms with new environmental conditions of dynamism, complexity and hostility, and a failure to satisfy customers. Wider political, legal and societal issues increasingly affect today's organisations. Local authority, building society, optician, legal and estate agency professions demonstrate how traditionally 'steady state' enterprises can now be threatened by decartelisation and other information freeing, 'perfect market' legislation.

New business planning and organising approaches are required if success is to be achieved or maintained wherever and whenever turbulent conditions prevail. For many organisations, entrenched in tradition, there is a need for early and substantial reorganisation towards improved environmental responsiveness, incorporating greater consumer satisfaction and more efficient operations.

Some organisations might still operate in conditions where change is slow and the environment easily understood. Others enjoy monopolistic or collusive oligopolistic positions. For all but the most strategically powerful of organisations, however, there is a need to amend strategies as the nature of the environment and the demands of environmental transactions change. Regular environmental changes require correspondingly regular strategic responses. Team culture planning attempts to design and implement an organisation wherein *all* personnel become involved in the day-by-day incremental adjustments necessary to maintain and improve the organisation's competitive (or wealth producing) position. In this chapter we explain how organisational analysis and the implementation of quality improvement campaigns can unleash a massive force for continuous incremental improvement. The chapter covers:

- Corporate planning versus team culture incrementalism
- What is team culture planning?
- Components of organising and the concept of organising 'fit'
- Quality and team culture
- Quality and strategy
- Quality, motivation systems and motivation theory

## Corporate planning versus team culture incrementalism

'The second path ... involves increasing labour value. For managers this path means continuously retraining employees for more complex tasks, automating in ways that cut routine tasks and enhance worker flexibility and creativity, diffusing responsibility for innovation, taking seriously labour's concern for job security and giving workers a stake in improved productivity via profit-linked bonuses and stock plans. For workers this second path means accepting flexible job classifications and work rules, agreeing to wage rates linked to profits and productivity improvements, and generally taking greater responsibility for the soundness and efficiency of the enterprise. The second path also involves a closer and more permanent relationship with other parties that have a stake in the firm – suppliers, dealers, creditors, even the towns and cities in which the firm resides.... Today's and tomorrow's winning hand is becoming increasingly clear – quality and flexibility. Essential to them both are (a) smaller units and (b) highly skilled workers serving as the chief source of incremental improvements in products and services.' (2)

The growing attention paid to *corporate planning* concepts and techniques over recent decades is a reflection of the increasingly difficult nature of creating strategy (see Table 11.1). However, although corporate planning and contingency planning skills remain essential to the modern management strategist, they are no longer viewed as providers of complete answers to today's strategic problems. Table 11.2 highlights the shortcomings of corporate planning.

**Table 11.1 General trends in organisational environments**

| Previous scenario | Present scenario |
| --- | --- |
| Sellers markets | Buyers markets |
| Slow technological development | Rapidly changing technology |
| Standardised products | Customised products |
| Less demanding labour | Aspiring labour |
| Consistent consumer demands | Changing tastes |
| Mass markets | Smaller, differentiated markets |
| Little competition | Much strong and hostile competition |
| Little societal involvement | Much governmental and pressure group interference |

Comparisons between some of the perspectives inherent in corporate planning philosophies and systems and the most typical of today's planning needs reveal many mismatches. For example, whilst corporate planning emphasises 'one-off', major, long-term strategic developments which are systematically designed and implemented, reality dictates that strategic development is more often an *incremental*, evolutionary process. Rather than being a top management or specialist planning function, strategy is actually taking place through the daily adjustments of personnel throughout the organisation as they handle operating situations. A major determinant of organisational success, therefore, is the organisation's ability to make useful incremental adaptations.

**Table 11.2 Strategic shortcomings of systematic corporate planning**

| Corporate planning perspective offers | Environment requires | Example |
|---|---|---|
| Strategic creativity as a top management and specialist planner function | People at all levels to get involved in the strategic process. The environment calls only for *somebody* to make decisions and take action. | Sensing and communicating strategic information e.g. the buying debt clerk who is first to spot a major supplier bank-ruptcy or the sales assistant the first to hear about a competitor price or product change

Contributing operational knowledge and expertise to the decision-making process

Creating strategy through action (e.g. the enterprising sales rep who, against the odds, captures an important new customer) |
| The primacy of shareholder/owner objectives | Attention to the range of stakeholders and continuous stakeholder ranking order changes | Note the potentially adverse effect on customers' (and thence owners') interests from a dissatisfied workforce |
| Clear, precise, objectives to provide a blueprint for future actions | Broader, long-term objectives which allow for flexibility in achievement and quickly made, subjectively decided and expressed responses | Much 'merger mania' type decision-making made 'off the cuff' but related to broader, long-term power, profitability and security objectives |
| Major 'one-off' decisions | Experimentation and modifications to ideas and plans. 'Bet hedging' and contingency planning | Trial and error pilot tests in a sample store before deciding on mass production/distribution of a new product |
| Mid to long-term resource commitment projects | Many short-term developments | Consider, for example, the new product innovation record of the IT industry |
| Clean sheet into the future | Modified approaches moulded in the light of the recipes, values and power structure in and around the organisation | Note the difficulties encountered in the 1980s by Fleet Street strategists over the implementation of preferred strategic developments |

**Table 11.2 continued**

| | | |
|---|---|---|
| Separation of planning from doing and the sequential nature of doing following planning, systematically | Many planning/doing, on the spot decisions/ actions, the involvement of 'doers' in planning and the iterative interaction as plans are tested, checked and reconsidered/modified | On the spot negotiations with customers<br><br>Quality circles<br><br>Remodifications of products based on post launch monitorings |
| Projection into the future via the use of formal, often quantitatively based, computerised planning models | Incremental adaptation often necessitating 'gut feel' subjectivism | The everyday business of the organisation<br><br>Research findings which suggest that many firms do not plan formally<br><br>The requirements for major fashion retailers to anticipate next year's fashion trends |

In *Images of Organisation*, Gareth Morgan draws attention to the theoretical progression which links corporate planning and team culture planning:'The brain thus offers itself as an obvious metaphor for organisation, particularly if our concern is to improve capacities for organisational intelligence. Many managers and organisation theorists have readily grasped this point. But for the most part they have limited their attention to the idea that organisations need a brain or brain-like function – e.g. in the form of corporate planning teams, think tanks or centralised research and decision-making units – that will be able to think for the rest of the organisation and integrate overall organisational activity. ... In contrast, it is far less common to think about organisations, *as if they were brains*, and to see if we can create new forms of organisation that disperse brain-like capacities throughout an enterprise rather than just confine them to special units or parts. This is a challenge for the future.' (3)

The challenge identified by Morgan is also, of course, a challenge for the management strategist (who remains as the *central* brain of the organisation). It is he or she who has the job of creating a brain-like *organisation* – one which senses the need to adapt existing activities to meet changing circumstances and which changes accordingly. In this way the organisation emerges/re-emerges, day by day, with greater strategic pertinence and success potential.

## What is team culture planning?

Whilst corporate planning provides much help in decisions on long-term direction and which markets to serve and/or leave, team culture planning is a form of planning which attempts to provide solutions to more recently perceived planning gaps by creating an organising mode which makes and implements strategy efficiently as *ongoing, natural organisational* activities. Essentially, it attempts to create an organisation wherein the key strategic tasks of *sensing* and *satisfying efficiently* the needs of external stakeholders (particulary customers) becomes an accepted part of everybody's job.

Responsiveness is not to be seen as the sole province of certain upper echelons or specialist staff. Neither is it to be achieved by the implementation of any one particular technique or system. Rather, responsiveness emanates from attention to all the component parts of organising. Organising (or reorganising), then, is the means to responsiveness and team culture.

# Components of organising and the concept of organising 'fit'

Organisation theorists have provided us with useful categorisations of the components of 'organisation' – those components of the total organising mode which require individual attention if a comprehensively successful reorganisation is to be achieved (see, for example, 4 and 5). Planners of organisations should take into account the following 'components' when designing their organising mode.

## Job design

Job design should, in the context of the 'organisation job' (its product/market strategies) allocate various technical and decision-making tasks and duties to fall within the orbit of one person's job and plan the grouping and communicating links between one job and others.

## Structure

The sum total of the individual job designs creates the structure of the organisation – its 'skeleton' or 'basic framework through which the enterprise is administered' (6).

## People

The 'right' people (in terms of present and/or potential skills, attitudes and interpersonal styles) should be working in, and for the organisation.

## Systems

These are the processes and associated techniques which are employed to ensure that people have the necessary skills, motivation, resources and information with which to do their jobs well – and to ensure that people are actually doing their jobs well.

## Technology

Here we refer to the equipment, machinery and processes used by the organisation. In recent times, of course, much emphasis is being placed on the role 'new' information technology has to play in the attainment of organisational success.

## Resources

Fundamentally, the organisation must be financially and otherwise capable of attracting the people and other resources necessary to achieve success. The underlying resource strength of the organisation is often a forgotten factor in discussions which focus on successful people-motivating campaigns.

## Organisation strategy

We have already said that strategy is about earning the organisational living from its transactions with external stakeholders. People inside the organisation maintain their benefits through efficient interactions with customers, suppliers and society's various governments and publics. While many such transactions take place during the course of just one working day, the overriding organisation strategy seeks to achieve those basic organisation 'system' goals identified by Mintzberg (7) as efficiency and control of the environment. Strategy is concerned with the attainment of these basic desired ends. The previously mentioned components of organising are, of course, the means for creating and implementing strategy.

## Culture

The outcomes created by decisions in each of the above component areas and the methods employed to produce these outcomes will be instrumental in the creation of organisational culture – the basic, often unspoken, assumptions of 'the way we do things around here'. For many organisations the components of organising and 'the way we do things around here' will have to change to internalise a deep commitment to responsiveness.

Having provided categorisations of organising components, we now stress the need for organising 'fit'. Thus, the organising mode, in totality, should be congruent with the nature and needs of its environment and the component parts themselves should be in harmony with each other (see Fig. 11.1).

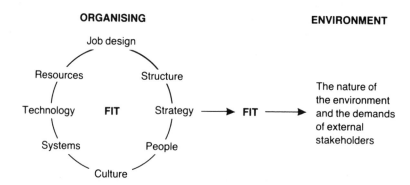

Figure 11.1 Organising 'fit' relationships

## Some examples of 'misfits' within organisations

(a) The introduction of new technology and the failure to prepare the people of the organisation for its efficient use, through prior communication, training or modified rewards.

(b) The appointment of a 'today' manager who has the necessary skills, attitude and management style but who is not provided with financial resources to enable him or her to put these talents to use.

(c) Jobs redesigned around 'teamwork' but with traditional individual bonus sytems maintained.

(d) Customers wanting variety and regular product modifications but technology designed to produce one standard model.

(e) Consumer groups exhibiting growing interest and hostility towards the organisation while organisational information systems pay no particular attention to the monitoring of their activities and demands.

(f) Customers showing increased quality consciousness – reward systems geared to quantity of output.

(g) Environments demanding responsive organisation modes – organisations maintaining previously effective bureaucratic forms.

'Misfits', of course, detract from the level of success which might otherwise have accrued. Anyone who has been in and around organisations will undoubtedly have their own 'misfit' anecdotes.

# Quality and team culture

How should the successful responsive mode be designed and implemented? Management strategists, having been alerted to the new planning needs and problems, can take comfort from the experiences of some proactive, enlightened British organisations which seem to have found the responsiveness solution.

Management literature provides a widening record of case studies which clearly illustrate how many organisations have hinged successful reorganisation on a planned approach to the production of greater quality – in terms of the products or services offered and of the productivity with which such offers are created – and to the establishment of a deep rooted quality ethos. Such organisations are now leading a general movement which focuses upon quality as the desired end of organising. Effective quality improvement programmes are contributing to the financial and general well being of these organisations by increasing, at one and the same time, productivity and product or service appeal. Importantly, their experiences reveal that a planned approach to quality improvement also provides an internal motivating and co-ordinating force.

Quality improvement campaigns are being used to achieve the desired end of organising and at the same time to provide the means for attainment of that end. Through their impact on the components of organising and on external stakeholders, 'quality'-based reorganisations are generating renewed success. Quality seems to provide the common link in the organising 'fit' equation.

# Quality and strategy

What are quality and value for money? There are two perspectives on quality:

(a) an external perspective which is related to the strategic need to satisfy customers (and clearly perceived by marketing personnel);

(b) an internal production-based perspective which arises from the other strategic need to produce goods and services efficiently.

These different perspectives both relate to the systems goals of efficiency and control of the environment but often exist in isolation of each other within the same organisation.

## The external perspective of quality

Initially, we look at the external perspective, concerned as it is, primarily with customer satisfaction. Quality is defined by the European Organisation for Quality Control as 'the totality of features and characteristics of a product or service that bears upon its ability to satisfy a given need'. Table 11.3 identifies the characteristics which make up 'quality'.

**Table 11.3 Characteristics of quality**

| CATEGORY | QUALITY CHARACTERISTICS |
|---|---|
| The product/service itself | * Performance<br>* Safety<br>* Aesthetic appeal<br>* Durability<br>* Reliability<br>* Costs and benefits<br>  arising from use |
| The organisation/customer interaction process | * Packaging<br>* Information<br>* Delivery<br>* Service – at point-of-<br>  sale and afterwards |

'Value for money' is related to quality but goes further to take account of price and customer expectations. Thus, value for money is assessed by the customer ultimately. He or she compares the package of quality characteristics he/she actually receives with the package he or she expected to get in return for the price agreed.

The organising end, therefore, is achieved in part (we still have to consider *productivity* quality) where value for money packages advertised attract a viable customer response and where the package is in accord with the customer's expectations.

## Think and discuss

Do some field research. Imagine you need to open a current account at a bank. Check out two or three branches of major banks and/or building societies.

(a) Identify features of each outlet's customer interaction strategy (including the product/service itself).

(b) Compare features between outlets.

(c) Which outlet would you prefer to open your account with and why?

## Some quality/value for money success stories

While British industrial performance stands accused, at national level, of quality failure costing the economy billions annually (see, for example, 8 and 9), at the micro level massive strategic benefits are flowing to quality-based organisers. US-based organisations such as IBM, Procter and Gamble, Revlon, and McDonalds have built their 'excellence' on organisational features such as flexibility, environmental responsiveness, closeness to customers and the provision of unparalleled quality, service and reliability – 'things that work and last' (10). In Britain, too, household names such as Sainsbury, Tesco and Timpson build success on similar attributes (see, for example, 11). Some brief illustrations might indicate how British organisations are using quality to develop successfully.

For example, some are using quality as a means to successful market penetration and/or diversification. For much of British industry, no longer able to compete on price, one recovery strategy might be via market segmentation and development into those higher quality (and higher value-added), customised specification segments which remain unattractive to the more advantageously cost structured but less flexible competition. An 'up market'/quality approach is being exhorted as an appropriate national strategy (12). For specific organisations, quality and the market changes it has facilitated have been a life saver.

## Case examples: new markets via quality

Greendale Electronics Limited, formerly struggling in low technology production, is now highly profitable in the higher value-added, high technology, electronic components manufacturing segment. Success has come from a new organisational attention to quality which extends to the point of refusing to make products to 'inferior customer specification'.

Managing Director Colin Wemyss argues that 'In the end, there is only one answer and that is quality. That is where we defeat them' – an assertion which is difficult to refute when backed by net asset growth from £23,000 to £538,000 and share price up from 5p to £1.65 over a five-year period.

A similar theme runs through the success story of BSC Cumbria Engineering where, after initial trauma and failure, improved quality assurance schemes have enabled a transition away from its steel fabrications base (and poor prospects) into commercial success in nuclear equipment manufacture.

Nearer to home, on the high street, further examples are available. Successful market segmentation provided a new lease of life for the long established menswear manufacturer/retailer, J Hepworth and Company Limited. An attractive image, backed by compatible product and service, captured, in the 1980s, the more affluent non-teenage women and men prepared to pay premium prices, to Next (a Hepworth 'offspring').

## Beating existing competition

The above examples illustrate the usefulness of improved quality to strategic redirection aspirations. In price competitive markets where existing players seek more incremental strategic changes to consolidate and develop their present market positions, new emphasis on quality can facilitate successful competitive differentiation. Organisations are paying more attention to improving the quality of their products and of accompanying services.

## Case example: service differentiation via quality

Connect's 1986 'We'll pay you' promotion campaign followed a nationwide poll which showed that 90 per cent of people felt that good delivery and aftersales service were vital factors in the making of an electrical goods purchase. Point-of-sale publicity material offered customers compensatory payments of £10 on any occasion when the organisation fails to:

(a)  deliver when it says it will;

(b)  keep its promise to make a repair call the next day;

(c)  keep a service appointment;

(d)  complete workshop repairs on time, or to keep the customer informed of any delay.

The impetus for this promotional tactic (and the underlying greater customer awareness and attention to quality) is 'competition'. In an industry where goods are often homogeneous and customers shop around, firms watch what is happening in the market place, follow the moves of competitors and, if possible, try to be the first with original marketing approaches. Quality of service is essential to competing effectively.

Practical applications of the quality concept also lie at the heart of mass market leaders' continued success. Famous name examples include Marks & Spencer and Thomson Holidays. Major mass market motor vehicle manufacturers like Ford and General Motors are also concentrating resources on the attainment of higher product quality and an improved quality image. Design, engineering and performance aspects are being pushed to the fore of marketing promotion. Developments in new technology too are helping the giants of industry to find the flexibility to offer smaller order contracts, more varied product lines and shorter lead times.

## Regaining lost ground

For many organisations the strategic challenge has not been one of taking the organisation into quality but more one of getting it back to quality.

### Case example: Jaguar's return to quality

In 1980 Jaguar Cars had luxury, style and performance but poor 'quality'. Its reputation for unreliability and poor delivery was 'killing a car that all the world wanted to love' (DoT, 1982). Incumbent Chairman, John Egan, reaffirmed the market position of the car: 'There is no middle ground for Jaguar. We are either among the best in the world – or we just can't exist.'

Dedication to quality (and initial massive investment) has produced a product now compatible with its market positioning and has stimulated car sales in excess of 40,000 per year (compared to 14,000 in 1980). A return to the old standard of reliability is acclaimed as the major regenerator of profitability and self-investment capability.

## Quality and strategy – the internal perspective

The external perspective of quality emphasises its usefulness as a means of seeking out and satisfying customers. Satisfying chosen markets, however, is only part of the strategic task; satisfaction has to be achieved efficiently. This is where the internal perspective of quality comes into its own, concerned as it is with quality of productivity.

In Chapter 10 we described productivity as a comparative ratio of benefits to costs – the greater the ratio the higher the quality of productivity. It is in this area of quality improvement where research has uncovered even more immediately impressive success statistics.

## Some quality/productivity success stories

Contrary to the traditional perception of quality control as an overall cost generator, it is apparent that significant net savings can in fact flow from concerted efforts to control quality. Look at the following examples:

(a) At Greendale Electronic £250,000 per year is reported to have been saved through reducing the level of rejects.

(b) BSC Cumbria Engineering reports savings of £40,000 per year following the introduction of a quality improvement programme.

(c) Jaguar cars recorded a decrease in warranty claims of 40 per cent in the four years from 1980.

In service industries, too, productivity benefits from better quality self-regulation are also apparent. Table 11.4 illustrates the results obtained by the Watney Mann subsidiary, Ushers Limited, which introduced improved quality control procedures in reaction to loss of trade which had been partly attributed to poor delivery service.

Other reports indicate that substantial 'bottom line' savings are generally available.

**Table 11.4  Ushers Ltd: How productivity improved with service (source: J. Bailey, 'How to motivate service',** *Management Today,* **Oct 1983)**

| Improvement areas | Year 1 | Year 2 | Year 3 |
|---|---|---|---|
| Own vehicle days | 5616 | 4847 | 4552 |
| Hired vehicle days | 298 | Nil | Nil |
| Number of calls | 49365 | 47945 | 49136 |
| Man days | 14521 | 11586 | 11252 |
| Barrels per vehicle day | 27.25 | 32.7 | 33.16 |
| Barrels per man day | 11.10 | 13.71 | 13.85 |
| Cost per barrel (% increase) | 10.0 | 4.63 | 3.02 |
| Sickness and absence (%) | 13.85 | 4.16 | 2.76 |

## Case examples: quality savings

(a) A precursor quality improvement programme instituted by ITT redeemed 'lost costs' equivalent to 5 per cent of sales income and prompted the claim in 1972 by chief executive, Harold Geneen, that 'because of our quality improvement programmes profits are £353 million higher this year than they would otherwise have been' (ITT Annual Report, 1972).

(b)  MacGregor (13) estimates that most companies can, by careful control of quality costs, increase profits by a factor of around two 'in accord with the experience of a number of well known companies'.

(c)  Mortiboys (14) claims that organisations should generally be able to achieve net savings of between 5 and 10 per cent of turnover.

(d)  The Department of Trade's experience of quality improvement programmes in the foundry and metal processing and motor vehicle industries suggests that net savings of 10 per cent and 3 per cent respectively (based on company turnover) should apply generally within these industries (12). Such individual savings, aggregated to the national level, would provide an enormous release of additional wealth and benefits. The Department of Trade (8) has estimated the potential savings to be £3 billion annually, while McRobb (15) put the figure at around £5 billion per year.

Importantly, preventative quality control, because of its propensity to reduce costs associated with quality appraisal and quality failure, is seen as the key to release the massive savings available. 'Building in quality' and 'getting it right first time' are 'in' slogans for today's quality improvers.

## Planning strategy through quality

Both perspectives of quality (internal and external) are usually to be found in any organisation. The team culture planner attempts, through a quality improvement campaign, to heighten the enterprise's concern for quality and to harness the twin success forces of customer satisfaction and improved productivity. In this way he extracts for the organisation the 'catch all' benefits illustrated in Fig. 11.2. Ideally, the planner attempts to achieve a situation where not only does a marketing/production dialogue take place easily and naturally but where *everybody* sees their job as encompassing both functions – responsibility for customer care and for the productivity effort – regardless of their functional or hierarchical position.

## Quality, motivation systems and motivation theory

### Motivation, needs and quality

Quality improvement campaigns hold high the principles of customer satisfaction and efficient productivity. Attaining these is the organisation's key task. As the people of the organisation embrace these principles personally, then sensing needs and changing accordingly become key tasks at the individual level too. In the quality conscious organisation people do not resist change. Rather they seek it as the necessary prerequisite to their meeting new customer situations and becoming more productive. When quality improvement becomes part of routine, continuous sensing of the environment and adaptation to it become an integral part of the way the organisation works. But why should the people of the organisation take to the quality philosophy? Why should it be that, according to Doran of IBM, 'The search for improved quality knows no boundaries ... it moves progressively into new operational efficiency and strategic effectiveness areas. At its most powerful it is a management stimulated release of commitment and creativity which generates energy and results that run far beyond mere conformance.' (16)

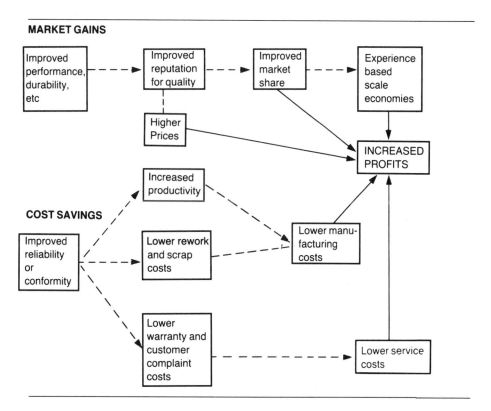

**Figure 11.2 The gains from improved service (source: Garvin, 'What does** *product quality really mean?'*, *Sloan Management Review*, **Fall, 1984)**

What is it that makes quality improvement campaigns such an important means of achieving reorganisation and enduring success? From the body of organisation theory, motivation theory offers many insights into questions such as 'Why do we join organisations in the first place?' and 'What determines the extent of commitment we show towards the successful performance of our jobs?' The 'today' management strategist knows that a well designed quality improvement campaign is a Pandora's box of 'catch all' motivational stimulants. Open it to the organisation and it will inevitably bring about the desired movement. We now examine why this is so.

Schein (17) has given us a classification of different perspectives as to what motivates employees. His classification traces the development of motivation needs theory as follows:

(a) *Rational-economic man.* This view sees man as a rational animal motivated mainly by basic needs and monetary rewards. The rational-economic man shows little propensity towards altruistic or intellectual self-development needs. Pay increases to match productivity increases are thus an appropriate way for practising managers to motivate subordinates.

(b) *Social man.* This view sees people predominantly motivated by social needs. Relationships at work, group interactions, management style, co-operation and teamwork are the important motivational issues according to the social man proponents. Team spirit and decision-making participation are crucial organising features.

(c) *Self-actualising man.* The self-actualiser is a seeker of self fulfilment who needs challenge, responsibility and a sense of pride in his or her work. Looked at from the self-actualising perspective, the subordinate has to be treated as a mature adult.

(d) *Complex man.* This view accedes to the reality of man as a complex animal whose needs are many and varied. Further, the relative importance of these needs change as the individual's situation changes. Today's 'contingency' theorists apply an 'it depends' approach to understanding the motivational needs of human beings.

## Quality improvement programmes and motivation

So how does the quality improvement campaign relate to the wide variety of need perspectives? Quite simply, it covers them all. The quality improvement campaign is the contingency theorist's dream and the team culture reorganiser's great ally. It avoids the need for lengthy motivation analysis and debate over which selection of needs to satisfy. The comprehensive quality campaign provides all things, motivationally speaking, to all people. We now explore this 'catch all' proposition from the perspectives of the rational-economic, social and self-actualisation models of man.

### The rational-economic appeal of quality
Quality improvement campaigns are particularly relevant for the rational economic man because:

(a) They promote greater awareness of the organisational and personal dangers of competitive failure. As an example, the quality improvement thrust at Lucas revolves around a series of competitive action plans and is characterised by a plethora of meetings, video presentations, in-house journal reports and other devices intended to keep personnel aware of organisational performance and external developments. Staff are encouraged, personally, to get involved in sensing and reporting activities. One result of this orientation is a clearer link between organisation performance, individual performance, security of employment, a regular pay packet – and the basic quality of personal life.

(b) They often link pay to performance. Many organisations appreciate that bonus payments linked to productivity increases can produce extra effort. Successful reorganisers often (though not necessarily always) link pay to productivity.

### Social man and quality
A range of social motivation forces are at work within the effective quality improvement campaign. For example:

(a) Task forces, quality circles, action groups and company slogans abound within the quality drive and work towards the achievement of team spirit. The culmination of the quality improvement effort occurs when the organisation acts as one team, striving towards one objective (the efficient satisfaction of customers) – to beat the one common enemy (the competition).

(b) The quality improver strives for an environment of healthy competition. Team spirit and camaraderie can lead to complacency. On the other hand, an over-competitive environment can produce damaging levels of conflict and non-cooperation. Because quality improvements can usually be made tangible they can be displayed to facilitate inter-department comparisons and the subsequent search for emulation or betterment. Visibility, 'the first committing aspect of behaviour' (18) is a key feature of performance control and motivation systems within the quality improvement programme. (However, the overriding tenor of the campaign should emphasise the overall team nature of the combined effort.)

(c) Many campaign emphasise the importance of fair treatment and status. People do not like to feel 'second class'. Conversely, we do like to feel valued by our colleagues. Quality campaigns often build up the status of operative personnel through enriching jobs to include more responsibility and planning involvement and by acknowledging the contribution of individual effort. Further, proactive organisations 'chisel away' at status differentials through more supportive, participative management styles and the removal of any 'them and us' organisation characteristics.

## Case examples: quality through – and for – everybody

(a) At Pedigree Petfoods everyone is an 'associate', clocks on and gets a weekly pay packet or cheque.

(b) Hindle Cockburn have adopted self-certification absence schemes (and have seen absence levels drop as a result).

(c) Cynics might argue that such moves are merely 'copy cat' cosmetics, but the evidence suggests that these more democratic 'touches' can work. David Jenkins, General Secretary of the Wales TUC, offers a positive perspective on the status differential reductionist movement: 'At Japanese and other good companies around here, everyone knows that the MD is paid more, but at least his status is not rubbed in.'

## Self-actualisation and quality

Aldous Huxley has observed that 'The secret of happiness and virtue is liking what you've got to do.' Much of the employee zeal exhibited in successful quality campaigns is due to increases in job satisfaction – enrichments of 'the job itself'(19). This is being achieved by including, or increasing, responsibility in jobs for:

(a) *Planning customer satisfaction and productivity system changes.* Task forces, quality circles, suggestion schemes, and Scanlon-plan type systems draw a widening spectrum of ordinary workers into the quality planning effort.

(b) *Actually ensuring customer satisfaction.* Hertzberg advocates the introduction of specific customer responsibility as a means of enhancing employee performance. Certainly, the quality improvement case studies support his advice and illustrate that, given encouragement, people actually prefer to produce results of which customers approve. For example, Watney Mann has stimulated improved performance through the allocation of specific customer responsibility to newly created teams of draymen and receptionists. As a further example, factory inspections by VIPs are handled by the workforce at ICL rather than by the management.

(c) *Sorting out problems.* Baliga and Jaeger (20) remind us how the Japanese production line sometimes stops completely as workers congregate around a problem – to help solve it and to use the occasion as a learning experience. In a complete reversal of their previously highly centralised approach, Lucas now work on the dictum that 'the centre's role is to help, not dictate' and that of 'whoever owns the problem manages the solution'. At shop floor level this means traceability and accountability for faulty or otherwise inadequate work.

(d) *Taking part in strategic planning.* The new roles created for ordinary personnel ensure that strategy is part of everybody's business. Thus strategy is continually being reshaped by the collective force of the many positive operational developments – as per the responsiveness planner's objective. Further, contributions are taken from all over the organisation towards those less incrementally implemented corporate planning type developments.

## Motivation, targets and quality

Writers such as McClelland (21) and Locke (22) suggest that there is a motivating force inherent in the setting of performance targets. Certainly, we have seen some effective interweaving of management by objectives systems and quality improvement programmes which have also suggested that most of us may be latent high achievers. People enjoy beating targets. One young manager summed up the motivational potential of target setting as he pointed towards the performance chart on his office wall and told us that 'The bonus is useful, of course, but this is the real "turn on". Charting ourselves against targets each week is a great motivator in itself.'

Another manager commented, 'The whole mood of the branch depends upon how Monday's computer print outs of the previous week's figures compare with the targets. If they are up, so are we. If they're down we have to shake ourselves out of despondency by discussing why they are down and how we're going to get back on schedule.'

Still another manager said 'For the first time we have information on what the organisation is doing, what we're supposed to be achieving and how well we're measuring up. I don't get any extra money for achieving targets but I do get a buzz out of the measurement process and I am tuned in to doing better.'

Management by objectives (MBO) systems seek to achieve organisation success through:

(a)  Providing motivation in the form of realistic performance objectives;

(b)  providing additional motivation through:

- relating pay and security to the attainment of targets;
- setting targets through a process of participation;
- allowing personnel to help plan work objectives and to have greater discretion in deciding how to perform work;

- furnishing swift and pertinent feedback on results;
- concentrating on key performance areas;
- emphasising results rather than actions or 'impressions'.

Effective MBO systems, then, share the same motivational features as those we have already outlined as being fundamental to effective quality improvement campaigns. Both proceed on rational, economic, social and self-actualising fronts. Put together, therefore, organisations can unleash their combined motivational power. The concept of quality also links neatly with the key performance area concept of MBO. Ensuring quality of customer satisfaction and quality of productivity are the two key tasks of the organisation as a whole and of each individual therein.

The quality concept, therefore, focuses on those areas of each job which concretely contribute to overall success. Because quality improvements are tangible (complaints levels and sales receipts can be measured, for example, as can reject and production levels) they can be displayed and monitored. Rapid feedback of results can then be applied to targets to complete the motivation cycle. When the speed and accuracy of new information technology is also interwoven with the MBO/quality improvement campaign 'mix' we have the means, 30 years after Peter Drucker's introductory text on the subject, to help MBO finally to come of age.

## For further study

1   Refer to the case study 'High Street Electrical plc' in the accompanying case study volume. Identify how top management is providing needs and process motivators to develop commitment in HSE staff.
2   Refer to the case study 'M & M Supplies' in the companion book. Describe how Pedigree, Jaguar and Greendale have designed and implemented their components of organising to improve responsiveness. Do their organising characteristics have common features? How have Jaguar's and Greendale's components of organising changed to ensure systems goals attainment?

## References

1   D Hall, 'How to get out of a Crisis', *Management Today*, February 1985
2   T J Peters, *Thriving on Chaos*, Macmillan, 1988, p 22
3   G Morgan, *Images of Organisation*, Sage, 1986, p 79
4   J Child, *Organisation: A Guide to Problems and Practice*, 2nd edn, Harper & Row, 1984, Ch 8
5   J R Galbraith and D A Nathanson, *Strategy Implementation: The Role of Structure and Process*, New York, West, 1978
6   A H Chandler, *Strategy and Structure*, MIT Press, 1962
7   H Mintzberg, *Power in and Around Organisations*, New York, Prentice-Hall International, 1984, Ch 16
8   Department of Trade, *A National Strategy for Quality*, DoT, 1978
9   J Holmes, 'How Quality Control made a Comeback', *Management Today*, November 1983
10  T J Peters and R H Waterman Jr, *In Search of Excellence*, New York, Harper & Row, 1982
11  C Adamson, *Consumers in Business*, London, National Consumers Council, 1982
12  A Mortiboys in *National Quality Campaign*, London, DoT, 1982
13  A MacGregor, 'Making Profit from Quality', *Quality Today*, June 1983
14  A Mortiboys in *National Quality Campaign*, London, DoT, 1982
15  R McRobb, 'Industry's Lost Costs', *Management Today*, May 1984

16  P Doran, 'How to Achieve Performance', *Management Today*, April 1986
17  E H Schein, *Organisational Psychology*, New York, Prentice-Hall International, 1965, pp 207–22
18  G R Salancik, 'Commitment is too Easy', in M L Tushman and W L Moore (eds), *Readings in the Management of Innovation*, Pitman, 1982
19  F Hertzberg, *Work and the Nature of Man*, New York, World Publishing, 1966
20  B R Baliga and A M Jaeger, 'Control Systems and Strategic Adaptation – Lessons from the Japanese Experience', *Strategic Management Journal*, 6, 1985, pp 115–34
21  D C McClelland, *The Achieving Society*, New York, Van Nostrand, 1961
22  E A Locke, 'Towards a Theory of Task Motivation and Incentives', *Organisational Behaviour and Human Performance*, 3, 1968, pp 157–89

## Recommended reading

R V Emerson, 'Corporate Planning – A Need to Examine Corporate Style', *Long Range Planning*, 18 (6), 1985, pp 29–33

M A Carpenter, 'Planning vs Strategy – Which Will Win?', *Long Range Planning*, 19 (6), 1986, pp 50–3

D A Garvin, 'What does 'Product Quality' really Mean?', *Sloan Management Review*, Fall 1984

P Doran, 'How to Achieve Performance', *Management Today*, April 1986

T J Peters, *Thriving on Chaos*, Macmillan, 1988

G Morgan, *Images of Organisation*, Sage, 1986, Chs 3 and 4

# 12 Team culture planning: creating a responsive team culture

Reorganising to a responsive team culture will inevitably require changes to the personnel working in the organisation. This process, of course, will already have been started by the introduction of a quality improvement campaign of the type discussed in Chapter 11. In this chapter we introduce the nature of personnel changes which successful reorganisers of the past decade have made to their workforces. The aim is to identify any principles of best practice in this area. We will see that significant personnel changes have taken place at all levels of the 'successful reorganiser' in its attempts to survive and/or grow. Our discussion examines the following topics:

- Chief executives, leadership and leadership theory
- Towards a 'today leader' typology
- Planning the workforce and its jobs
- Creating a responsive team culture

## Chief executives, leadership and leadership theory

The drive towards a newly responsive organising mode has, of course, to start somewhere. Schein (1) identifies a key leadership task as that of providing guidance when habitual ways of doing things no longer work or when a dramatic change in the environment requires new responses.

Research confirms the importance of the 'top man' to successful reorganisation. The one common and, in our view, most important thread running through successful reorganisations is the commitment to success and the leadership capability demonstrated by the top people of the organisation. Their passion for the installation of new values (invariably incorporating the quality ethos) provides the cornerstone upon which change is effected and ongoing success generated. Hogg of Courtaulds sums up the key culture creator/carrier function of the today leader: 'You create a climate which affects the structure, the way the company is organised, which in turn affects the way it does business.' (2)

### The top executive obsolescence cycle

According to Hall (3) 'There is no handy kitbag of techniques for transforming a company …. But one clear determinant of success is an acceptance of the need for change.'

All too often inertia (4) and introversion (5) mean that businesses do not sense environmental change and/or are unwilling to make the necessary adaptations. A major cause of this problem is an incumbent 'obsolete' chief executive who has, over time, built up a power base and entrenched his or her position. Some organisations seem capable of developing those potentially effective leaders who often exist – but who are equally often neglected and ignored – within the existing corporate framework. Some leaders show sufficient perception to realise the need for an infusion of new executive 'blood' (for example, Zilkha's alignment of Mothercare with Conran and Habitat and the introduction of Rose Perot into Roger Smith's General Motors). Occasionally, top executives seem capable of changing their own personal approaches to stimulate a new organisational response.

However, existing chief executives would, generally, be well advised to check their own situations. The available catalogue of reorganisation case studies shows a succession of new leaders – 'today managers' – replacing 'out-of-date' models. In terms of security of tenure, there has never been so pressing a time for personnel change at chief executive level and the encouragement of 'intrapreneurship'. The obsolescence cycle of top executives is summarised below.

## Stage 1
A leader is appointed who is best able to cope with the present organisational critical problems and uncertainties. For example:

(a) production problems produce production-orientated leaders;

(b) bureaucrats get top jobs when the greatest problems concern efficient administration;

(c) politicians are appointed where political contacts and skill are crucial.

## Stage 2
The leader widens and entrenches his or her power base in two ways. First by spreading power beyond its initial bases – for example, by creating allies in the boardroom, in external stakeholder groups and in departments and sub-groups of the organisation; second, by institutionalising his or her power. This is achieved in a variety of ways:

(a) by thinking, acting and publicising himself or herself as critical to organisation success even where this is no longer the case. New, critical contingencies and appropriate responses are not readily apparent to organisations whose leaders desire to maintain the status quo;

(b) by introducing new rules and procedures (for example, redirecting important information flows through the chief executive's office);

(c) by creating and/or giving precedence to functional activities associated closely with the chief executive and staffed by loyal subordinates;

(d) by taking steps to reduce the power and status of competing officials – often older staff in traditionally important roles;

(e) by using position power rewards and punishments to encourage acquiescence and loyalty and to discourage dissension and opposition.

## Stage 3
The chief executive's power base is accepted as part of the natural order of things.

## Stage 4

The critical contingencies change (in recent times, generally, through the appearance of more volatile and hostile environments and the associated difficulty in planning successful futures). The chief executive becomes obsolete because:

(a) the chief executive and the organisation do not keep abreast of changes in the environment. Often managers do not appreciate that things have changed;

(b) the chief executive exhibits complacency and satisfaction with his or her own approach, skills and attitudes and the existing organisation recipes for success;

(c) the chief executive, through long periods in successful conditions develops a high tolerance for mediocrity and the carrying of 'dead wood'. Cyert and March (6) describe how organisational 'slack' builds up during good times. Managers accustomed to such conditions often find getting back to efficiency difficult.

A widening strategic leadership gap develops and organisational performance, correspondingly, suffers increasingly.

## Stage 5

A shock event/crisis occurs (for example, a sudden liquidity crisis, a takeover bid, a major legal action, or adverse publicity over a social issue). The crisis is needed to destroy the existing power base and restart the top executive obsolescence cycle.

# Towards a 'today leader' typology

Present chief executives wishing to groom or appoint their successors (or board members charged with the task) might appreciate some help towards clarifying what goes into the make-up of a successful 'today leader'. In fact, the determination of what makes successful leadership has been something of a quest for organisation theory and its researchers. We propose now to use some previous theoretical contributions in this area to build a general model of the effective modern chief executive.

## Traits

Early attempts to understand leadership effectiveness concentrated on the attributes and characteristics of the leader. Not surprisingly, these studies produce a wide array of traits and abilities associated with effective leaders and, at best, provide only generally prescriptive indications of what to look for in the personal make-up of a would-be chief executive.

Stogdill (see Table 12.1) has reported the results of a review of 163 trait studies that were conducted between 1949 and 1974. Table 12.1 summarises the personality traits, abilities and social skills found most frequently to be characteristic of effective and successful leaders. Not surprisingly, perhaps, our studies of successful modern leaders reveal similar profiles.

We would also stress, however, the physical health and strength requirements of current top leadership positions. Physical fitness is a vital prerequisite to the intense physical and emotional demands which go with the job of 'first initiator' and 'first integrator'.

**Table 12.1 Personality traits, abilities and social skills associated with effective leaders (source: Reprinted with permission of the Free Press, A Division of Macmillan, Inc. from _Handbook of Leadership_, by Ralph M. Stodgill. Copyright ©1974 by The Free Press.)**

| Personality traits | Abilities | Social skills |
| --- | --- | --- |
| Adaptability | Intelligence | Ability to enlist co-operation |
| Adjustment (normality) | Judgement and decisiveness | Administrative ability |
| Aggresiveness and Assertiveness | Knowledge | Co-operativeness |
| Dominance | Fluency | Popularity and prestige |
| Emotional balance and control | Academically able* | Sociability |
| Independence (non-conformity) | | Social conformity |
| Originality and Creativity | | Tact and diplomacy |
| Personal integrity (ethical conduct) | | |
| Self-confidence | | |

*Kiernan and Company research (1984) indicates that 66 per cent of top managers hold a degree or HNC or HND. This compares with 44 per cent ten years earlier.

Above all, perhaps, the culture creator has to actually 'be there' – at least during the early stages of his or her change campaign – to lead by example, to select his or her core team of cultural aides and to provide the centrifugal force for effective redirection. Illness and illness-enforced absence has no place in the culture creator's itinerary.

## Interpersonal style

Much leadership theory is concerned with the effect of leadership style on the performance of subordinates. Theoretical interpersonal continuums tend to show concern for subordinates at one extreme and preoccupation with the task to be performed at the other. Debate over whether managers are capable of adopting different styles to accommodate different situations has endured in this area of theory (See Table 12.2).

Our own research shows clearly that today's effective leaders are capable of alternating styles. Whether one particular style remains fundamental (i.e. the manager always has a 'home base' style) is still open to discussion, but in practice successful reorganisers demonstrate task- _and_ people-centred approaches.

**Table 12.2 Leadership interpersonal style continuums (7)**

| Source | Style orientation continuums | | |
|---|---|---|---|
| Douglas McGregor | Theory X | Theory Y | |
| The Iowa Studies | Authoritarian | Democratic | Laissez-faire |
| The Ohio Studies | Initiating Structure | Consideration | |
| Blake & Moulton | Task centred | People centred | |
| F E Fiedler | Low least preferred co-worker scorer | High least preferred co-worker scorer | |
| Description of typical leader behaviour | Directive, critical, feels subordinates need to be coerced, carrot and stick approach, concern with planning, goal setting, meeting schedules and production | Supportive, fosters participation, delegates authority friendly, creates environment for mature responses | No policy. Allows total freedom in planning, doing and evaluating work |
| Comments on efffectiveness of each approach | Best for attaining high quantity | Most satisfying for subordinate, creates high creativity and quality, produces lower labour turnover, workers more likely to continue in absence of leader | Lowest effectiveness on all counts |

The desire to achieve 'core' objectives (including quality and its associated states of consumer satisfaction and efficiency of operations) produces forcefully directive styles. 'Today' chief executives continually extol the need for subordinates to adhere to these fundamental concepts and they will take a hard line on these issues if necessary. Here are some examples.

(a)  Greendale Electronics operates a quality management system to BS.5750 and 'on these standards and their application, Colin Wemyss is quite inflexible'.

(b)  The road to Jaguar's recovery has been built in part on new methods of quality control, tighter discipline and a 30 per cent reduction in workforce levels.

(c)  At Pedigree Petfoods success is based on 'quality assurance as a way of life – the control of every ingredient, every process, every machine, systematically'.

However, the successful acceptance and application of quality concepts depends, ultimately, on the internalisation by subordinates of these key values. Paradoxically, the state of internalisation owes much to favourable reactions to open, communicative and (according to one chief executive we know) 'a more Christian approach to working with people'. Open door policies, informal methods of contact, requests for help on organisational problems and the treatment of subordinates as mature equals are hallmarks of the 'people-centred half' of the modern management strategist.

At the same time, again, our team culture reorganiser has to be prepared to use a range of punishments and to be psychologically strong enough to survive battles with 'old hands' resentful of the new regime and its innovatory approaches. Often, also, he or she has to be up to the task of slimming down the workforce.

## The today leader and the issue of centralisation

The modern top man's interpersonal style is reflected in the structure of his organisation. Rather than achieving one or the other of those sets of advantages which flow to centralised and decentralised organisation structures respectively, the planned approach to responsiveness obtains the advantages of both.

Peters and Waterman (8) have noted the pertinence of 'loose-tight' organisational properties to successful organisation performance: 'The excellent companies are both centralised and decentralised. For the most part they have pushed autonomy down to the product development team. On the other hand they are fanatic centralists around the few core values they hold dear.' In the responsive organisation decentralisation is practised within these core cultural principle constraints. Performance measurements as fundamental barometers of success and as control mechanisms are not forgotten either.

The new today leaders, as usual, go for all they can get – this time in the form of structural benefits. One perspective, or approach to organising structure, is (as in so many other issues) for them inadequate.

### Case examples: delegating autonomy – and accountability

(a) At BTR where Sir Owen Green notes 'above a certain business size something seems to go wrong', the top level executive body behaves 'very like a small hungry firm with eyes fixed firmly on the prime purpose of business – to increase the wealth of shareholders at a rate faster than inflation'. Operating companies are expected to act as if they are 'stand alone' companies to achieve allocated targets in their own chosen way.

(b) Gill at Lucas says, 'There's a strong correlation between decentralisation and success.' Each Lucas business unit is given responsibility for working out its own 'competitive action plan'. Around 40 units have been disposed of, however, for 'not coming up to scratch'.

(c) At Courtaulds decentralisation has brought a 'light-footed approach to the market' from individual, more entrepreneurial and accountable, subsidiary companies.

## Strategic style

Ackoff (9), Miles and Snow (10) and Clarke and Pratt (11) provide us with managerial typologies of strategic planning/adaptation styles (see Table 12.3). Examination of the 'today' chief executive against a backcloth of these typologies reveals a strategic planning superman – a modern leader who appreciates that current environmental pressures necessitate, more than ever, a 'bag of tools' approach.

**Table 12.3  Top leader strategic style typologies**

| Source | | | | Typology |
|---|---|---|---|---|
| R L Ackoff (1970) | *Satisficer* | *Optimiser* | *Adaptiviser* | |
| – Planning types | Seeks to do well enough but not as well as possible. Unsystematic adaptation via strategic choices from a limited range of present operations assoc- iated strategies. Pre-occupation with finance and 'hard' extrapol- ations. Politically sensitive – keen not to 'rock the boat'. Not strong on control. | Seeks to do as well as possible. Uses mathematical models and techniques. Sets objectives in quantitative terms. Emphasises financial resources. More useful in materials/equip- ment planning rather than people planning. Monitors/controls performance Greater applic- ability in operational areas. | Emphasises *part- icipation in* planning process more than its results. Seeks to eliminate need for 'retros- pective planning' (planning to rectify previous planning mistakes). Emphasis on 'pros- pective planning' (efficient contin- gency and respon- siveness planning to cater for uncertainty and to ensure attainment of desired future outcomes). | |
| Miles and Snow (1978) | *Defenders* | *Prospectors* | *Analysers* | *Reactors* |
| –Strategic Adaptation types | Seek primarily to improve efficiency. High expertise in limited area of operation but no search for opportunities outside this area. | Continual search for market opps. Experiments with potential responses to emerging environmental trends. Creators of change and uncertainty but strong concern for innovation makes them less than efficient. | Operate routinely and efficiently where they can. Copy better ideas of competitors swiftly. | Perceive change but unable to respond effectively. Lack a consistent strategy/ structure relationship so make adjustments only when forced. |

**Table 12.3 continued**

| Clarke & Pratt (1985) | Champion | Tank Commander | Housekeeper | Lemon Squeezer |
|---|---|---|---|---|
| – Entrepreneurial/ Administrative types | Entrepreneur who fights for and defends 'seedling' businesses. Provides a wide range of management skills, himself. Wins orders from customers, cash from financiers | Systematic and adept at acquiring and using resources. Needs good supporting team – particularly finance director. Good at market segmentation and promotion. | Sets businesses and systems in order Manages precisely and economically. Encourages new developments. Skills of careful planning, control over detailed costs sound personnel policies. Looks for steady long-term success. | Tough innovative cost cutter and productivity improver. Reduces manning levels. Divests ailing parts and re-channels funds into more promising areas and aggressive acquisitions. |

The 'today' manager goes for efficiency by optimising as far as possible, particularly in areas of production and general cost efficiency. He or she emphasises financial targets and performance. However, the today manager is also a skilled politician capable of giving, taking and satisficing up to a point (pragmatism is rarely allowed to dilute endeavour towards customer satisfaction and productivity improvement). Above all the today manager is the supreme adaptiviser – the expert at creating team spirit, organisation-wide. He or she is a guru – creating, through participative management style and other motivational methods a 'committed and vital force for change' (12).

Further, the today manager exhibits high levels of entrepreneurial flair combined with skill in the design and implementation of more systematic approaches to business planning. While the strategic superman might make use of more traditional corporate planning and contingency planning concepts and techniques perhaps his or her greatest planning strength lies in the understanding of, and abilities in, team culture planning – rare and secret characteristics still at a premium in a world which often requires organisation-wide sensitivity and swift reactive capability as the foremost means for successful adaptation. Substantial salaries are available to people with this rare and transferable talent.

## The all-round strategist

Some 'today' leaders exhibit the full range of typology characteristics in a comparatively short period of time. One chief executive we know had:

- sold one-third of his organisation's retail outlets;
- sold a significant portion of the organisation's customer accounts;
- opened new 'out of town' superstores;
- developed new markets geographically;

- changed the company's basic product/market strategy;
- introduced new personnel policies leading to a significantly different personnel profile;
- invested heavily in new information technology and the associated control systems;
- attracted the finance (from an illiquid, unprofitable, bargaining position) to perform the above changes – all within the first twelve months of taking office!

Other leaders have been forced to concentrate their attentions on one aspect of their strategic armoury and await the chance to use other sides of their strategic personality.

Hogg, for example, forced to preside over and engineer a retrenchment era which encompassed a 50 per cent staff reduction (from the 100,000 employees 1979 level) reflects on his first two years at Courtaulds as 'an appalling period' and emphasises that while his image had been one of 'destroyer' he was, all the time, thinking as, and waiting for the opportunity to use his talents as a builder – a role he had successfully played with other organisations.

## Functional skills and biases

In functional terms the story remains the same. Here, the role played by our successful leader is one of generalist. The accountancy-orientated top people are, more recently, being replaced by leaders with wider perspectives.

### The all-round functional leader

In functional terms the responsiveness strategist seems to be an expert in all fields. Examples might include:

(a) Lister at ICI Fibres: with planning and general management experience;

(b) Hogg at Courtaulds: Oxford First in English, the analytical training provided by an Harvard MBA programme and extensive professional development;

(c) Davies formerly of Next: who with a wealth of retailing experience involves himself with all aspects of the business from grappling with warehousing to computers;

(d) Conran at Habitat-Mothercare: who may still like to call himself a designer, but whose business and general managerial talent is just as considerable.

Today leaders can look at any one aspect of the business and come up with clear and logical solutions. Our findings on the versatility of these successful managers are confirmed by the Kiernan report: 'The man who rises to the top in 1984 has gained his experience with several different companies in a number of different disciplines (usually more than two disciplines and most commonly including marketing and production).'(13)

## The commitment to quality

Underlying all the varieties of generalist approaches exhibited by the 'today' managers is a common core value. The newer breed of successful top leaders is committed to quality – quality of product/service offer, quality of productivity and quality of work life. They know, too, that 'making things that work and last' (8) lies at the heart of success.

Conran typifies the stance taken by the today leader: 'Our policy simply amounts to a belief that if reasonable and intelligent people are offered products for their home that are well-made, well-designed, work well, are of decent quality and at a price they can afford, they will like and buy them.'

Improved satisfaction of external stakeholders facilitates improved satisfaction of the workforce. Improved satisfaction of the workforce should produce greater effort towards the further improvement of external stakeholder satisfaction. At the heart of the 'today' leader's success is a greater understanding of people. He/she knows broadly – and finds out specifically – what they want – whether 'they' be customers, suppliers, the government or the workers. Attention to the concept of quality enables him/her to set in motion an ever-improving stakeholder satisfaction cycle.

## The leader situation

The leaders we have considered devote much attention to the development of mutual respect, trust and co-operation. Usually subordinates speak of their successful reorganiser chiefs with respect and often with admiration and warmth. Through the use of a range of motivational and control mechanisms the leader attracts amenable 'new blood' to the organisation and moulds existing personnel to new ways of thinking and working. Invariably, successful reorganisation produces, as an end result, supportive and loyal subordinates. Staff who stay initially but find themselves unable to come to terms with the new regime and culture, often leave to find more conducive organisation homes.

Growing accedence to the leader's desire owes much to the improving job satisfactions and prospects which have been made available – rewards which the leader bestows but which are often viewed as having been created through new approaches. Furthermore, the strength of commitment exhibited together with the leader's articulation and interpersonal skills often combine with a growing reputation to produce a charismatically based force towards the acquiescence and respect of subordinates. Charisma and reputation sometimes combine to form organisational and leadership legends.

Ultimately, however, the reorganiser must have sufficient formal position power together with attendant rewards and punishments to make – and force through, when necessary – desired changes. The old management adage of 'authority should accompany responsibility' remains potent, and begins its application at the highest organisational level. If the new culture creator is to succeed he or she must be granted the power necessary to effect changes. Of course, the entire thrust of the reorganisation campaign is comprised of personal and positional influencers and all the components of organising. The successful leader arranges all aspects of organisational life in such a way that the ecology of the organisation acts as a less overt but comprehensive and powerful force for manipulation. In this way the leader ensures the success of an indoctrination process intended to induce organisation-wide internalisation of his new cultural paradigms and eventually to achieve the Utopian state where he or she can predict accurately: 'There are a number of people inside the organisation, any of whom could do my job now because the organisation has a momentum of its own.' (Sir Owen Green of BTR, 1986)

In *A Theory of Leadership Effectiveness*, F E Fiedler (14) researched the relationship between leader type, the 'favourableness' of the work situations and the effectiveness of performance. His model identifies three components of 'situation favourableness'. In descending order of importance these are:

(a) *Leader-member relations.* The harmony, respect, co-operation, etc., that exists between leader and subordinates;

(b) *The task structure.* A highly structured task might be one of well defined duties working in a 'closed box' environment such as much production line work, a low-structured task is one which requires discretion and creativity on the part of the job incumbent, e.g. the R & D inventor;

(c) *Position power.* The power/backing which the leader obtains from the organisation.

Fiedler's work suggests that more autocratic, task-orientated styles are more effective in highly favourable and highly unfavourable situations (people-orientated styles are most suitable for managing the mid-favourableness situations) (see Fig. 12.1).

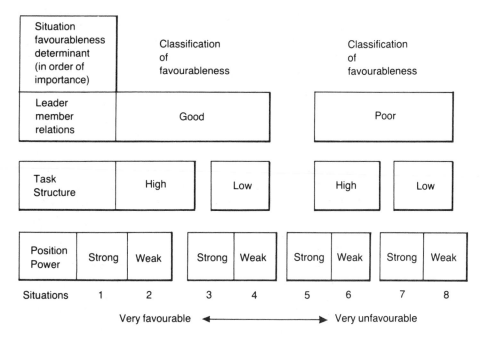

**Figure 12.1 Fiedler's classification of situation favourableness (F E Fiedler, *A Theory of Leadership Effectiveness*, McGraw Hill, 1967)**

## Think and discuss

1   Analyse the situation of a leader you know. How might he or she improve the situation?

For further study

Refer to the case study 'High Street Electricals plc' in the accompanying case study book. Analyse and evaluate David Monks' leadership situation. How has he improved the favourableness of his situation?

## Recruiting the 'today' chief executive

For those who might be called on to take the first step towards the creation of a responsive team culture through their involvement in the selection of a today chief executive, we offer a resume of this section in the form of a personnel selection checklist using Rodger's (1952) 'Seven Point Plan' framework (see Table 12.4).

At this point also, however, we would remind readers of the two-sided nature of the employment contract. The today leader should expect to receive full support from the board towards the provision of adequate financial resources in order to exercise and demonstrate his or her management strategy talents.

**Table 12.4 Selection criteria for appointing the 'today leader' (adapted from Rodger, _The Seven Point Plan,_ National Insitute of Psychology, 1952)**

| Personnel specification categories | Desirable personnel characteristics (generalised) |
| --- | --- |
| Physical make-up | Fit and healthy; young(ish) - less than 50 |
| Attainments | Educated and probably, though not necessarily, qualified to degree or HNC/HND level; public school, grammar school background not necessary unless it has bearing on any important social skills and contacts. Past record, professionally, should show success in senior management positions and experience of a range of disciplines and a number of organisations. |
| General intelligence | High |
| Special aptitudes | Keen and understanding of the marketing concept and the importance of quality<br>Effective interpersonal style<br>Adept at using strategy-making techniques<br>Logical and creative thinker<br>Good at coping with stressful conditions<br>Eloquent conversationalist |
| Interests | Social interests which incorporate mixing in the 'right circles'<br>Physically active |
| Disposition | Capable of influencing others<br>Steady, dependable and self-reliant<br>Flexible and open-minded<br>Ambitious and passionate for success |
| Circumstances | Financial and emotional stability<br>Backing of family |

# Planning the workforce and its jobs

Jobs, people and power structures tend, in unresponsive enterprises, to reflect older, out-of-date 'critical problems'(15). The new leader has to change this propensity to introversion, inertia and maintenance of the status quo. Once installed the leader has to set about the task of re-orientating the organisation towards responsiveness. A first priority then is to redesign the organisation to incorporate jobs which offer customised, specialist and more comprehensive attention to the handling of current critical problems. These jobs and the people who fill them become the driving forces of the organisation.

## The top team

In all but the smallest of organisations the leader will require assistance towards the goal of organisation-wide responsiveness. The establishment of a 'top today team' can be helpful here. Chosen most ostensibly for the contribution each member can make to heading and organising particular functional areas of the enterprise the team (including the chief executive) will often provide a mix of marketing, finance and operation management biases and skills. Equally importantly, however, the top team will provide the chief executive with an even broader perspective and base force for the function of management strategy and the creation and carriage of cultural change. Together these strategically compatible people will act as a cohesive force for deciding product/market objectives and for redesigning the organisation. They will also, by their words and actions, provide the necessary top level example of commitment to organisational success through the provision of customer care, value for money and productivity.

## Middle level culture carriers: customer relations departments

The impetus towards the successful implementation of the customer care/quality improvement programme can be further stimulated by the introduction of middle level culture carriers. Manufacturers have, for example, usefully introduced quality improvement task forces to oversee the implementation and continued operation of the quality improvement effort.

In retail situations also we have seen major improvements flow from relatively inexpensive resource, power and status enhancements of customer relations functions.

Middle level customer care/quality improvement jobs and people mixes, then, like the quality improvement campaigns of which they are an integral part, should not be viewed as costs which must be incurred to appease new societal demands. Implemented and operated efficiently they can be massive net benefit generators.

### Case examples: creating customer care departments

(a) Jaguar Cars attributes much of its improved efficiency to a systematic monitoring and analysis of complaints. As a result warranty claims and costs are now a fraction of their 1980 levels.

(b) Mitchell (16) describes how the central customer complaints department of a motorway motel chain spotted, investigated and subsequently resolved a source of customer dissatisfaction (over sandwich fillings) which had been largely ignored at the disaggregated branch level.

(c) More generally, quality improvement steering groups and customer relations departments are inspiring greater productivity through their exhortations, support and monitorings in a host of operational areas: see, for example, Doran's (17) account of the change taking place at IBM and Havant, or Clarke's (12) account of similar activities at ICL.

(d) Wigfalls in the electrical goods retail industry has used its central customer relations department to communicate quality performance results via the organisation's in-house journal, by 'head patting' (commending useful consumer reception examples) and 'wrist slapping' (reproaching the guilty parties in poorly handled complaints situations). Wigfalls has also used the customer service department to provide a ready source of advice and support for staff with quality/customer care associated problems. Junior/newer managers are particularly appreciative of the access to a more seasoned reference source. The department, headed by a respected veteran manager, provides an interface between top policy requirements and operational activities, and acts as a forum for communications and exchanges of views and ideas on quality improvement.

(e) We have seen a range of successful and unsuccessful customer relations departments which indicate the need for such functions to be headed by personnel with status, position and expert power and interpersonal skills.

(f) A successful example was found in a national electrical goods retailer where the customer relations manager was a well respected organisation veteran who had previously occupied a number of positions within the firm and who, visibly, had access to the chief executive's ear.

(g) Another useful customer relations function was found in a national finance house whose first appointment to the newly created department was a young, ambitious and successful sales manager who, enjoying the full support of his chief executive, was keen to do a good job in tidying up his organisation's approach to customer relations. Success in this post was perceived as a preliminary objective for his further career advancement.

(h) Conversely, however, in another retail organisation, we found a customer relations manager who enjoyed a less advantageous position. He was nearing retirement after spending some years in the job he had initially applied for because of his academic interest in legal matters. Although he worked from head office his job was generally recognised as being peripheral to the mainstream activity of selling goods in volume. Store managers were unsure of the authority vested in the customer relations manager and unclear about organisation policy over the the seemingly opposed functions of securing sales and offering fair and generous attention to dissatisfied customers. Needless to say, the situation which emerged here was one where the customer relations manager seemed to flit in and out of complaint situations without making any real impact on the overall situation. Eventually, legally based interventions from consumer protection agencies forced the firm to re-examine its existing approaches.

## The sensors

Today's organisations need to have people in touch with the environment. It is sound practice for organisations dealing with environmental players who have the capability significantly to enhance or damage success prospects to allocate people to the task of ensuring successful relationships or, alternatively, swift remedial action if the powerful stakeholder threatens to exercise power in a negative way.

Such reasoning has been fundamental to the creation of political action departments, public relations functions, special account sections and supplier liaison duties. To an outsider looking in, the need for such appointments might be obvious. To successful organisations advice which recommends such attention to this area of job design is already out of date and superfluous. Unfortunately, for all too many British organisations languishing in introversion and inertia a 'Catch 22' situation prevails. The organisation's shortage of sensing functions helps to maintain an ignorance of the need to design and implement them. Fortunately, the 'today leader' brings with him the necessary overview to appreciate the need for specialist sensors.

## Technical specialists

Catering for new critical problems inevitably involves the recruitment of technical experts from outside the organisation. The building societies, for example, in the late 1980s, were grappling with the problems of recruiting and integrating consumer credit, insurance and estate agency specialists to provide expertise not immediately available within their depths of mortgage loan skills and expertise. Information technology has had similar impact on personnel policies. New skills require the injection of new people with different ways of thinking and doing business.

## New jobs for old

The management strategist will have achieved excellence when the enterprise is not merely 'spiced' with quality specialists but when it is filled with a viable force of quality commitment – when a new quality-based responsiveness culture has become embedded. Of course, pertinent organising modes will generate such a culture. The checklist below provides advices on how jobs might be designed and people paid to generate commitment from rank and file personnel to the team effort.

Frederick Hertzberg (18) differentiates between *motivation* and *movement*. Motivation, for Hertzberg, is about enduring commitment to job success. Movement, on the other hand, starts and stops as rewards and punishments are applied and removed. Commitment is to be induced through *job enrichment*. Designers of jobs can build in to jobs enrichment and hence (in to the worker) commitment. To create commitment each job should:

(a)  be subject to direct feedback on performance results;

(b)  incorporate a client relationship (the worker should feel responsible to a customer);

(c)  incorporate a learning function;

(d)  offer the opportunity for the worker to schedule his or her own work;

(e)  provide the worker with a sense of unique expertise;

(f)  allow the worker some control over the resources involved in the work;

(g)  subject the job holder to personal accountability for his or her work.

Drennan, (19) drawing from experience of organisation practice, suggests that pay incentive schemes tend to be devisive because they:

(a)  motivate only the minority (the top 20 per cent performers) and 'turn off' the majority;

(b)  create fencing matches between manager and subordinate in performance appraisals;

(c)  create resentment from middle of the scale high performers who see top of the scale recipients effectively 'retired in their jobs'.

Further, traditional pay systems tend to produce 'more than deserved' awards as managers seek to avoid confrontation and unpleasantness and create never to be taken away new bases for additional pay rounds.

Pay systems, therefore, should be redesigned to incorporate the following features:

(a)  Reduce the length of pay scales to avoid a belief that pay increases are automatic and not related to performance.

(b)  Define a *limited* amount of cash which managers can allocate among their subordinates to take care of merit awards. This focuses prior thinking towards establishing who deserves a merit award.

(c)  Build into the reward system the prospect of *success for the majority*. This characteristic should encourage *everyone* to stretch and expend that extra effort. 'Tips' here, include:

- make the money incentives endlessly renewable. They should not die out when individuals reach the top of the scale;
- pay *lump sums*. £500 paid out just before Christmas has much more impact than £10 per week. 'One-off' payments, too, do not become enduring entitlements;
- the winning posts (targets/objectives) should be clear and unambiguous;
- the system should encourage the holding of appraisals;
- the system should avoid discrimination in favour of particular types of personnel;
- incentives should be based on *future* performance rather than *past* service.

## Younger employees

A new team culture can usually be obtained more quickly and easily with younger employees. Younger people are less set in the ways of previous occupational settings and so are more amenable to the management strategist's preferred ways of doing things. Generally they are ambitious for the rewards of higher office. Again this makes for the greater pertinence of such rewards as stimuli for acquiescence and commitment to the new ways of doing things. Younger people too, as we noted in our chief executive profile discussion, are generally fitter, quicker and more creative. Thus, they are more up to the new demands for speedy and flexible thought and action and more naturally in tune with the new vibrancy of a responsive life.

It is likely, therefore, that the younger chief executive, once established, will redirect retirement, redundancy, recruitment and promotion policies towards an injection of youth into the enterprise. This is why (where demographic variables allow) reorganisation towards responsiveness often reduces the average personnel age of the organisation.

## Fewer employees and a changing structure of employment

The search is on continually in the responsive organisation to obtain more for less. Cutting back on the size of the labour force is one obvious way of saving money. Figure 12.2 shows the categories of permanent and temporary employees.

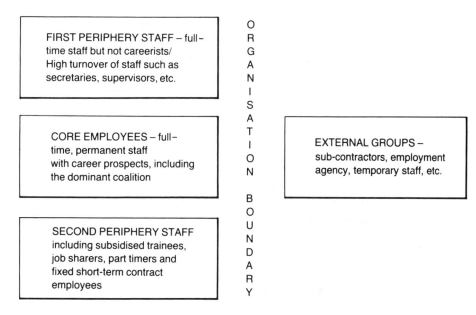

**Figure 12.2 Permanent and temporary employee categories**

Stagnation in the world's economy, competitive failure and the impact of information technology are factors which have combined to create the present trend, at micro and macro level, towards smaller British workforces. It seems likely that the effective reorganiser must always have in mind the need to 'trim to the bone' the costs of operation. Responsiveness reorganisation is characterised by a net shedding of jobs. Increased stakeholder satisfaction levels are visible in the successfully responsible enterprise, but, invariably, fewer people share the organisational success cake.

The changing permanent/temporary structure of employment is also providing fewer employment opportunities. Within this overall trend, structural changes in permanent/temporary employment patterns are also taking place. It is evident that firms are not only looking to reduce the size of their total workforce but are also seeking to reduce the proportion of full-time employees therein.

Modern day success is being built, at least in part, on new approaches to labour force structuring which emphasise the benefits to be obtained from greater use of 'second periphery' and externally based supplies of labour (see Fig. 12.2). In particular, such policies should generate savings in areas such as:

(a) *Lower wage and associated wage costs.* Government subsidised trainees, for example, cost less than those employed directly by the firm. Casual workers often have no rights to holiday and sickness pay or occupational pensions.

(b) *Lower, or non-existent, severance costs.* Permanent employees on the books for a number of years have legal rights to termination of contract payments and, in appropriate cases, redundancy compensation. These combined 'pay offs' often add up to a significant financial liability.

(c) *Savings in office accommodation and associated costs.* Many employers are now prepared to consider temporary workers in those higher level occupations for which permanent employment has previously been the norm. As the use of sub-contracted or employment agency-based personnel increases, so does the possibility of making savings in office accommodation expenses. New employment policies implemented by Rank Xerox have resulted in former employees, now based in their homes, selling their services to the company. This has facilitated, amongst other benefits, the sale of an office building previously housing 50 employees and costing £30,000 per year to run.

(d) *Saving some labour associated costs.* The removal of slack costs associated with the carrying of buffer levels of labour during quiet times to ensure effective response to upsurges in demand. In this respect the use of temporary labour is akin to the 'just in time' stock control efficiency methods which are also presently taking root in business.

Of course, temporary employment policies have their negative side. In particular, employers need to keep in mind the 'effective' side of the productivity equation. Greater efficiency from reduced labour costs can be more than negated by a subsequent failure to satisfy customers or to produce goods and services efficiently. Temporary staff might be less motivated, inadequately trained and more difficult to control. In order to avoid the adverse effects of these potential workforce characteristics, modifications will have to be made to present systems of training, motivation and control.

More generally, organisations becoming reliant on the use of temporary labour might be well advised to consider the impact of any reversal of present governmental policies towards state assistance in this area. Concern has been expressed, for example, over the effect such policies are having on the proportion of unemployment-related costs to be borne by society generally, compared to those attaching to the private sector. While employers are taking advantage of state subsidies, temporary workers, in turn, look to the state for support during the troughs in company workloads.

Despite these caveats, however, it seems that we are moving inevitably towards the era of the temporary, part-time, relief, job sharer. The today management strategist will undoubtedly fuel this trend to the extent that he or she sees it working towards the firm's advantage.

## Creating a responsive team culture

Culture is 'those deeply rooted beliefs about the more effective ways of achieving external adaptation and internal integration' (1). Through attention to the components of organising, strategists can create an organisation ecology which acts as a massive force for indoctrination. Recent success stories indicate that people at work can be manipulated to acquire the belief that working together, for the organisation, is natural work behaviour and that constant change is the necessary prerequisite to the ongoing major task of satisfying customers more efficiently.

'Today' management strategists are creating such cultures. A look back over this chapter should reveal how practising management strategists are putting into practice the principles of norm enforcement and the group development processes identified below and in the illustration of the Sherif summer camp experiment which follows.

### Why norms become entrenched [20]

(a) Norms are likely to be strongly enforced if they ensure group success and survival.

(b) Norms are likely to be strongly enforced if they reflect the preferences of supervisors or other powerful group members.

(c) Norms are likely to be strongly enforced if they simplify, or make predictable, what behaviour is expected of group members.

(d) Norms are likely to be strongly enforced if they reinforce specific invididual members' roles.

(e) Norms are likely to be strongly enforced if they are referred to regularly.

(f) Norms are likely to be strongly enforced if they help the group avoid embarrassing interpersonal problems.

(g) Norms are likely to be strongly enforced if group cohesiveness is developed.

### Think and discuss

Identify some of the ways in which strategists referred to in Chapters 11 and 12 have practised some of the above norm enforcing principles.

### Stages of group development [21]

(a) Stage 1 – Forming: finding out about the task, rules and methods; acquiring information and resources; relying on the leader.

(b) Stage 2 – Storming: internal conflict develops; members resist the task at the emotional level.

(c) Stage 3 – Norming: conflict is settled, co-operation develops, views are exchanged and new norms developed.

(d) Stage 4 – Performing: teamwork is achieved, roles are flexible, solutions are found and implemented.

## Case example: the Sherif summer camp experiments [22]

In 1949 Sherif and Sherif selected a sample of 24 boys, all around twelve years of age, and took them away on an 18-day summer camp holiday. As part of the experiment, designed to demonstrate group formation, the boys were split into two groups of twelve each and all activities were organised separately. The effect was striking. The two collections of twelve boys turned into two close knit groups each preferring not to mix with members of the other group. The gap between the two groups widened as games and competitions between them were introduced.

Initial 'name calling' developed into actual fights during a party called to let 'bygones be bygones'. Efforts to unite the camp were generally rebuffed. On one occasion, however, the full party was taken on a bus outing during which the experimenters engineered a bus breakdown in the desert. Faced with a common objective – to get themselves out of the crisis – and a common enemy – the environment – the boys were soon working together to get the bus mended and the journey recommenced.

The success which the management strategist achieves in creating an effective team culture will depend to some large extent on the management strategist him/herself. Table 12.5 offers the views of management gurus on how and why leaders create culture.

**Table 12.5 Two management guru's views on leadership and culture**

Charles Handy (23)

Charles Handy offers the following leadership and culture principles:

1    Leadership has to be endemic. *Everyone* with pretentions to be anyone must begin to think and act like a leader.
2    Leaders shape and share visions with others.
3    The vision must be different from traditional views and ways.
4    It must make sense to others. It should create the 'Aha effect' – 'Aha – of course, now I see it'.
5    It must relate clearly to the work of subordinates – a grand design which seems to have little relevance is no good.
6    It must be understandable. It should not take two pages to be read or be too full of numbers.
7    The leader must live the vision – it must come from his/her inner system of belief.
8    The vision must be shared with people who are listened to and trusted. In this way it will become their vision too.

Edgar Schein (24)

Edgar Schein informs us of the most powerful mechanisms for culture embedding and reinforcement:

1    What leaders pay attention to, measure and control.
2    Leader reactions to critical incidents and organisational crises (at these times does the leader stick to his/her espoused principles)
3    Deliberate role modelling, teaching and coaching by leaders.
4    Criteria for allocation of rewards and status.
5    Criteria for recruitment, selection, promotion, retirement and examination.

# Team culture planning: conclusion

There is an urgent need for UK organisations to plan, formally, to be responsive to the nature and needs of their environments. This requires the use of a range of planning techniques and activities. Centrally, however, the management strategist needs to create an organising mode which is, itself, capable of taking care of incremental strategic development – responding effectively to the daily changes which occur at operational level and continually working to satisfy external stakeholders and improve productivity. Emphasis on quality is, for many firms, generating massive benefits through increased levels of customer satisfaction and productivity. Quality improvement campaigns are having important impacts on all the components of organising, those constituent parts of the organisation which require to be designed to match the environment and to be in harmony with themselves. While reorganisation towards responsiveness requires attention to all the components of organising, we have concentrated on only some of these components – strategy, concerned as it is with the achievement of the organisation's basic end objectives; motivation systems, concerned as they are to ensure that the people of the organisation are committed to the achievement of strategic success; the management strategist who seems to require particular skills and styles in order to be a 'today leader'; and the workforce and the jobs which need to be redesigned and arranged to provide the flexible responsive team approach for strategy today.

More sophisticated organisations have already reorganised towards responsiveness and are reaping the benefits. Other, more 'out of touch' and tardy enterprises would be well advised to start the reorganisation process now – before it is too late. Specifically, steps to be taken include:

(a) Check out the organisation for fits and misfits between the components of organising, and the organisation and its environment.

(b) Consider how the three qualities of responsiveness (quality of product/service, productivity and work life) might be better achieved (the productivity planning process will already have furnished useful information for use here).

(c) Draw up a plan which makes the necessary changes to the components of organising, which gives existing productivity drives a quality campaign perspective, and which reinforces a responsive team-orientated culture.

(d) Implement the plan, monitor performance and communicate results.

Analysis of a number of case studies describing successful team culture building exercises is summarised in the checklist below. By highlighting characteristics and attitudes in personnel which are common to companies which promote a responsive team culture, this checklist can act as a diagnostic tool for establishing the state of responsiveness/team orientation which exists in an organisation.

(a) Our leader is effective, youthful and has drive.

(b) We care about three *qualities*: quality of product/service; quality of productivity; quality of work life. We know what is expected of us, work wise, for the achievement of these qualities.

(c)  We are constantly reminded that caring about quality is personally rewarded.

(d)  We are *marketing led.*

(e)  We have experts in critical areas of the business.

(f)  We are a team.

(g)  We all take part in sensing and communicating information.

(h)  Information technology streamlines and makes more effective our information systems and decision-making processes.

(i)  Generally, we are looking to move up-market as far as the image of our organisational product/services is concerned.

(j)  We have a customer relations function which tends to champion the consumer in dispute situations.

(k)  We employ a form of management by objectives.

(l)  Management and staff get on well together. Management is friendly, relaxed and approachable – provided no one steps outside the *core values* of the organisation.

(m) The ongoing search to improve productivity infers that manning levels are constantly monitored and amended.

(n)  We expect to enjoy work, to be successful and to take a fair share of the wealth created by the organisation.

(o)  Financial resources are found to fund investments which are perceived to be critical to the future survival and success of the organisation.

(p)  *All* the components of organising are arranged and implemented to reinforce/indoctrinate the above principles.

## Think and discuss
Refer to your own organisation (or one of your choosing).

(a)  Identify some problematic misfits. How might a more harmonious blend of organising components be achieved?

(b)  Identify the cause of any motivational problems. How might these situations be improved?

(c)  Evaluate your organisation's success in achieving the three qualities of team culture responsiveness planning.

## For further study
1  Refer to the 'Rutshire Consumer Protection Department' case study in the accompanying case study book.
   In hindsight it is possible to comment that the problems experienced by Rutshire's Consumer Protection Department were due to shortcomings of organis-ational 'fit'.
   Selecting any *three* of the following areas and using theoretical and practical perspectives, explain why these problems occurred. What action, in the chosen

areas, would you have advised to promote more effective harmony between internal organising components and between the organisation and its external environment?

(a) Recruitment and selection.

(b) Organisation structure/culture

(c) Motivation and control systems

(d) Management style

(e) Power and influence

# References

1  E H Schein, 'Towards a New Awareness of Culture', *Long Range Planning*, Fall, 1984

2  C Hogg, quoted in 'Courtaulds Fashions a Comeback', *Management Today*, May 1986

3  S Hall, 'How to get out of a Crisis', *Management Today*, February 1985

4  A M Pettigrew, *The Politics of Organisation Decision-making*, Tavistock, 1973

5  I D C Ramsay, *Rationales for Interventions in the Consumer Marketplace*, London, Office of Fair Trading, 1984

6  R M Cyert and J G March, *A Behavioural Theory of the Firm*, Englewood Cliffs, New Jersey, Prentice-Hall, 1963

7  For a wider discussion (with references) of these leadership style continuums see G A Cole, *Management Theory and Practice*, D P Publications, 1983.

8  T J Peters and R H Waterman Jr, *In Search of Excellence*, New York, Harper & Row, 1982

9  R L Ackoff, *A Concept of Corporate Planning*, New York, Wiley Interscience, 1970

10  R E Miles and C C Snow, *Organisational Strategy, Structure and Process*, New York, McGraw-Hill, 1978

11  C Clarke and S Pratt, 'Leadership's Four-part Progress', *Management Today*, March 1985

12  L Clarke, 'Making Change at ICL', *Management Today*, May 1986

13  Kiernan & Co., *Research into Top Leader Profiles*, Kiernan, 1984

14  F E Fiedler, *A Theory of Leadership Effectiveness*, McGraw-Hill, 1967

15  G R Salancik and J J Pfeffer, 'Who gets Power – and How They Hold on to It: A Strategic-Contingency Model of Power' in M L Tushman and W L Moore (eds), *Readings in the Management of Innovation*, Pitman, 1982

16  J S Mitchell, *Marketing and the Consumer Movement*, New York, McGraw-Hill, 1978

17  P Doran, 'How to Achieve Performance, *Management Today*, April 1986

18  F Hertzberg, 'One More Time: How do you Motivate Employees?', *Harvard Business Review*, Sept–Oct 1987, pp 109–20

19  D Drennan, 'Down the Organisation', *Management Today*, June 1988, pp 129–38

20  D C Feldman and J H Arnold, *Managing Individual and Group Behaviour in Organisations*, McGraw-Hill, 1983, pp 447–9

21  B W Tuckman, 'Development Sequence in Small Groups', *Psych Bulletin*, 1965

22  C B Handy, *Understanding Organisations*, Penguin, 1976 (adapted from Sherif and Sherif, *An Outline of Social Psychology*, 1956)

23  C B Handy, *The Age of Unreason*, Hutchinson, 1989

24  E H Schein, *Organisation Culture and Leadership*, San Francisco, Jossey-Bass, 1985, Ch 10

# Recommended reading

C B Handy, *The Age of Unreason*, Hutchinson, 1989

T J Peters, *Thriving on Chaos*, Macmillan, 1988

E H Schein, *Organisational Culture and Leadership*, San Francisco, Jossey-Bass, 1985

# 13 Innovation planning

The ability to produce new organisational offerings and/or to change the way the enterprise does things to enhance productivity is, for many organisations, a keystone of their competitive success. As innovation becomes an increasingly critical competitive tool most organisations need to pay more formal attention to the planning of their innovation function. In this chapter we seek to help readers become acquainted with theoretically prescribed steps for the creation of a specialist force to ensure that the enterprise's products/services and processes continue to lead in (or at least keep pace with) a competitive and changing market place. Our discussion is structured under the following headings:

- Why innovation planning?
- Creating a corporate-wide innovative culture
- Restructuring to create a separate creative/innovative function
- Enlisting key personnel for the success of the innovative function
- Activating the functional force for creativity and innovation
- Taking control of the creative process
- Entwining the innovative function with the innovative corporation

## Why innovation planning?

As organisations change to maintain successful existences they innovate. Strategy *is* innovation and organisations have always needed to be innovative. Why then has there been an emergence of interest in innovation in recent times? Why are business theorists and practitioners paying separate and special attention to the problem of how to innovate? The answer, of course, lies in the increasingly critical role innovation is playing in the determination of competitive advantage and organisational success.

'In the past when competition was not so fierce, updating occurred infrequently. When it did, most firms competing in a particular market tended to change the essential features of their products (and/or services and/or processes) at about the same time ... responsibility was commonly delegated to the technical department whose job was to ensure that products remained the rough equal of competitive products. Today in *more and more* markets the situation has changed or is changing very fast .... The pace of change for product design and quality is accelerating across *a wide front*, with ... few markets being unaffected by this new form of competition.'(1)

Put simply, firms have now to make more change, more often – if they are to survive and prosper. Thus, managers who have hitherto paid little attention to the function of innovation should now check their situations. New critical problem areas tend to emerge without organisational personnel, immersed in the traditional ways of doing things, noticing.

Case examples: gaining competitive advantage through innovation

(a) Yamasaki has established its worldwide position with a product line of 50 models compared with the usual manufacturer's 10 to 15 – which it still builds in one-third of the standard time.

(b) Lucas' remarkable return from the brink is due, in part, to the slashing of manufacturing lead times from 55 to 12 days.

(c) Black & Decker's success strategy demands the capability to make a vast variety of products – from lawn mowers to workbenches to power drills – in huge volumes and also to be able to switch rapidly between them in response to volatile market demand.

(d) At Amstrad, updating old products ensures continuing cash generation from which completely new product lines are funded.

(e) George Davies at Next exhorted, 'The only way forward is to change. But as captives of their own industry most organisations resist change. They defend their one goal lead. They only change when they are going broke, when they are 5-0 down. We must not defend Next.'

(f) In 1982 Yamaha president, Mr Kioke, told shareholders 'In two years time we will be number one in the world.' Honda's reaction was swift. During the next 18 months it completely replaced its range twice. And many of its 100 new models were significant innovations in motor cycle design. In the face of falling market shares and a loss-making situation Koike had to admit, 'We cannot match Honda's product development or sales strength and would like to end the Honda–Yamaha war.'

This chapter brings together some prescriptions, from the theory of management strategy, which indicate how organisational *creativity* (thinking up new things) and organisational *innovation* (actually *doing* new things) might be given a boost. The CREATE framework below and the accompanying discussion contain general prescriptions which are intended to help readers gain insight for more situation specific innovation planning exercises.

## How to create and innovate creative innovation

(a) Step 1: *C*reate a corporate-wide creative/innovative culture.

(b) Step 2: *R*estructure to create a separate creative/innovative function.

(c) Step 3: *E*nlist key personnel for the success of the creative/innovative function.

(d) Step 4: *A*ctivate the functional force for creativity and innovation.

(e) Step 5: *T*ake control of the creative process.

(f) Step 6: *E*ntwine the creative/innovative function with the creative/innovative corporation.

## Creating a corporate-wide creative/innovative culture

The means for creating an organisation which 'creates and implements strategy efficiently as ongoing *natural organisational* activities', and where 'the key strategic tasks of sensing and satisfying efficiently the needs of external stakeholders (particularly customers) becomes an accepted part of everybody's job' has already been outlined in Chapters 11 and 12. In brief, reorganising towards responsiveness involves changes to the components of organising (jobs, people, systems, technology, etc.) and the installation of a quality-orientated culture. Importantly, a corporate-wide desire to seek productive change is an essential underpinning to the creation of a more specialist force for innovation (2).

## Restructuring to create a separate innovative function

If innovation is to be an essential strand of the firm's competitive strategy then it must be given the chance to flourish. It needs its own plot within the already fertile, responsive, organisation from which to take root and grow. This means differentiating between the innovatory vanguard and the rest of the business. In small businesses this will often have to be achieved via mainstream personnel taking time out from their normal duties. After-hours sessions with external consultants is one way of creating an innovation specific function in such organisations. Larger firms continue to experiment with a variety of 'innovation units' ranging from temporary cross functional teams, to full-time innovation task forces and on to new venture units and divisions.

While a separate specialist function for innovation can attract benefits (see below), Bart (3) has suggested that differentiation *within* an existing business unit might be preferable to the creation of a totally separate unit. This structural arrangement, he argues, attracts more easily the support and resources of the wider organisation and avoids the hostility which might otherwise be exhibited towards a new 'special' unit. More distinctly separated functions might be best introduced only for innovations unrelated to mainstream business and/or for essential projects in which existing departments show little interest.

### Advantages of a separate unit for innovation

The following checklist is adapted from Bart's work in this field (3).

(a) *Speedier new product development*. New venture units can speed up the development and launch of new products. IBM, for example, claims that such a unit was responsible for the swiftest production of any new product (personal computers) in its history.

(b) *Appropriate attention*. Existing products drive new products out unless a device such as a separate innovation unit exists to remind senior managers, forcefully, of the importance of new products/services and processes to longer term prosperity.

(c) *No glass fishbowl*. IBM and Levi Strauss each incorporate a separate company to handle new innovatory developments. This has helped reduce the extent of nervous, and interfering, line managers and has maintained the privacy and breathing space necessary to allow new developments to evolve successfully.

(d) *Entrepreneurial environment*. A new unit can adopt different perspectives to the traditional 'today's business' dominated units. A smaller unit can make quicker decisions and stay more 'nimble-footed' in terms of changing market needs.

(e) *Motivated and communicative environment.* Smaller teams with easier to perceive common goals can more easily develop the interactive and cohesive mode essential to group creativity.

# Enlisting key personnel for the success of the innovative function

Management strategy has identified a number of key roles which contribute to successful innovation. These are:

(a)  top leaders;

(b)  a sponsor;

(c)  a champion;

(d)  a team of contributors.

## Top leaders
Innovative companies are led by innovative leaders – people like Egan, Davies and Conran who, believing in change themselves, set the innovatory targets for the enterprise and play the leading role in installing the innovative culture throughout the corporation.

## A sponsor
This contributor is a manager high enough up the organisation to marshall its resources for the furtherance of the venture unit's activities and, when necessary, to protect the unit from attacks by other vested interests within the enterprise. The sponsor is well placed to make a number of critical contributions to the successful development of the unit. He or she should *oversee* its activities, *set its general objectives*, provide *resources* and *protection* and *monitor progress* at important stages of the development process. The sponsor acts, ideally, as a *redirector* if ideas from the venture group do not fit the demands of the organisation's competitive strategy; as an *auditor* to maintain a commercial perspective in the face of any technically motivated enthusiasm; and as a *controller* (of budgets and time schedules). While management strategy has tended to emphasise the importance of *champions* (see below) to successful innovation, the input of a sophisticated sponsor, capable of performing the above roles without ever taking a position of 'hands on controller', is often the critical success factor.

## A champion
This contributor is the middle manager in charge of a project who believes so strongly in an idea that he or she will push it into successful reality, regardless of obstacles.

## A team of creative contributors
This force for innovation is often comprised of functional specialists (marketing, personnel, production, research and development, for example) who bring their individual expertise to the *team effort*.

Traditionally, new products have been developed using the *relay* approach. Today's need for speedy innovation requires that the unit's functional experts work *together*, attending to tasks simultaneously in a more expensive – but quicker – *rugby* formation.

Team members including the champion, should perceive innovation unit membership as a worthwhile challenge and career step. If a new venture manager's budget is less than that for his previous assignment, for example, the new project (according to research) is more likely to fail. Team contributors should be sufficiently experienced to tackle the job in hand effectively but not so senior as to fear failure – and the consequential loss of hard earned reputation, position and prospects.

3M *recruits* (rather than assigns) volunteers to work in new venture units. Recruitment is more likely to locate committed champions and to avoid the risk of employing managers who would rather be contributing elsewhere. If no recruits come forward 3M usually drops the potential project.

According to theory, 'tell tale' signs of the creative individual are available to guide those doing the recruiting. These signs are illustrated below (4). The creative individual:

(a)  shows constant dissatisfaction with the current state of things;

(b)  seeks change and new experiences;

(c)  is intelligent, conceptually fluent and flexible;

(d)  is prepared to live with and to utilise co-existing states of order and disorder, rationality and intuition, masculinity and femininity;

(e)  is aware of his/her own strengths and weaknesses.

## Case example: 'I do not want to see that project in the labs'

Life is not easy for entrepreneurs, not even at Hewlett-Packard. At 26, frustrated oscilloscope designer Chuck House accepted the challenge from a senior manager looking for volunteers to take on the development of an electronic lens for the Federal Aviation market. House and his team quickly built a monitor, incorporating the lens, which was half the size and weight of other monitors, 20 times as fast, produced a brighter display but used less power.

It did not, however, provide a picture clear enough to enable air controllers to read identifying code numbers on the planes they were monitoring. House's supervisors encouraged him to give up the project. House, however, had spotted other market opportunities – and he now had a prototype. At this point he crossed the threshold from engineer to champion entrepreneur. During the next months he undertook a number of 'champion' activities including:

(a)  taking the prototype with his family on holiday so that he could introduce it to potential customers en route;

(b)  breaking the Hewlett-Packard rule of *never* showing customers prototypes (arguing that the project had all but been scrapped anyway);

(c)  winning begrudged additional (but limited) time and finance for his project from supervisors;

(d)  arguing with the marketing people who had surveyed the 'traditional market' and predicted a total market take-up of only 32 units. House said they had surveyed the wrong market segments and that anyway their estimates had not included the two units his father had promised to buy, personally;

(e) gaining his team's support in the quest to find new customer segments and to have the product out of the lab and into production within a year – following a literal (and creative) translation of top executive Dave Packard's stipulation that 'when I come back next year I don't want to see that project in the lab';

(f) maintaining the support of his immediate superior, Dan Howard, who put himself 'on the line' in the process.

In double time House produced three versions of the product and all achieved glory in their first year. The moon monitor supported man's first trip to the moon. The medical monitor was used in the first artificial heart transplant. The large screen model helped win a special effects Emmy Award. Within a few years project products were generating over $10 million in annual sales (5).

## Think and discuss
Identify the key personnel involved in the above innovation project. Describe their roles in making this project successful

# Activating the functional force for creativity and innovation

The creation of specialist jobs and the appointment of specialist personnel provide the 'garden' and 'seed' for the growing of the innovatory force. Its germination and nurturing remain as important tasks to be attained via the organising system which develops for the innovation function. The components of organising (people, systems, structures, technology and resources, etc.) pertinent for these tasks must be arranged and applied to achieve a 'balancing act' – to create an environment which is loose enough to stimulate creativity and, at the same time, tight enough to generate useful innovations. Tasks for creative innovation planners include:

(a) *Balance rewards.* Too little reward makes innovation unit membership unattractive – too much makes innovation over-expensive.

(b) *Balance failure/success expectancies.* Too much failure cannot be tolerated – too much *fear* of failure will make staff poor innovators.

(c) *Balance control systems.* Too much sponsor intervention will stifle creativity – too little can result in wasteful 'drifting' and/or chaos.

(d) *Balance pressure and ambiguity.* Too much pressure (in terms of tight resource or time budgets/deadlines) will constrict creative developments, too much ambiguity (in terms of the objectives to be achieved) can produce waste and harmful tension – and yet creativity thrives on *effective* mixes of tension and ambiguity.

(e) *Balance individualism and team work.* Many highly creative people prefer to 'beaver away' alone, jealous of their secrets – yet synergy is to be had from sharing creativity. Further, individual autonomy must be harnessed to the *organisational* cause.

Management strategy offers some tips on how the innovation unit's components of organising might be usefully designed and arranged. Thus, strategists keen to create a specialist force for innovation might make their customised plans in the context of the following prescriptions.

## Information systems for innovation

Information systems for innovation need to *process* and to *create* information. Effective systems exhibit the following characteristics.

### They emphasise the link between competitive strategy and innovation

Rather than being left to get on with *any* innovation the bright people within the innovation unit should be clearly informed of the nature of the organisation's basic competitive strategy and of the need for unit efforts to be directed towards the enhancement of the enterprise's competitive position. A written business plan should be produced at the outset to guide and monitor unit activity.

### They emphasise comparisons with competitors and the need to beat competitive performance

Information which provides insights into competitor performance provides two major forces for the innovatory thrust. First it concentrates attention on beating the competition (rather than on just doing better). Second it provides a rich source of externally generated and tested innovations which *can be copied and improved on.*

### They help create the creative environment

In successfully innovative companies information/communication systems are informal and intense (people talk – and argue – everywhere, anytime, naturally). Communication is given physical supports. Information systems maintain pressure and ambiguity. (See the following illustrations.)

### Case examples: Creating successful creativity

(a)  A senior HP manager claims 'we're really not sure how exactly the innovatory process works. But there's one thing we do know: the easy communications, the absence of barriers to talking to one another are essential. Whatever we do, whatever structure we adopt, whatever systems we try, that's the cornerstone – we won't do anything to jeopardise it.'

(b)  Informal interest in what innovatory units are doing acts as a control mechanism – unit personnel are aware that they are being watched and judged.

(c)  In Peters and Waterman Jr's (5) 'excellent companies' detailed and practical steps give communication physical support. Blackboards are standard furniture, rectangular tables have replaced smaller round tables to increase the range of mealtime contacts, and people work in close physical proximity to each other.

(d)  IBM ordered, from catalogues, several million dollars worth of micro processors so that personnel in IBM labs could 'play with them'.

(e)  Bechtel urges that every project manager spends 20 per cent of his or her time experimenting with new technologies.

(f)  Honda's middle managers continually rejected product development teams' ideas and exhorted 'start all over again' – as part of the process of creating the Honda City.

(g)  Some theorists advocate the use of creativity stimulating techniques such as 'brainstorming' to aid the innovation process.

## They move new ideas quickly from grassroots level to sponsor level

The length of time taken between idea generation and market launch correlates with innovatory success or failure. Effective innovatory information systems enable new ideas to surface from the 'mire' of today's business systems to seek quick endorsement from sponsors.

## They emphasise the importance of information for decision-making

Underpinning successful innovation is the use of knowledge – what Pearson (7) calls 'knowing your business cold'. Thus the successful innovatory firm of today knows its competitors, its customers, its capabilities and its competitive strategy-aligned innovation strategy.

## Management style for innovation

The innovatory culture like any organisation culture is much shaped by its leaders. Management style for successful innovation is open, supportive, interactive and goal-orientated. From our discussion so far, it should be obvious that leadership sophistication – from leaders at all levels – is a vital ingredient in the development of innovation-based competitive advantage.

## Reward systems for innovation

Reward systems, too, have a particularly important role to play in the innovatory organisation. Pay, promotion and recognition – as well as job satisfaction – have to be sufficiently attractive if the right people are to be recruited to join and to be motivated to work for the new unit. Thus, the reward package on offer must make the inherent risk of failure worthwhile. Pepsi Cola attacks the risk of failure problem head on through policies which enable people involved with *failures* to obtain promotion. Other organisations guarantee returns to former positions. If conflict is to be avoided and organisation-wide co-operation gained, care needs also to be taken to ensure that rewards for unit personnel are harmonious with those on offer in other parts of the enterprise.

## Resources for innovation

Any of the organisation's planning activities should address the problem of how to achieve more for less over time. Innovation unit planners, however, must accept that returns from work in this area will be more futuristic and less certain than is the case in other planning areas. The nature of this type of work involves, more than any other, failures as well as successes. This means that management strategists seeking to use innovation as a cornerstone of competitive advantage must be prepared to provide adequate resources (and courage) to facilitate experimentation and failure. Here again managerial sophistication is required. Many potential winners have failed because insufficient time, money and other resources have been made available during development and/or at the product/process launch stage. Conversely, however, simply opening the resource floodgates can create unit complacency over the organisation's need to make profits. Tightening the purse strings, too, can sometimes motivate innovators to succeed.

On the question of how to allocate resources between competing projects, management strategy's advice is 'do not spread resources too thin'. Sponsors should be prepared to say 'no'. Success is most likely to flow from applying a *concentration* of resources into prioritised projects. Some attractive projects may be best 'left on ice' until adequate resources are available for their successful development.

## Taking control of the creative process

Creativity breeds new ideas and new projects. Successful innovation is achieved when such ideas and projects degenerate into real competitive advantage. Industry-wide there is no shortage of new ideas and projects. There is, however, a comparative shortage of successful innovations. *Most* new products, for example, fail to secure a viable market position. As a result of this failure rate problem theorists (8) have advocated the introduction of a systematic screening process better to control innovation and to improve the chances of actually attaining success in the market place.

This step-by-step approach provides a heavy rational counterbalance to the unstructured nature of the creative innovative process. It provides a 'key tasks' basis for the innovation project's written business plan, creates for the sponsor his/her control/intervention points and facilitates 'pulling the plug' (thus avoiding further wasteful resource inputs) at different stages in the development process. Stages in this control mechanism are as follows.

### Stage 1: Preliminary screening
At this point new ideas are evaluated against a range of decision criteria such as fit with competitive strategy, market potential and organisational resource capability. Early 'intention to buy' research of potential customers can assist 'go' or 'drop' decisions here.

### Stage 2: Profitability analysis
Soon after the preliminary screening, decision-makers should estimate the financial viability of the development investment under review.

### Stage 3: Product/process development
A decision to 'go' at Stage 2 should stimulate early prototype developments, continual testing of the evolving product and work on packaging for the market ready innovation. Previous 'go' decisions will have been vindicated if, at the end of Stage 3, the innovation unit has produced a refined prototype which:

(a)  is seen by consumers as successfully embodying attractive attributes;

(b)  performs safely under normal use and conditions;

(c)  can be produced for the budgeted manufacturing costs.

### Stage 4: Test marketing

If market launch and/or market penetration is likely to be costly; if the product/process is revolutionary rather than evolutionary; and if the organisation has the time available, then test marketing makes sense. This involves the *actual selling* of the product, in the context of its likely marketing mix, to target customers. New products might, for example, be 'tried' in selected stores and selected cities. Information gleaned from this exercise can be used for decisions to 'firm up' sales forecasts, rectify product problems, amend planned marketing mixes and, even at this late stage, to drop the innovation.

### Stage 5: Commercialisation

All that remains now is the planning of marketing campaigns based on decisions on target customers, marketing mixes, market entry strategies and entry timing. (See Chapter 7 for a fuller discussion of these stages of marketing planning.)

## Entwining the innovative function with the innovative corporation

Strategists who have undertaken innovation planning in the context of the above prescriptions will almost certainly have provided for the harmonious blending of the new function for innovation with the rest of the corporation. A responsive organisation, for example, will be amenable to the idea of a specialist force for innovation. Organisation-wide requests for 'recruits' will have conveyed the organisation-wide ownership nature of the new unit. Care over reward policies will have avoided problems about inequity and favouritism. Nevertheless, a final check needs to be made to ensure that the new function is not damaging the total organisation system. Old-time Apple Computer staff, for example, felt overlooked and resentful of the rewards and freedom enjoyed by Macintosh personnel. In the euphoria of creating a force for innovation top managers can forget that the most important form of innovation (most of the time) is that which has rank and file personnel, throughout the organisation, doing their today jobs a little better each day. The final stage of the CREATE process, therefore, is designed to check out total organisational morale, including that of those important people 'left minding the store'.

## Innovation planning: conclusion

The problem of how to enhance organisation creativity and innovation is one for the attention of our practising management strategists. For an increasing number of British managers this problem is intensifying as innovation plays a bigger role in the sorting out of competitive positions. The issue of how to innovate now demands special and formal attention. While the actual process of creativity and innovation thrives on the application of intuition in the face of ambiguity, planning to create a *specialist force* for innovation is, according to the theory of management strategy, best undertaken from a more rational, deductive base. Drawing from theory, this chapter has offered a CREATE model for the benefit of those managers who might be seeking such a base from which to plan and implement their own campaigns to create and innovate creativity and innovation. This model prescribes that creative innovation is to be enhanced by plans and decisions which:

(a)  create a corporate-wide creative/innovative culture;

(b)  restructure organisation to create a separate creative/innovative function;

(c)  enlist key personnel for the success of the creative/ innovative function;

(d)  activate the functional force for creativity and innovation;

(e)  take control of the creative process;

(f)  entwine the innovative function with the innovative corporation.

## Case study: the development of the Honda City

In 1978, the management of Honda Motors was worried that the company was losing its vitality. Its basic models, such as the Civic and the Accord, had reached 'middle age' at a time of major generational shift in the Japanese market. For the first time, Japanese born after World War II outnumbered those born before and during the war. Honda's top management decided to let the younger design engineers develop something for their own generation. The project began with the catch-phrase, 'let's make an adventure'.

The youngest people on Honda's design staff were selected as members of the City development team. Their average age was only 27. Former president Kiyoshi Kawashima and other top managers promised there would be no interference with the team's operation. One of the team members recalls, 'it was surprising and wonderful that the company dared to entrust younger staff like us with the design and development of a new model.' Even so, the company did not just abandon them, but rather sought to impress them with a high degree of responsibility.

Mr Nobuhiko Kawamoto, vice president in charge of R & D describes how Honda's top managers approach research projects: 'We usually control the tasks of researchers quite tightly, and then loosen the control from time to time. Ideas with great potential often emerge from this process. What we have to do is to watch these creative spurts carefully, notice them when they are good, and then develop them. Of course, too much freedom doesn't work. But sometimes we take the chance of giving researchers basic goals and responsibilities, and then letting them go by themselves. In other words, we put them upstairs, remove the ladders, and say, "You have to jump from there. We don't care if you can't." I think human beings display their greatest creativity under pressure.'

Some say Honda not only puts researchers upstairs without a ladder, but also 'sets the first floor on fire'.

Mr Kawamoto appointed Mr Hiroo Watanabe, a chief researcher who was 35 years old at the time, to be the leader of the team. Mr Kawamoto explains, 'it's hard to get enough cooperation if you only have young staff members. Therefore I chose a skilled senior as their leader.'

The autonomous team faced some challenging goals. The overall assignment from headquarters was to 'create something different from the existing concept'. This involved two major targets: creating a popular, fuel-efficient car (a top management goal) and designing a low-priced but not cheap model (a self-imposed team objective). The team eventually saw two ways to achieve these goals.

They first attempted to develop a 'mini Civic' by shortening the car 100mm in front and back. Although the original instructions from top management – on a single sheet of paper – had been general and ambiguous, management resolutely rejected the compromise. Team leader Watanabe recalls, 'No matter how we refined development plans of this kind, Mr Kawamoto rejected them again and again, saying we have to start all over from the very beginning. We didn't know what to do, but we couldn't tell them that a fresh start was absolutely impossible. So we were finally persuaded to try it.' Top management thus forced the team forward but maintained the loose power balance between the two groups. Mr Watanabe, who had reached a conceptual dead end, went to Europe, where he was inspired by the Austin Mini to lead the team to create a 'luxurious mini' model.

The second means of reaching the team's goal involved challenging an idea that was dominant in the automobile industry: that a car should be 'horizontally long and vertically short'. At the time, most automobile manufacturers were looking for fuel economy with lightweight materials and aerodynamic designs. Consequently, vertically short designs were prevalent. After a month of heated discussions, the team began to move in another direction. Their new policy involved what Mr Watanabe called 'automobile evolution theory': 'The theory is that the ultimate form of the automobile requires us to maximise human space by minimising machine parts. We decided that the automobile was evolving toward this ideal form, and that Honda should lead this evolutionary movement. The first step was to design a tall model that would challenge the 'common sense of Detroit' which permitted car designers to pursue beautiful forms at the expense of space for human use .... It takes a technological perspective to see the significance of a taller model .... It is a cube that can be more lightweight, lower priced, and more solid.'

Based on this theory, the development team chose a 'horizontally short and vertically tall' car as its target. The 'luxurious mini' became the core of their design policy. The challenge was to design a machine-minimum (minimum space devoted to the machine) and man-maximum (maximum space for human use) automobile. These seemingly contradictory goals required the creation of a new viewpoint. One of the team members recalls, 'I feel, however illogical it sounds, that the success of this project owes a lot to the very wide gap between the ideal and the actual. We could not achieve the ideal goal by an incremental improvement of the actual. Revolutionary reformation was necessary, and, in order to achieve this, new technologies and concepts were generated one after another.'

The group then, was given autonomy and was simultaneously forced to challenge long-held assumptions. These alone were not sufficient for the realisation of creative concepts, however. The importance of also having a group of people with heterogeneous backgrounds cannot be overstated. Any group can create a wider variety of concepts than the average individual. This potential is best realised when group members are extremely heterogeneous with respect to jobs, orientations and behaviour. In the phase of concept formation, the City development team was a hybrid, except in that all of the members were genuine car maniacs. In fact, many worried that the team would be unable to reach consensus.

The group needed to introduce, challenge, process and integrate a wide range of information and ideas. One of the methods used was *tamadashi kai*, or meetings to create and share information. *Tamadashi kai* are not formal, and every meeting was held at a different time and place. Each was entirely devoted to discussions and aimed at clearing some hurdle into which the project had run. The participants in these meetings were not just the team members. When necessary, the staffs of related departments were invited as well. All participants were required to be equally involved and absorbed in the lively discussion regardless of titles or qualifications. However, criticism was taboo. As Mr Watanabe says, 'To criticise is ten times easier than to propose a constructive option. The discussion would have been useless if participants had reminded silent for fear of being criticised.' Several times, Mr Watanabe held day-and-night discussion sessions, most often in rooms at small taverns or inns near the research lab instead of at luxurious hotels. In ceaseless discussion from morning to midnight participants had to use all their wits to challenge existing paradigms.

During the development process, the project team comprised people from the development, production and sales departments. The team made use of a quick information creation system based on a hybridisation of the three departmental positions. The system performed the following functions: procuring personnel, facilities and budget figures for the production plant; analysing the automobile market and the competition; and setting a market target and determining sale price and production quantity. This system, which collects, creates and implements information, is called the 'SED system'. It is also used to develop about 45 new motorcycle models each year. The SED system was established when Mr Kawashima was president of Honda. Its initial aim was to manage development activities more systematically by integrating the knowledge and wisdom of ordinary people instead of relying on a 'hero' like founder Soichiro Honda.

The operation of the system is quite flexible. The three areas, Sales, Engineering, and Development (SED) are nominally distinct, but there is a built-in learning process that encourages invasion into others' areas. The actual work requires researchers to collaborate with their colleagues. Mr Watanabe comments, 'I am always telling the team members that our work is not a relay race – that's my work, and yours starts here. Every one of us should run all the way from the start to the finish. Like in a rugby game, all of us should run together, passing the ball left and right, reaching the goal as one united body.'

This process leads to a high level of information sharing. In a project team, members share a huge amount of managerial information received through conversations with top management, they also share market information concerning the competition. Moreover, as the division of labour is rather unclear and flexible, members can meddle wherever they like. There is thus no information lag between top management and the team leader. Also, since whatever the various members are doing is out in the open, each knows almost instinctively what his or her co-workers have in mind. This information sharing among project members reflects a distinctive aspect of Honda's broad corporate culture. The company is already famous as an originator of the 'large room' system, and all its meeting rooms are glass-plated so that what is going on can be seen from the outside. As the degree of information sharing increases, individuals identify themselves with the team as a whole, and begin 'self-controlling'. 'Basically speaking', says Vice President Kawamoto, 'organisational management is no longer necessary if each individual properly performs what is expected. Once a goal is given and roles are specified to a certain extent, our staff works quite well.'

Every participating member grows up by casting off his older skin in the process of successful project development. Prominent success helps other members to follow, saying, 'Hey! Look at what those guys have done.' After the successful completion of a project, participants are assigned to other projects so that the knowledge they have acquired can be transferred throughout the organisation. An engineer comments, 'I think it's pretty difficult to articulate really meaningful know-how in text, figures, or other measurable forms. The knowledge is alive because … it changes continuously …. The best way to transfer it is through human interaction.'

On the other hand, Honda dislikes easy imitations of recent successes, and sometimes even goes so far as to destroy its own accumulated knowledge. 'The most severe criticism for us is to say, "It looks like something else", states Mr Hinoshi Honma, a chief engineer. The concept of 'Tall Boy' (the nickname for the City model) was created by destroying the concepts that dominated Honda and the automobile industry in general at the time. A special engine, suspension and radial tyre were developed exclusively for the new car. All other parts were also designed for the City, to avoid giving customers an image of a 'mini Civic'. About 90 patents were applied for during the project, which clearly indicates the 'unlearning' of accumulated knowledge and the acquisition of new knowledge.

Middle management plays a key role in this process of abandoning the old and generating the new. The Honda City case clearly shows the critical importance of Mr Watanabe, the middle manager selected as project leader. His role had several key aspects: providing direct information links to top management; transforming top management's general vision into directions for the team's activities and for pursuing the creating of meaning; managing 'chaos' and keeping it within tolerable limits; and providing the context for integration across specialities. While Honda pays tribute to the energy and drive of the young researchers who generated the new product idea, top management clearly recognises the strategic role of its middle management project leaders as well.

Mr Katutoshi Wada, head of the Human Resources Development Centre at Honda, characterises Honda management as follows: 'Mr Soichiro Honda, the founder of our company, did not articulate this, but we now realise that an organisation has a kind of culture, with dreams on the one hand and a realistic methodology on the other. Taken together, the dream is always larger than the reality, qualitatively as well as quantitatively. The solution to the gap between the two comprises the essential mission of Honda management. We are perpetually engaged in an effort to mediate and solve the contradictions generated by a naive romanticism and a hard realism. Without coupling such romanticism and realism, it would be difficult to manage our company well. Neither a dreaming child nor an adult who has lost all his dreams can produce good management. Good management can be achieved only by matching the dream of a child with the realism of an adult.'

(Source: 'Toward Middle-Up-Down Management', by I. Nonaka, in *Sloan Management Review*, Spring 1988, pp 9–18)

## Think and discuss

1 Refer to the Honda City case study. What aspects of the CREATE framework seem to have been applied in the innovation of the Honda City?

2 Think about your own organisation (or one of your choosing). Describe innovations which have affected the competitive structure of the industry in which your organisation operates.

How has your organisation responded/taken advantage of the innovation(s) identified?

What changes would you make to improve your chosen organisation's innovatory performance?

## References

1   A Johne and P Snelson, 'Innovate or Die', *Management Today*, November 1987
2   W Richardson and D Morris, 'Reorganising Towards Responsiveness', *Management Monitor*, Spring 1987
3   C Bart, 'New Venture Units: Use them wisely to manage innovation', *Sloan Management Review*, Summer 1988
4   S Cooke and N Slack, *Making Management Decisions*, Prentice-Hall International, 1984
5   T J Peters and R H Waterman Jr, *In Search of Excellence*, Harper & Row, 1982
6   G Pinchot, 'How Entrepreneurs Innovate', *Management Today*, December 1985
7   A E Pearson, 'Tough-Minded Ways to Get Innovative', *Harvard Business Review*, May–June 1988
8   See, for example, P Kotler, *Marketing Management, Analysis, Planning and Control*, 4th edn, Prentice-Hall International, 1980, Ch 13

## Recommended reading

P F Drucker, *Innovation and Entrepreneurship*, Heinemann, 1985
G J Pearson, 'Promoting Enterpreneurship in Large Companies', *Long Range Planning*, 22 (3), 1989, pp 88–97
T J Peters, *Thriving on Chaos*, Macmillan, 1988

# 14 Shock event planning

As modern environments become more dynamic, turbulent and unpredictable, management strategists need to address the problem of *how to plan for the 'unplannable'*. Shock events – and unexpected opportunities – are becoming more commonplace despite improvements in organisational planning skills. In this final chapter we introduce some of that theory only recently made available in the literature of management strategy, which seeks to indicate how shock events might be more effectively handled. In this chapter our discussion examines:

- The growing incidence of shock events
- The dimensions of shock events
- Planning shock event effectiveness
- Complete planning sophistication – shock events and strategic success

## The growing incidence of shock events

'I'm sure you're aware of the constantly increasing potential for crisis in organisations. Indeed, the largest have become house-hold words. Tylenol was the worst case to date of a nationwide product tampering incident; Bhopal was the largest industrial accident in history, Chernobyl the largest nuclear accident .... The increased crisis potential of organisations, if not of our entire society, is striking. Since 1900, there have been 29 major industrial accidents in the world .... The clinker in the preceding statistic is that half of those disasters occurred within the past eight years.' (1)

A modern planning paradox is one which has strategists improving their ability to spot environmental change, understand futures and plan desired outcomes, while environments continue to throw up even bigger and more frequent shocks. Below we have identified some of the increasingly 'commonplace' surprises which threaten today's organisations.

(a) major 'global' accidents

(b) terrorism

(c) kidnappings

(d) hostile takeovers

(e) sabotage/product tampering

(f) 'the people should know' – investigative journalism

(g) product/plant/equipment defects

(h) political upheaval

(i) pressure group activity

Table 14.1 provides some specific examples of modern, disaster type, shock events and some of the alleged organisation failures which enabled them to happen.

**Table 14.1 Shock events (source: student assignment MBA III)**

| Event | Nature | Organisation failure |
|---|---|---|
| Lockerbie | Aircraft destroyed | Failure by Pan Am to act on warnings of possible terrorist attack: lax security |
| King's Cross | Underground fire | Poor maintenance and cleaning; lack of staff training and emergency procedures (3) |
| Hillsborough | Football club crush | Crowd control failures; faulty crush barrier (4) |
| Flixborough | Nyro plant explosion | Improper repair to plant; lack of supervision and control |
| Summerlands Leisure Centre | Fire | Use of inflammable Oroglass as cladding material |
| Challenger | Space shuttle explosion | Design faults; poor assembly; conditions unsuitable for launch (13) |
| Herald of Free Enterprise | Car ferry capsize | Bow doors left open; lack of checks; poor management |
| Kegworth | Air crash | Wrong engine shut down; failure to follow procedures |
| Chernobyl | Nuclear Plant explosion | Poor design; test procedures not followed (6) |
| Three Mile Island | Nuclear plant contamination | Safety systems failure; poor instrumentation (7) |
| Bradford FC | Football club fire | Old timber construction; accumulation of rubbish |
| Aberfan | Waste tip collapse | Tip constructed on spring; no checks by NCB |
| Piper Alpha | Oil platform explosion | Relief valve failure; lack of safety control systems (8) |

Organisation life tends towards being 'what happens while you're busy making other plans' (2). Management strategy, of course, is based on the basic optimism that, regardless of the nature of the problem faced, a more theoretically based and systematically approached search for a solution *will* produce desired outcomes. As we move through the final, uncertain, decade of the century the theory of management strategy is endeavouring to provide frameworks to help solve the newly critical planning problem of shock events. This final chapter introduces some of the prescriptions emanating from this most recent (and least adequately served) area in the theory and practice of management strategy.

Figure 14.1 illustrates a theme which has run consistently through this book – that of *environmental change, turbulence and hostility*. Society is creating a business environment which is wider, more diverse, more complex and more novel. More new, less observable, less understandable, *less reliable* factors and situations imply *surprising* and *dangerous* events.

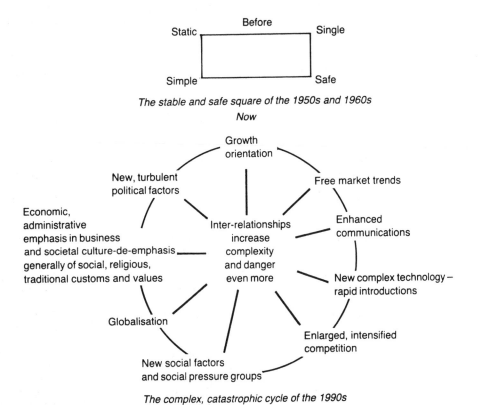

Figure 14.1 Why the increasing incidence of shock events?

## The dimensions of shock events

Igor Ansoff (9) acknowledges the 'newness' of shock event planning theory and the growing need for surprise management systems: 'So far as I am aware, few, if any firms have developed and committed themselves to a formal surprise management system ... the system presented here is only a proposal for handling surprises and a prediction that firms will begin to adopt surprise management systems.' Importantly, perhaps, Ansoff also describes the dimensions of a shock event. Thus in shock event situations:

(a)  the issue arrives suddenly, *unanticipated*;

(b)  it poses *novel* problems in which the firm has little prior experience;

(c)  failure to respond implies either a *major financial reversal* or loss of a *major opportunity*;

(d)  the response is *urgent* and cannot be handled promptly enough by the normal systems and procedures.

This analysis of the nature of the shock event phenomenon is important because it identifies the problems which shock event planners need to address. Shrivastava et al. (10) remind us that organisational activities create harmful as well as beneficial effects and that as industrial technologies become more complex they also become potentially more harmful. The authors provide a domain for studying industrial crises by describing their key characteristics and suggest that general characteristics are discernible in such different crisis situations as e.g. Bhopal, Tylenol and the Challenger shuttle incident. These key characteristics include:

(a)  *triggering events* which create damage inside or outside the organisation;

(b)  *large scale damage* to human life and environment;

(c)  *large economic costs,*

(d)  *large social costs.*

Crises are triggered by interacting sets of human, organisational or technical failures and can escalate, in certain environmental situations, into full-blown crises.

Industrial crises are also characterised by an involvement of *multiple stakeholders.* This often causes numerous long-drawn conflicts over responsibility, liability and recovery costs. Short-term responses from stakeholders are directed towards mitigating destruction and social disruption, and preventing future crises of a similar nature from occurring. Such responses are made under severe time pressures, inadequate and conflicting information, conditions of breakdown of social and organisational systems, intense media scrutiny and an emotionally charged environment. More long-term responses focus on causes of crises, conflict resolution, compensation and rehabilitation of victims, and on technological and organisational improvements. Efforts are also made to change environmental conditions, enhance infrastructural services, and change regulations governing industries.

While much organisational activity is directed at mitigating the effects of the crisis few efforts, according to Shrivastava et al., are expended towards eliminating the original causes. This focus on symptoms rather than causes leaves the enterprise vulnerable to similar crises which can deepen and extend the original problem. The Hillsborough disaster illustration, below, describes this tragedy in the context of Shrivastava et al.'s model of the characteristics of industrial crises. Such general models are useful because they point strategists towards potential sources of problems and, hence, towards plans for their avoidance and/or management.

## Case example: profile of a shock event – the Hillsborough disaster

'Industrial crises are situations in which organised industrial activities [rather than nature] are the source of major damage to human life, and national and social environments. They often occur in an economic crisis characterised by insufficient growth, unemployment, fiscal deficits, budgetary and competitive pressures on individual organisations and an inadequate industrial infrastructure. Crises invariably extend beyond the organisation of origin to encompass a broad range of economic, social and political agents and forces ... Industrial crises have a number of key defining characteristics' (10) as introduced, below, in the context of the Hillsborough football stadium tragedy.

(a) *Triggering events*. These represent sudden destructive events which have a very low probability of occurrence, but there are often warnings of their occurrence. Given their low probability assessments, these warnings are often not taken seriously. For example, when challenged about the pertinence of allocating the smallest part of the Hillsborough ground to the largest section of fans, the police decided not to change its policy. Similar control procedures had worked well the previous year. Generally inadequate and potentially unsafe football stadiums were being maintained despite clear and regular warnings from a sequence of inquiries into previous football stadium disasters. Only a few years earlier at another semi-final match at Hillsborough members of the crowd had been injured due to overcrowding. It is difficult to isolate *one* triggering event, however. In the Hillsborough disaster, and more generally, perhaps, it might be more useful to identify the 'coupling causes' (11). These might include, for example, society's change to a football hooligan culture; the erection of strong, secure, crowd control barriers; the decision not to reorganise ground and ticket allocation arrangements; a police control method change outside the gates; impatience of a crowd of boisterous supporters (some of which had missed the first goal of the previous week's match due to a delay in entering the ground); the decision to open external gates; the failure to close doors to Stand C.

(b) *Large scale damage to human life and environment*. The Hillsborough tragedy resulted in 95 dead and more than 200 injured. Grieving friends and relatives were still taking legal action in 1991, seeking compensation for the enduring physical and emotional effects the incident had produced on themselves. One injured fan was still comatosed two years on from the incident.

(c) *Large economic costs*. Costs incurred in dealing with the disaster and its aftermath include those for police, ambulance, health and fire authorities, counselling services and inquiry investigations and reporting. The Hillsborough inquest, alone, sat for 93 days. By mid-1991 more than £19 million compensation had been agreed and more claims remained in the legal pipeline. The government made available £100 million to help clubs improve their grounds. By the end of the century all grounds will need to be all-seated.

(d) *Large social costs.* Families and communities have needed to be reorganised and rehabilitated following the tragedy. The South Yorkshire Police, particularly, have been subjected to immense social and political pressures.

(e) *Causes of crises: human, organisational and technology (HOT) factors and regulatory, infrastructural and preparedness (RIP), factors.* HOT factors lead to the triggering event and include operator and managerial errors (these accusations were levied at particular police officers involved in the Hillsborough incident); policy failures; inadequate resource allocations; strategic business pressures leading to a neglect of safety issues; communication failures; misperceptions of the extent and nature of hazards; inadequate emergency plans; and cost pressures. Each of these factors can be viewed as having played a part in the Hillsborough tragedy. For example, 70 fewer police attended the event than had been the case for the previous year's match; communication systems between individual police officers and the control room failed at crucial times; officers in the control tower seemed initially to be unable to perceive the crowd spillage onto the pitch as anything other than a crowd invasion control problem. The Sheffield Wednesday organisation is not a cash rich organisation (although it has since embarked on a £3 million ground improvement programme) and needs to take potentially expensive investment in safety choices in the context of an overall business decision-making process. Neither did it seem, perhaps, to see itself as a leisure/entertainment provider with a primary duty to provide comfortable, safe, enjoyable and motivational benefits to its customers. Rather it provides a venue for people, who must be controlled (by the police), to watch soccer matches. Technical problems include defective equipment and faulty design, each of which played a part in the tragedy. (Are secure, rigid, and difficult to open/remove crowd fences and barriers, well designed, for example?)

Regulatory failures allow disasters to happen. Despite the recommendations over safety matters by a number of soccer tragedy inquiries little special regulatory attention has been paid to the enforcement of improved standards. Infrastructural (water, electricity, transportation, communication, etc.) back up, however, was rapidly available to provide positive help quickly. 'Hiccups' in the operationalisation of support services, nevertheless, occurred. Ambulances, for example, initially created their own traffic jam. The telephone receptionist for the fire service was unable to respond to the first request for help until the request had been formulated in a way acceptable to the computerised recording/administrating system she managed: 'My training is not to assume what an address is, it is up to me to ascertain that from the person calling.' The fire service computer would not recognise the Hillsborough ground as a place. Preparedness failure is apparent, to some large degree, in the Hillsborough example.

(f) *Multiple stakeholder involvement and conflict.* From the above it is obvious that multiple agencies, stakeholder groups and individuals have been involved in the tragedy and its subsequent long-drawn conflicts over responsibility, liability and recovery costs. Media coverage of these proceedings has been intense. Stakeholder support activity has been forthcoming from both the government and voluntary sectors.

(g) *Responses to crises.* Immediate responses attempt to control technical problems producing damage and to rescue and help affected persons. These responses have to be made under severe time pressures, inadequate and conflicting information, breakdown of normal social and organisational systems, intense media sensitivity and an emotionally charged environment. Longer term responses focus on inquiries into causes and consequences, conflict resolution, compensation claims, rehabilitation services and improvements to organisational, technological, infrastructural and environment situations. New regulations are often improved. Again, the general description provides a pertinent framework within which the specifics of the Hillsborough incident fit.

(h) *Crisis resolution.* Decision-makers atttempt to mitigate the effects of a crisis. Organisations and technological improvements are sought. Economic compensation is offered to victims. Social recovery requires the re-integration of victims into social systems and the normalisation of social relations. Business recovery is sought perhaps through product/market and financial changes. Once more the Hillsborough model is in accord with the general model.

(i) *Focus on symptoms not causes.* Decision-makers tend to view recovery from damages as the resolution of the crisis. However, few efforts are made to eliminate the original causes. The focus is on symptoms rather than causes. This appears to have been the case during the history of the soccer industry and, so far as the outcomes of the Hillsborough tragedy are concerned, the 'court is still out'. We must wait to see whether real, significant cause eradicating improvements are to be made within society and the football industry.

(j) *Befores, during and afters.* It is worth stating the obvious that shock events begin well before, and often distant from, the final triggering event. There are intense periods during which the initial incident impacts, and longer periods during which aftermaths unfurl and have to be managed (12). Models such as that above by Shrivastava et al., and case study accounts of disasters such as that of the Hillsborough tragedy (4) help us to plan to be better avoiders and managers of the 'befores, durings and afters' of shock events.

# Planning shock event effectiveness

The effective 'shock event planner' is the organisation which eradicates or reduces substantially the problems created by shock events and/or which takes advantage of the opportunities which such events 'throw up'. Effective shock event planning, therefore, involves changing an organisation to reduce the extent to which shock events are novel and unanticipated and to improve the speed with which they are effectively managed (see Fig. 14.2). Successful organisational change reduces the enormity of the adverse impact which might otherwise apply, and/or improves the flow of benefits which the enterprise attracts from taking advantage of unpredicted opportunities. In this chapter we concentrate on the problem of planning for *adverse* shock events.

## Making shock events less unpredictable

The 'denovelising' process can begin with the realisation that *structural similarities* underpin the countless potential specific shock events. Mitroff (1) for example, advocates the development of a crisis portfolio – the grouping of crises according to their structural similarity. Thus, '*breaks*' consist of defects in products, plants and

| Shock event dimensions | | Planning tasks for shock event effectiveness |
|---|---|---|
| Novel | → | Make *less novel* through organisational change |
| Unanticipated | → | Make *less unanticipated* through organisational change |
| Urgent | → | Change the organisation to make it a *quicker* and more effective manager of shock event situations |
| Major impact | → | Change organisation so that it *reduces* the adverse impact of shock events |

**Figure 14.2  Planning effective responses to shock events**

people, etc. 'Psycho' consists of extreme anti-social acts such as terrorism, kidnappings and sabotage. 'External information attacks' include counterfeiting, loss of information and rumours while 'exterior economic attacks' incorporate extortion, hostile takeovers and boycotts, etc. 'Mega damage' is created by environmental accidents. These 'families' of shock events have been modelled by Mitroff as being located on a matrix (see Fig. 14.3) which measures the extent of severity of the event on the one axis and the extent to which the events are technical/economic or human/social in causation on the other. (Mitroff asserts that virtually all crises are created by a mixture of human and technical elements.)

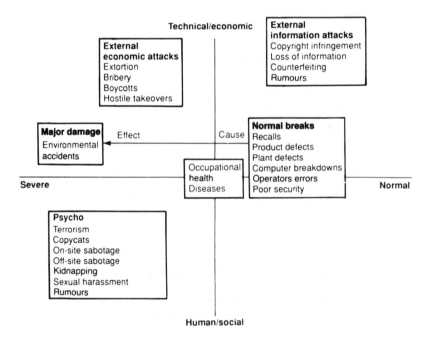

**Figure 14.3  Crisis families**

The crisis planning activity is enhanced by the choosing of at least one crisis from each of the families and subsequently 'planning' for that crisis. In this way the organisation develops understanding and skills which 'denovelise' *any* specific shock event. Simulated shock event aftermaths can also provide useful training vehicles for equipping the organisation to respond with some familiarity to real crises.

## Making shock events less unanticipated

A bomb which goes off, demolishing the works canteen, will be, for the organisation concerned, a shock event. A bomb which goes off, similarly, 30 minutes after it has been discovered will still be a shock event – but less so. Its potential adverse impact will have been reduced, thanks to the notice gained – through clearing the canteen of people, for example. While shock events are by definition unanticipated, different degrees of 'unanticipation' can apply. The firm which gets wind of a takeover bid only two days before offer letters are received is, nevertheless, in a less serious state of shock than one whose first indication of the takeover is the bid letter itself. To quote Mitroff: 'Long before its actual occurrence a crisis sends off repeated and early warning signals. Crisis managers must be alert to those signals.'

Reputedly, the space shuttle disaster of 1986 had been *forecast* in a series of memos which never reached the top of NASA (13). Information is the means to anticipation. Therefore, organisational systems must be geared to a more systematic analysis of shock event information signals. Internal occurrences (machinery breakdowns, labour force unrest, etc.) and external events and trends (political events, shareholding changes, pressure group activity, etc.) need to be recorded, analysed and evaluated in the context of their implications for potential shock events. Information gathering might commence in areas commended for investigation by the firm's crisis portfolio exercises. Because much shock event information is of a very weak signal nature, spotting shock events before they occur will often depend upon the availability of creative, motivated personnel who will pick up weak information, feel 'uneasy' about it and then pass on these feelings and/or search further for signal amplifications.

## Managing shock events urgently

Successful anticipation, of course, gains time and so reduces urgency. In those situations where unanticipated shocks do, however, arise, quicker and more effective responses are likely from the organisation which has prepared in advance. Ansoff (9), who bases his prescriptions on a study of military and business surprises, suggests that the 'strategic surprise system' should be in place in advance of a shock event and should comprise:

(a)  An emergency communications network which crosses normal organisational boundaries to take and give out information, organisation-wide, rapidly.

(b)  A repartitionment of top management to provide:

- one unit concerned with maintaining organisation morale;
- one unit to concentrate on 'business as usual'; and
- one unit to take charge of the response to the shock event. This unit is likely

to be more effective if it is headed by a strong, aggressive, power-orientated risk taker (14).

(c)  A task force which has direct links with the shock event management unit and authority to cross normal organisational lines. The top management unit should decide overall strategy – the task force should have the authority to implement strategy in pertinent fashion as situations unfurl. Members of this group should be trained under simulated crisis conditions. Training should seek to build up analytical and creative skills for the making of quick decisions. Intellectual training also needs to be supplemented by *emotional* preparation – many shock events bring, in their wakes, tragedy and recriminations.

## Reducing adverse impacts – learning from actual crisis

Effective planning across the interrelated quests to make shock events less novel, less unanticipated and more effectively handled will, of course, reduce the costs and/or increase the benefits which might otherwise flow to an organisation from a shock occurrence.

Quarantelli (15) provides many useful, more specific tips to help the shock event planner to be more effective. Quarantelli has researched crisis management to provide material for *disaster planners*, who must respond urgently to such disasters as floods or earthquakes at national or international level. His research indicates that *similar* types of problem accrue in *different* crisis management situations. Attention to these potential problem areas, therefore, might alleviate the difficulties which face those involved in responding to crisis and can provide some preparatory groundwork which enables more effective crisis responses. Quarantelli's recommmmendations are of relevance to management strategists who must plan for unexpected crises within the business environment.

According to Quarantelli, crisis planners should pay particular attention to the communication processes, and the decision-making authority and co-ordination issues which arise during a crisis. More specifically, the following *actions for disaster planners* can be taken directly or inferred from Quarantelli's findings.

(a)  Identify different *means* of communication which might be capable of supplementing or even replacing traditional systems (telephone, postal, etc.). Often, traditional systems are damaged and/or overloaded during times of crisis.

(b)  Identify and create links with *other* organisational personnel (people in the police, fire, health departments, etc.). Establish information flows between your organisation and theirs.

(c)  Train staff to work with unfamiliar officials and groups. Identify ways in which your organisational personnel might make themselves easily known (badges, uniforms, etc.).

(d)  Identify those organisations most likely to be contacted by the public during an emergency. Again, create contacts and inter-organisational information systems.

(e)  Designate an organisational office as contact point for enquiries. Decide from where that office will, itself, obtain information and, so far as possible, what questions it will and will not answer. Train staff from this office to deal with enquiry overload situations and to deal with highly emotional enquirers.

(f) Identify a range of potentially useful general communication media. Train pertinent staff in how to devise and present clear, succinct and comprehensive messages to *publics*.

(g) Identify personnel who might *emerge* as important decision-makers during an emergency (middle managers and personnel on site, for example, might have to make, temporarily, top management decisions). Train these people in decision-making under crisis conditions. Let them know where and how they might find help from the organisational hierarchy in a crisis situation. Establish, so far as possible, which personnel (all things being equal) will have authority for decisions over particular disaster-related tasks. Establish 'preferred hours on duty' limits. Establish delegation systems to avoid personnel burnout and to ensure that important information is passed on when officials go off duty.

(h) Pre-plan *co-ordination* (rather than *control*) systems. Liaise with other organisations to develop a common understanding of what co-ordination means.

(i) Train organisation officials to ask rather than tell, request rather than order and delegate or decentralise rather than narrow and centralise – these options being, generally, the more appropriate crisis management behaviours.

(j) Expect real crisis management to require *different responses* to those covered in pre-planning. Underpin all organisational activities intended to improve disaster management with exercises designed to improve personnel skills in resolving non-routine, conflict-generating situations through creativity.

## Case study: managing natural disasters

Within days of eye witness accounts of unusually heavy rains in Sudan, a British relief plane had landed in Khartoum. The ensuing Sudan Emergency Appeal, launched by the Disasters Emergency Committee (DEC) was the first of a trio of nationwide appeals which together raised more than £14 million for Sudan, Bangladesh, the Caribbean and Nicaragua in just four months. DEC is normally geared-up to run just one appeal at a time, so running three simultaneously really put its system to the test – particularly given the UK postal strike which took place in the middle of the campaign.

According to DEC Secretary, Pam Pouncy: 'Disasters are by definition, impossible to predict or plan for and we cannot afford to have people waiting for them to happen. As far as possible we have to set things up in advance – contact lists, action schedules, lines of rapid communication and financial arrangements, so that when a disaster happens everything is in place.' A schedule of key tasks is implemented with great speed in the event of a disaster. Operational staff advise DEC's five full Committee Members (British Red Cross, CAFOD, Christian Aid, Oxfam, and Save the Children) who decide whether an appeal should be launched. If a positive decision is made, the DEC Secretariat alerts the broadcasting authorities, the banks and the Post Office which provide collecting points for donations at all branches, as well as special Post Office boxes. Endorsements from the BBC and IBA, which give free air-time to the DEC, are obtained, a launch date is agreed and journalists begin work on the appeal scripts. The DEC's advertising agency is briefed and a co-ordinated publicity drive is implemented. Each charity informs its own network of members of the impending appeal. Special accounts are opened for the handling of donations, for communicating with donors and for disbursing the funds. In the field, agencies work with locally based partner organisations and their own field teams. After the Nile flooded the country's communications system, precarious at the best of times, failed completely and British agencies used long-wave radio transmitters to maintain contact until electricity was restored in Khartoum. Back in London, 'desk officers' with day to day responsibility for operations, met regularly.

An important stage of the key task implementation is that which has fund raising and publicity staff meeting to agree a common explanation of the causes of the disaster. The 'message' to the public has to convey complex aid issues (civil wars were additional aid problems in the Sudan, for example). At the same time, it needs to convey a vivid, immediate picture of need to which people can respond instantly. *Facilitating* instantaneous responses is also important. During 'Smile Jamaica', groups of volunteers manned over 200 lines at various regional centres. Telephoned credit card donations were introduced in 1987 and in each subsequent appeal more donors have opted to use credit card lines.

(Source: adapted from S Faulkner, 'Coping With Crisis', *The Administrator*, February 1989)

## Think and discuss

Identify the extent to which DEC seems to have developed theoretically prescribed systems for managing crisis.

## Complete planning sophistication, shock events and stategic success

In Chapter 1, and subsequently, we have noted how each of the planning subsystems in our complete model interact and overlap. Improved effectiveness in one planning activity will invariably produce 'spin off' benefits for better planning in other areas. As we move towards the end of this book's exploration of how a 'complete' business planning system might be achieved we can note, particularly, the synergistic nature of the complete planning process. If the organisation's shock event planning system is the *final* system to receive management strategy-based attention then a useful foundation for its successful development will already be in place. For example, communication and information systems will already be 'highly tuned' and capable of handling more effectively, weak signals. Slack created by productivity/efficiency drives and by successful market operations will be available for the creation of shock event systems, for the resourcing of shock event teams and for their *deployment* in emergency. The organisation will be responsive to the need for co-operative and extra effort during the crisis. It will be able to draw important resources from its range of loyal stakeholders. A creative force for dealing with the problem should be readily available. In short, 'complete' planning sophistication is a breeder of *teams* which *reduce* the size and scope of shock events and which *survive* those disasters which do occur as a prerequisite to *renewing the drive for strategic success*. Complete planning effectiveness is the basis of sustained strategic success.

# Case study: surviving a shock event

In 1963 the young Cassius Clay arrived in London predicting that Henry Cooper would 'dive in five'. His fight with Cooper was to be the next successful stage in the long-term plan which had already achieved an Olympic title for Clay and which would assuredly lead to the World Boxing Heavyweight title. Clay's team was steeped in managerial and technical expertise and experience. Clay himself was the perfect boxing product.

Dedication to the attainment of his dream stimulated a conscientious approach to training which honed his natural ability and growing strength. Inside the ring Clay was the fastest-moving – and thinking – heavyweight of his time – perhaps of all time. His ability to clown, dance, box and fight – as his mood or the needs of the particular fight changed – had proven too effectively innovative for his opponents to date. When he stepped into the ring to face the ageing British champion, Henry Cooper, a long and successful future seemed to be unfurling before him.

Cooper almost destroyed the dreams. 'Enery's famous 'left hammer' hit Clay in the fourth round and very nearly provided one of the biggest shock events of recent sporting history. It amost robbed the world, too, of the delights of the renamed Muhammed Ali's reign as three times world champion. However, Cooper's moment of glory was to be short-lived. A dazed Clay found the strength to drag himself off the canvas and to survive the remainder of the round. Mysteriously Clay's glove split during the ensuing interval. Valuable seconds were gained for his recuperation as the glove was changed. In the fifth round a newly aggressive Clay dominated throughout and, in accordance with his pre-fight prediction, the fight was stopped in his favour in that round.

## Think and discuss

1 Identify or speculate on the factors which helped Cassius Clay survive the above shock event.
2 Consider the appropriateness of similar factors for the resolution of a less foreseeable shock in the context of an industrial organisation which suddenly loses half its sales turnover.

# Shock event planning: conclusion

'There seems to be an inexhorable systemic logic in societies that makes industrial crises almost inevitable. Industry technologies are becoming progressively more complex and harmful. Organisations are becoming larger in size and scope ... [and can create] harm on a global scale.' (15) Shock events should be considered by today's managers as 'normal events' (11).

As modern environments produce shock events with increasing force and regularity it makes growing sense for today's firm to pay formal attention to improving its shock event capability. A shock event planning system will work best if it is built onto an already almost complete 'complete' planning system. In terms of this book the following shock event planning steps provide the final link in our quest to prescribe a complete business planning system and to help develop, in our readers, more comprehensive management strategist skills. Thus, shock event planners should:

(a) Build a 'complete' planning platform for the shock event planning exercise.

(b) In the corporate planning process ask the question 'is there anything about the way we do business which might conceivably damage society – what are the harmful effects of our system of organising?'

(c) Make shock events less novel by developing a crisis portfolio and grouping potential crises into families which share similar economic/technical, human/social roots. Choose at least one crisis from each of the families and plan to meet each of these crises. Simulate shock events and practise the organisation's responses.

(d) Make shock events less unanticipated by redesigning information systems to better locate and consider shock event implications. Encourage personnel to get involved in sensing, following up and communicating shock event signals.

(e) Prepare for rapid but effective responses to shock events by installing an emergency communication network which crosses normal organisational boundaries; make ready management units to take care of business as usual, staff morale and the actual crisis, respectively; create a shock event task force to work, without regard for normal organisational boundaries, for and with the crisis management unit.

Train the crisis management network members to make quick analyses of situations. Train these members also to handle the emotional problems which often accompany shock events.

## Case study: Review of Perrier's recall of its product

(Source: D Butler, 'Perrier's Painful Period', *Management Today*, August 1990, pp 72–3 – A review by Bill Richardson)

Daphne Barret, a crisis management specialist, sums up the nature of a shock event: 'We created a crisis management strategy for Perrier UK five years ago. Every year this was reviewed in the light of developments. Everyone knew what they were supposed to do, but obviously you hope it will never happen. In spite of this, we never, ever imagined a worldwide withdrawal. We'd never dreamed of a problem of such magnitude.' Shock events are *unexpected, sudden,* occurrences of potentially *major adverse effect.* This article provides a glimpse (only) of the prior planning and the related organisational activity which helped Perrier handle the major crisis which arrived on the 10 February 1990.

Perrier is the 'designer' water – chic, sophisticated and pure. At the beginning of 1990 its leadership in the mineral water market was massive and unassailable. With 32 per cent of the market it was above 2½ times the size of its nearest rival, Evian, (although 'own label' products took a 27 per cent and growing share of the market). In February 1990, however, a control test on mineral water, carried out in North Carolina (and using Perrier because of its acknowledged purity) found minute traces of benzene in the Perrier water. The minute quantities recorded did not represent a health risk but, fearing a backlash by the health lobby because of benzene's carcinogenic links, the US subsidiary immediately withdrew all products.

In the UK Wenche Marshall Foster, chief executive of Perrier UK was at first unconcerned. Trading Standards officers in Britain tested Perrier water continuously and had found no impurities, previously. The view was that the US problem was likely to be of a localised, product tampering type. Nevertheless, Perrier UK swung its crisis management plan into action. The problem arose in the US on the Saturday morning. The first UK crisis management meeting took place *that very same evening.*

The organisation had prepared plans for such an event. In theory all that had to be done now was for the plans to be operationalised. A first problem, however, was due to the timing of the incident. Perrier UK wanted to test its own products quickly but finding authorising officials of the Ministry of Agriculture, Fisheries and Foods on a Saturday evening proved difficult. The organisation went through its pre-planned procedures – never believing that a UK-based crisis would occur. It set up ten emergency telephone lines, met with the Ministry and began testing its product.

Meanwhile, a confused spokesman for the company, *in Paris* hypothesised that the benzene could have originated with a 'greasy rag'. Although incorrect, this hypothesis could not be refuted or even commented on by an information-lacking London. Speculation about grease ran rife in the press, further damaging Perrier's reputation for purity. Tests revealed that benzene was, in fact, contaminating the UK product. Barret, acting in her consultancy capacity, would have preferred an open stance immediately and Perrier UK's crisis plan included an immediate withdrawal of all products. However, the French headquarters insisted that, instead, a late afternoon statement would be made, in Paris, on behalf of the company as a whole. The UK subsidiary complied with the French directive but dispatched couriers to all major UK supermarket buyers warning them of an impending product withdrawal.

The Parisian press conference was a shambles. The company had expected the French press only. However, the incident was international news. Hundreds of journalists besieged the headquarters in Paris. People could not get in or out and the lifts jammed.

Perrier UK adopted a different strategy. The problem with the press conference medium, explains Barret, is that 'You have a client who is as shocked as everyone else, who doesn't know much more than the journalists, facing questions fired from all directions under a barrage of flashlights.' Obviously such situations are not conducive to the presentation of a calm, 'we're in control', facade. Instead, Marshall Foster (the chief executive) worked throughout the evening and night talking to journalists individually. This helped produce a generally sympathetic press reaction.

On Thursday, 15 February, full-page adverts were run in every national newspaper telling people about the withdrawal, where they could return their bottles and how to get refunds. During this period the 24-hour hotlines were inundated with calls.

A plan to recycle 50 per cent of the 40 million bottles which had been withdrawn and to use the rest for landfill failed to recognise the strength of feeling this would generate. Friends of the Earth was particularly alert. Rumours spread quickly. People with placards demonstrated and *Today* newspaper launched a campaign to stop the landfill strategy. British glass manufacturers, of course, were not over-interested in taking the *green* glass from Perrier. Eventually the company crushed and stored the glass for gradual use over the course of the next year.

As a result of the benzene scare several retailing chains asked to inspect the production plant. Perrier's label, boasting 'naturally carbonated natural mineral water' came under scrutiny. While the water is naturally gassy, mass production and the need for product uniformity has led to an industrial process whereby the water and gas are collected separately underground, and mixed at the bottling site. Sainsbury, a massive Perrier customer, felt that the processes might invalidate the lablel's claim and expressed concern that consumers might be being misled. It refused to restock until the label was altered. As a result of this squabble, the EC commenced a review of the labelling requirements for all bottled waters. Apart from the very real effects of the loss of a customer with 18 per cent of the UK's retail food outlets the investigations sparked off by the crisis were undoubtedly damaging to the image of naturalness and purity which has been built up over many years.

Despite the many problems experienced by Perrier UK and candidly described in this article, the underlying picture which can be discerned is one of a sophisticated, well-prepared, quick moving, speedily communicative and highly sensitive organisation which *because of its prior activities* in shock event planning, handled this crisis more effectively than it would otherwise have done. 'A crisis always gets worse', believes Marshall Foster. This article suggests that in the context of potential disasters a proactive approach can make 'worse' better, than it would otherwise have been. Perrier's recovery also owed much to a natural advantage. The problem of long-term damage to market share was ameliorated by the inability of the competition to exploit the gap left open by the product withdrawal. Increased consumer demand over the past few years has meant that almost every producer has a source of water which is only just enough to meet existing production levels. In the short term, at least, the competition could not increase its supply significantly. Further, 'Perrier' is almost synonymous with 'sparkling water' and by knocking it, the competition risked undermining the whole sector. The industry's competitive structure, therefore, was significant in helping Perrier to move back towards pre-crisis sales volumes. This article suggests that Perrier's crisis management capabilities were also instrumental in the rapid and successful way in which Perrier has 'bounced' back from a major catastrophe. While its response to the disaster was clearly far from perfect it seems likely that a totally unprepared organisation would have handled the situation less effectively – perhaps even to the extent of adding to the initial damage. The article, therefore, acts as a reminder to all organisations operating in our shock event world that disaster planning makes sense.

## Think and discuss

1   What organisational arrangements need to be in place before a shock event strikes? Use the Perrier example to set your thoughts and discussions in a real world context.
2   Which factors were most important in helping Perrier regain its market position? Did its organisational arrangements help?
3   Choose an organisation and design a shock event system for it.
4   Contribute to the enhancement of your present or future organisation's planning systems, and strategic success.

## References

1   I I Mitroff, 'Crisis Management: Cutting through the Confusion', *Sloan Management Review*, Winter, 1988, pp 15–20
2   A line taken from John Lennon's, 'Beautiful Boy', *Double Fantasy* LP, 1980
3   B Mortimer, 'Diary of Disaster', *Employment Gazette*, 97 (2), February 1989
4   Rt. Hon. Lord Justice Taylor (Chair), *The Hillsborough Stadium Disaster, Final Report*, HMSO, 1990
5   Ibid
6   J H Gittens et al., *The Chernobyl Accident and its Consequences*, HMSO, 1987
7   Health and Safety Executive, *The Accident at Three Mile Island*, H and S E, 1979
8   Lord Cullen (Chair), *Public Inquiry into the Piper Alpha Disaster*, HMSO, 1990
9   H I Ansoff, *Implementing Strategic Management*, New York, Prentice-Hall International, 1984, pp 24–5

10  P Shrivastava et al., 'Understanding Industrial Crises', *Journal of Management Studies*, 4 July 1988, pp 285–303

11  C Perow, *Normal Accidents: Living with High Risk Technologies*, Basic Books, 1984, discusses 'interactive complexity and tight couplings' as systemic causes of major accidents.

12  D Smith, 'Beyond Contingency Planning Towards a Model of Crisis Management', *Industrial Crisis Quarterly*, 4, 1990, pp 263–75 discusses crises in the context of their 'three distinct phases'.

13  Report of the President's Commission on the Space Shuttle Challenger Accident (Washington DC, GPO Superintendent of Documents, 1988)

14  C B Handy, *Understanding Organisations*, Penguin, 1976, p 179

15  E L Quarantelli, 'Disaster Crisis Management: A Summary of Research Findings', *Journal of Management Studies*, 25 (4), July 1988, pp 373–85

# Recommended reading

E L Quarantelli, 'Disaster Crisis Management: A Summary of Research Findings', *Journal of Management Studies*, 25 (4), July 1988

# Index